T0330123

International Trade and Food Security

NUS CENTRE FOR INTERNATIONAL LAW

The NUS Centre for International Law series aims to provide critical analysis on issues of international law relevant to the region, including ocean law and policy, ASEAN law and policy, trade and investment law and international dispute resolution. The series will examine international law issues from a legal, political and policy perspective, and will serve as a valuable reference for international and regional organizations, government officials, scholars and practitioners. More information about Centre for International Law can be found at www.cil.nus.edu.sg.

Titles in the series include:

International Trade and Food Security

Exploring Collective Food Security in Asia

Edited by

Michael Ewing-Chow

WTO Chair, Faculty of Law, National University of Singapore

Melanie Vilarasau Slade

Senior Research Fellow, Centre for International Law, National University of Singapore

NUS CENTRE FOR INTERNATIONAL LAW

Edward Elgar
PUBLISHING

Cheltenham, UK • Northampton, MA, USA

Published by
Edward Elgar Publishing Limited
The Lypiatts
15 Lansdown Road
Cheltenham
Glos GL50 2JA
UK

Edward Elgar Publishing, Inc.
William Pratt House
9 Dewey Court
Northampton
Massachusetts 01060
USA

A catalogue record for this book
is available from the British Library

Library of Congress Control Number: 2015950287

This book is available electronically in the **Elgar**online
Law subject collection
DOI 10.4337/9781785361890

ISBN 978 1 78536 188 3 (cased)
ISBN 978 1 78536 189 0 (eBook)

Typeset by Servis Filmsetting Ltd, Stockport, Cheshire

Printed and bound in Great Britain by
TJ International Ltd, Padstow, Cornwall

Contents

v

PART III

PART IV

Figures

Tables

Contributors

Clemens Boonekamp, Former Director in the WTO of both the Trade Policies Review and the Agriculture and Commodities Divisions and presently Associate Partner at the Ideas Centre in Geneva (Switzerland).

Roehlano M. Briones, Research Fellow at the Philippine Institute for Development Studies (The Philippines).

Ramon Clarete, Dean of the University of the Philippines School of Economics (The Philippines).

Diwakar Dixit, Economic Affairs Officer of the Agriculture and Commodities Division of the WTO (Switzerland).

Michael Ewing-Chow, WTO Chair, Faculty of Law, National University of Singapore (Singapore).

Lee Ann Jackson, Counsellor in the Agriculture and Commodities Division at the World Trade Organization and Secretary to the Committee on Agriculture (Switzerland).

J. Jackson Ewing, Director of Asian Sustainability, Asia Society Policy Institute (United States), Adjunct Fellow at the S. Rajaratnam School of International Studies (RSIS) Centre for Non-Traditional Security Studies (Singapore).

James McVitty, Policy and Advocacy Manager at Fonterra (Singapore).

Evan Rogerson, Director of the Agriculture and Commodities Division of the WTO (Switzerland).

Julia Tijaja, Former Research Analyst at the Fung Global Institute (now the Asia Global Institute; Hong Kong) and presently Assistant Director and Senior Economist at the ASEAN Secretariat (Indonesia).

C. Peter Timmer, Thomas D. Cabot Professor of Development Studies, *emeritus*, Harvard University, and Adjunct Professor, Crawford School of Economics and Government, Australian National University, Canberra, Australia (United States).

Melanie Vilarasau Slade, Senior Research Fellow, Centre for International Law, National University of Singapore (United Kingdom).

Abbreviations

AoA	Uruguay Round Agreement on Agriculture
ACIA	ASEAN Comprehensive Investment Agreement
AFSIS	ASEAN Food Security Information System
AMS	Aggregate Measurement of Support
AMIS	Agriculture Market Information Systems
APTERR	ASEAN Plus Three Emergency Rice Reserve
ASEAN	Association of Southeast Asian Nations
ASEAN+3	ASEAN plus China, Japan and South Korea
ASEAN+6	ASEAN+3 plus Australia, India and New Zealand
AEC	ASEAN Economic Community
AFTA	ASEAN Free Trade Area
ATIGA	ASEAN Trade in Goods Agreement
BIN	Built-In Agenda at the WTO
BIT	Bilateral Investment Treaty
CoA	WTO Committee on Agriculture
CFS	Committee on World Food Security
CSR	Corporate Social Responsibility
DDA	Doha Development Agenda at the WTO
DSM	Dispute Settlement Mechanism
EAERR	East Asia Emergency Rice Reserve
EU	European Union
FAO	Food and Agriculture Organization
FTA	Free Trade Agreement
GATT	General Agreement on Tariffs and Trade
GFCs	Global Food Chains
GVCs	Global Value Chains
IFPRI	International Food Policy Research Institute
IIA	International Investment Agreement
ISA	Investor-State Arbitration
LDCs	Least Developed Countries
MNCs	Multinational Corporations
MPS	Market Price Support
NAMA	Non Agricultural Market Access at the WTO
NFIDCs	Net Food Importing Developing Countries

OECD	Organisation for Economic Cooperation and Development
OTDS	Overall Trade-Distorting Support
PSE	Producer Support Estimate
QRs	Quantitative Restrictions
SPS	Sanitary and Phytosanitary
SSM	Special Safeguard Mechanism
STDF	Standards and Trade Development Facility at the WTO
STEs	State Trading Enterprises
TF	Trade Facilitation
UNHLTF	UN High Level Task Force
VFA	Vietnam Food Association
WFP	World Food Programme
WTO	World Trade Organization

Introduction: Setting the stage: The problem with self-sufficiency and the need for collective food security for a global crisis

Michael Ewing-Chow and Melanie Vilarasau Slade

The 2008 food crisis exposed the vulnerabilities of the global food system and their direct impact on human wellbeing. The sudden increase in commodity prices pushed over a hundred million people into chronic hunger.[1] Some scholars have also suggested that the high prices contributed to the unrest in North Africa and the Middle East which led then to the continuing political instability in the region that started with the Arab Spring.[2] Though following the crisis the number of hungry is reported to be declining, the Food and Agriculture Organization of the United Nations (FAO) estimates that 805 million people were still suffering from chronic hunger in the period 2012–14.[3] Instability in the region was also increased by the 2011 food price increases and the sudden perceived failure by regional governments to provide essential food security to the population.[4]

As if the devastating effects of food price volatility on the most vulnerable and the current inequality of food distribution together with the potential for increasing political instability were not sufficient incentives for action, the world's population is growing by around 77 million people every year. By 2050, there will be more than nine billion people reliant on the earth's natural resources.[5] It is estimated that to feed the global population will require 60–70 per cent more food from the 3 per cent of the

---

[1] FAO estimates set the figure at approximately 115 million, principally due to higher food prices. See FAO, *The State of Agricultural Commodity Markets*, (FAO, 2009).

[2] M. Lagi, K. Z. Bertrand and Y. Bar-Yam, 'The Food Crises and Political Instability in North Africa and the Middle East', New England Complex Systems Institute (September, 2011) available at http://necsi.edu/research/social/food_crises.pdf.

[3] FAO *The State of Food Insecurity in the World 2014* (FAO, 2014).

[4] Above fn 2.

[5] United Nations, *World Population Prospects: the 2012 Revision* (UN, 2013).

world's surface which is arable land.[6] This makes it likely that we will face more crises than less in the future particularly when production disruptions caused by climate changes are anticipated.

The world will also undergo rapid urbanisation accompanied by increases in income levels and changing food preferences. McKinsey estimate that as urbanisation proceeds on an unprecedented scale, new and expanding cities could displace up to 30 million hectares of the highest quality agricultural land by 2030.[7] Another concern is that over 80 per cent of available arable land is subject to high political risk and/or infrastructure challenges: a potential deterrent to the much-needed investment in agriculture.[8] Globally there is forecast to be a 40 per cent shortfall in sustainable water by 2030,[9] and agriculture accounts for around 70 per cent of global water use.[10] Climate change is now poised to bring its own set of challenges to a sector which remains highly susceptible to, and dependent on, favourable and predictable weather conditions.

This dire situation is generally acknowledged. However, despite the urgent need for an effective response to these challenges, there is little consensus as to the appropriate policy mechanisms required to bolster the resilience of global food systems.

A critical point of contention is the role which international trade should play in the pursuit of food security and, conversely, the extent to which self-sufficiency policies can be relied upon to achieve food security globally.[11] Given the systemic impact of national food security policies, the existence of such fundamental divisions is of grave concern and threatens to undermine the pursuit of collaborative solutions.

One of the few areas of consensus among food security specialists is the complexity of this field and the need for a multidisciplinary approach to its study, which takes into account the broad range of stakeholders involved in our global food system. This book aims to contribute to the debate on the topic of international trade and food security, and to do so from a multidisciplinary perspective. It will take as its focus the Asia region, with a

---

[6] UN estimate cited in several sources including http://unesdoc.unesco.org/images/0021/002154/215492e.pdf and http://www.fao.org/fileadmin/templates/wsfs/docs/expert_paper/How_to_Feed_the_World_in_2050.pdf.

[7] McKinsey Global Institute *Resource Revolution: Tracking global commodity markets* (MGI, 2013).

[8] Ibid.

[9] See for example: http://unesdoc.unesco.org/images/0023/002318/231823E.pdf.

[10] See for example: http://www.oecd.org/tad/sustainable-agriculture/49040929.pdf.

[11] This includes divisions among international organisations dealing with food security issues. A high-profile example of this division can be found in the unresolved debate between former WTO head Pascal Lamy and former UN Special Rapporteur on the Right to Food Olivier de Schutter.

particular emphasis on the ASEAN region where national self-sufficiency policies co-exist with regional agreements to enhance food security, thus creating an ideal case study to explore tensions between national and regional or 'collective' approaches to food security particularly as they relate to developing countries where some of the most vulnerable live.

Cognisant of the pivotal role which legal systems can play in supporting systemic solutions to the food security challenge, in October 2013 the Centre for International Law (CIL) at the National University of Singapore, supported by the WTO Chairs Programme, hosted an international conference on food security and invited contributions from specialists in a variety of fields, including economists, policymakers, lawyers and academics, all with a particular interest in Asia. The Food Security Conference was held conjunctively with the 2nd Singapore Trade Dialogue in October 2013 and was attended by senior Asian trade officials prior to the 9th World Trade Organization (WTO) Ministerial Conference held in Bali, Indonesia in December 2013. The outcomes of the CIL Food Security Conference were the starting point for this publication, through which we hope to encourage and contribute to a constructive discussion on the ways in which food security can be strengthened across the Asia region and globally.

In Asia, two of the principal regional food security challenges are pricing volatility and the impact of environmental changes including climate change. This book addresses these challenges.

Common to each of the contributions are some terms and fundamental assumptions which will be outlined here. These include our understanding of 'food security'; its critical link to 'rice security' (the main staple crop) in Asia; the impact of the 2008 food crisis and of the food security policies implemented in its aftermath.

We trust that, with this context in place, the views, analysis and conclusions of each of the contributing authors will be more easily understood.

FOOD SECURITY

What is Food Security?

Food security exists when all people, at all times, have physical and economic access to sufficient safe and nutritious food that meets their dietary needs and food preferences for an active and healthy life. This definition, agreed at the 1996 World Food Summit[12] was adopted by the FAO and

---

[12] Rome Declaration on World Food Security, done at Rome, 13 to 17 November 1996. The World Food Summit where the Declaration was agreed took place from 13 to 17

has become the normative definition of food security. Intrinsic to this definition are the elements of *availability, utilisation,* and *access,* along with the need for *stability* of all these elements over time: a requirement particularly relevant in the era of pricing instability in the global food market.[13]

The transition from the concept of national food security to that of individual food security has been a gradual one, in which the focus shifted from the State to the individual[14] much as it did in the shift between the theory of mercantilism to that of comparative advantage and free trade.

The World Food Conference (1974) defined food security in terms of food supply, ensuring the availability and price stability of basic foodstuffs at the international and national level 'Availability at all times of adequate world food supplies of basic foodstuffs to sustain a steady expansion of food consumption and to offset fluctuations in production and prices.' Put simply, the term was used to describe whether a country had access to enough food to meet dietary energy requirements. The potential gulf between availability of food at national level and access to food by individual households within a given country was acknowledged in the 1980s, most notably in the literature of Amartya Sen. The concept of food security is therefore far from being a static one.[15]

Nonetheless, this book will take as a starting point the 1996 definition of food security together with its four main elements (i.e., availability, stability, utilisation, and access). While this definition is not without its limitations, it remains the definition which has generated the most international consensus. Further, it highlights that progress towards the achievement of global food security must be measured on the basis of whether each individual enjoys food security now and in the future. Logical though this may seem, as we will explore further in this book,

---

November 1996. This historic event, convened at FAO headquarters in Rome, comprised five days of meetings at the highest level with representatives from 185 countries and the European Community. For more information see: http://www.fao.org/wfs.

[13] In P. Pinstrup-Andersen, *Food Price Policy in an Era of Market Instability: A Political Economy Analysis.* (Oxford University Press, 2014).

[14] See Amartya Sen, *Poverty and Famines: An Essay on Entitlement and Deprivation* (Clarendon Press, 1981). This led to the FAO redefining food security in 1983 as: 'Ensuring that all people at all times have both physical and economic access to the basic food that they need.'

[15] Indeed, the concept remains fluid: the FAO's *The State of Food Insecurity in the World 2001* (Rome: FAO, 2001) provides the following definition: 'Food security [is] a situation that exists when all people, at all times, have physical, social and economic access to sufficient, safe and nutritious food that meets their dietary needs and food preferences for an active and healthy life.' As described in a subsequent report by the FAO '[t]his new emphasis on consumption, the demand side and the issues of access by vulnerable people to food, is most closely identified with the seminal study by Amartya Sen. See *Trade Reforms and Food Security: Conceptualising the Linkages* (FAO, 2003).

current food security policies focus on ensuring self-sufficiency on a national level rather than – and at times to the detriment of – achieving food security for 'all people' globally.

Food Security in Asia: Rice Security is Food Security

Rice is a highly sensitive product in Asia. Over 90 per cent of the world's rice is produced and consumed in the Asian region. Until recently, the trend in Asia showed an increase in production and export, but a decrease in consumption[16] as growing prosperity and urbanisation contributed to a decline, particularly in middle- and high-income Asian countries like Japan and the Republic of Korea, in favour of more Western diets. More recently it seems this declining trend may have stabilised or even reversed, in particular in China, India and Indonesia, contributing to a rise in global consumption.[17]

Nevertheless, according to FAO statistics, in 2007 more than half of the ASEAN countries still took around 50 per cent of their daily calories from rice.[18] Further, approximately one-quarter of the Asian population is still poor and there is considerable unmet demand for rice in countries such as Afghanistan, North Korea, Nepal and Vietnam. It is in these countries that rice consumption could grow faster.[19] This means:

> Increasingly, rice is consumed by the poor, who usually must buy most of their rice in rural and urban markets. Almost by definition, having a surplus of rice to sell to the market raises a family above the poverty line in most Asian countries. This reality, of course, makes rice more, not less, important to food security in Asia.[20]

---

[16] S. Ito, E. Wesley, F. Peterson and W. Grant, 'Rice in Asia: Is it becoming an inferior good?' (1989) 71 *American Journal of Agricultural Economics* at pp. 32–4.

[17] Based on PSD online database (USDA) and FAOSTAT population database (FAO) cited in Samarendu Mohanty 'Trends in global rice consumption' in IRRI publication 'Rice Today' January–March 2013 available at http://irri.org/rice-today/trends-in-global-rice-consumption.

[18] This includes Cambodia, Indonesia, Laos, Myanmar, Philippines, Thailand and Vietnam. In particular, about 64 per cent of the daily calories intake is from rice in Cambodia and Laos. Source: Authors' own calculations based on FAO Statistics.

[19] M. K. Papademetriou, 'Rice production in the Asia-Pacific region: Issues and perspectives', in M. K. Papademetriou, F. Dent and E. Herath (eds), *Bridging the Rice Yield Gap in the Asia-Pacific Region*, RAP Publication: 2000/16 (FAO, 2000): http://www.fao.org/docrep/003/x6905e/x6905e04.htm#RICE%20PRODUCTION%20IN%20THE%20ASIAPACIFIC%20REGION%20ISSUES%20AND%20PERSPECTIVES%20M.K.%20Papademetriou*.

[20] C. P. Timmer, 'The changing role of rice in Asia's food security', in *Food for All: Investing in Food Security in Asia and the Pacific – Issues, Innovations, and Practices* (Asian Development Bank 2011).

Southeast Asia, the main focus of this book, is heavily dependent on rice: in 2007, rice accounted for 85.9 per cent of cereal production and 32 per cent of the total agriculture.[21] The ratio of production to domestic utilisation for ASEAN as a whole in 2014 is estimated at 120.82 per cent. While in aggregate ASEAN is a rice self-sufficient region, some countries in the region still need to import rice for their own consumption.[22]

Worryingly, the potential for volatility of the price of rice across Asia is still high. Indeed, pricing volatility in food markets has been described as the 'new normal' and rice pricing in particular remains highly vulnerable to political decisions by regional governments.[23]

The combination of this volatility with reliance on this staple crop by the poorest sectors of society in Asia makes a large part of the Asian population, especially those in the least-developed countries, particularly vulnerable to spikes in the price of rice. Together these factors mean that, at present, achieving food security in the Asian context is inextricably linked to achieving a state of rice security.

Challenges to Food Security: The 2008 Food Crisis

The ability of the current food system to ensure collective food security was severely tested by the 2008 food crisis, revealing a number of serious deficiencies and systemic flaws.

In 2008 the upturn in international food prices that began in 2006 escalated to a surge of food price inflation on a global scale. The crisis has been described as follows:

> As food prices began to rise, commodity-exporting nations placed export restrictions on price-volatile crops grown nationally, such as rice, to protect their food security. Export restrictions, reduced import tariffs and other trade distortions drove up international commodity prices, resulting in shortages of food on the global market and causing panic for many emerging economies suffering from a dearth in natural resources.[24]

Additional factors included an increased use of food crops for biofuel, high oil prices, an inflow of speculative funds into the agricultural com-

---

21 Ibid., at Table 1 rice and the structural transformation: 1961–2007.
22 ASEAN Food Security Information System Project, Report on ASEAN Agricultural Commodity Outlook No. 12, June 2014.
23 See in particular Clarete et al *Rice Trade and Price Volatility: Implications on ASEAN and Global Food Security* ADB Economics Working Paper Series No. 368, (Asian Development Bank 2013).
24 B. Robertson and P. Pinstrup-Andersen, 'Global land acquisition: neo-colonialism or development opportunity?' (2010) 2(3) *Food Security*, at pp.271–83.

modity futures market and an increasing demand for food in emerging economies such as China and India which generated increased demand for feed. The FAO contends that all these factors contributed to the spike in food prices and that 'it was the combination of them that was crucial'.[25]

Whatever its causes, the effect on commodity price levels was dramatic. FAO figures show that while there was an increase of 9 per cent in the price of rice from 2005 to 2006 and 17.5 per cent from 2006 to 2007; from 2007 to 2008, the rice price skyrocketed by 83 per cent.[26] The effect on global food security was no less dramatic. The FAO calculates that in 2007 and 2008, mainly because of high food prices, an additional 115 million people were pushed into chronic hunger.[27]

In most cases the short-term policy responses adopted to deal with the food price spike fitted into longer-term policy frameworks and were driven by long-term policy objectives, such as national food security or stabilisation of farm revenues.[28] Unfortunately, these policies tended to aggravate the food price spike globally rather than alleviate it. The dramatic effect of the 2008 food price spike on the rice market is a good illustration of the effect of national self-sufficiency policies on global prices. By way of a short summary of events in the rice market, India's decision in October 2007 to ban rice exports, except for Basmati, was quickly followed by Vietnam and other major players, and speculation that Thailand would follow suit. This had an immediate impact on prices leading to panic purchases of rice, especially by large rice importers such as Philippines, which further aggravated the situation. Speculators, sensing a crisis, then swooped in to take advantage of this, leading to even higher prices.[29] The International Food Policy Research Institute (IFPRI) concluded that 'three-quarters of the increase in the price of rice occurred in 2008 – almost certainly because of adverse policy responses, such as export bans, from some major exporters'.[30]

Yet the food security policies of many food-producing nations remain premised on the assumption that the only way to guarantee their national

---

[25] FAO, fn 1 above.

[26] See FAO Rice Price Update (January 2010), online: http://www.fao.org/es/esc/en/15/70/highlight_533.html.

[27] FAO, above fn 1.

[28] D. Jones and A. Kwiecinski, 'Policy Responses in Emerging Economies to International Agricultural Commodity Price Surges', OECD Food, Agriculture and Fisheries Working Papers, n. 34, (OECD Publishing 2010).

[29] See, inter alia, Dawe and Slayton, 'The World Rice Market Crisis of 2007–2008' in David Dawe (ed.), *The Rice Crisis: Markets, Policies and Food Security* (London, (FAO and Earthscan 2010), pp.18–24.

[30] D. Headey and S. Fan, *Reflections on the Global Food Crisis*, International Food Policy Research Institute (IFPRI) monograph 165 (IFPRI, 2010) at p.32.

food security is to focus on achieving some level of self-sufficiency. They believe that if they do not produce enough domestically, during a shortage, no one else will be willing to trade food with them or will only trade food at exploitative prices. As a result, the agricultural policies of many nations focus on providing their domestic producers with increased incentives to produce food domestically by way of subsidies and/or protecting them from foreign competition through barriers such as quotas, tariffs and standards targeted to limit foreign imports.

The problem with this response is that it fails to fully appreciate the systemic impact such policies have on global food production. Incentives in one nation may create disincentives in others to produce food. For example, subsidies may distort food prices sufficiently to reduce the food production in the country importing the subsidised food. With the increasingly unpredictable weather patterns caused by climate change (anthropogenic or otherwise), focusing on domestic production alone seems to be a rather more risky strategy than previously imagined. Indeed, the 2008 food price spikes were triggered by unanticipated weather affecting crop yields. The extended drought in the Murray-Darling region of Australia reduced rice yields by 98 per cent,[31] unseasonal rains wiped out crops in Kerala, India,[32] and Cyclone Nargis destroyed the rice fields in the Irrawaddy Delta of Myanmar.[33] Recently, on World Food Day, Christiana Figueres, Executive Secretary of the UN Framework Convention on Climate Change (UNFCCC), said:

> Aside from permanent shifts in climatic conditions which will affect farming, climate change is causing more and more extreme weather, for example tropical storms, floods and droughts which can push subsistence farmers and others living in food insecurity into dire circumstances.[34]

We can no longer predict with certainty the likelihood of food production of any particular nation or region.

---

[31] 'Drought in Australia reduces Australia's rice crop by 98 percent' *The New York Times*, 17 April 2008 see http://www.nytimes.com/2008/04/17/business/worldbusiness/17warm. html?n=Top/News/Science/Topics/Global%20Warming.

[32] 'Crops lost due to unseasonal rains in Kerala' *The Economic Times*, 8 April 2008 at http://articles.economictimes.indiatimes.com/2008-04-08/news/28439839_1_unseasonal-rains-paddy-production-crops.

[33] 'Cyclone fuels rice price increase', BBC News, 7 May 2008 at http://news.bbc.co.uk/1/hi/business/7387251.stm.

[34] UN Press Release, 16 October 2013, Efforts to end world hunger must be aligned with tackling climate change warns UN's top climate change official Christiana Figueres on World Food Day available at: http://unfccc.int/files/press/press_releases_advisories/appli cation/pdf/pr20131610_m4c_food.pdf.

It may even be that geographical borders in an increasingly interconnected and unpredictable world are becoming less helpful parameters for food security policymaking. The rise of global value chains (GVCs) have resulted in many food production systems being increasingly influenced by multinational corporations (MNCs) rather than individual nations. These MNCs straddle multiple nations and have sophisticated chains of production dependent on the incorporation of different inputs from a number of different sources. A break in the chain where it is weakest may trigger a cascade of events that national food security policies alone may not be able to control.

Even if a nation were sufficiently large, controlling and isolationist to organise its food security policies in a way that secured its own security, recent events in the Middle East have once again highlighted the difficulty of securing the borders from people fleeing crises. Climate change and food shortages will inevitably cause major movement of people and we can anticipate that no one nation will be able to manage the attendant problems on their own.

All of these new factors of climate change, GVCs and potential growth in the number of political refugees and climate migrants suggest that we need to rethink food security. We can no longer think of it as national self-sufficiency but rather instead we need to understand the problem as one of global collective food security. We need to understand how trade, investments and information may all be able to play a role in addressing this major concern.

Too often, governments interpret 'all people' to be limited to their territory and citizens, ignoring the universal scope of the concept of food security and the systemic impact of national food security policies. To bring this back to the fore, we, the Editors developed the term 'collective food security' to refer to a state where the systemic impact of national policies is acknowledged and the focus shifted to ensuring food security can be achieved globally rather than nationally.

Just as trade is an essential element of food security policy; it is also an essential requirement of a sustainable global food trade system that it enables the achievement of food security for all. This is not a selfless endeavour but rather a fundamental requirement in order to ensure the viability and sustainability of national food security policies.

We suggest therefore that the debate should be refocused: In a globalised food system, compliance with WTO rules may not be an undue restriction but rather a virtuous discipline, which reduces volatility-enhancing trade distortions. The 2008 food price spikes were aggravated by a cascade of export restrictions by major crop exporters that increased panic and thereby unilateral responses. A collective response to future crises is needed and may be possible even under the current WTO rules.

This book will endeavour to explore this premise in three parts:

The first section presents the realities of the current global food trade system. It explores international trade rules, and provides an overview of GVCs in agriculture in an effort to place current food security initiatives in their global context. It then explores national and regional food security initiatives in ASEAN, examining the contrasting efforts towards greater cooperation and greater self-reliance, and assessing the impact of international trade rules on these initiatives. Thus, in Chapter 1, Evan Rogerson and Diwakar Dixit describe the WTO's contribution to the liberalization of trade in food, from the Uruguay Round to the latest Bali Decisions. In Chapter 2 Julia Tijaja provides an overview of Global Food Chains, exploring trends that could impact on national food security policies. Chapters 3 and 4 explore regional tensions in ASEAN between national and regional food security. Roehlano M. Briones, Michael Ewing-Chow and Melanie Vilarasau Slade separately examine these food security initiatives, contrasting efforts towards greater regional integration with national self-sufficiency initiatives, and exploring the impact that WTO rules.

This second section focuses on one of the most significant challenges faced by the current system: market shocks and pricing volatility. It explores the causes and effects of pricing volatility in agriculture (across sectors including rice and dairy) and the potential for policy solutions, including stockholdings, transparency initiatives and market-based mechanisms. In Chapter 5, C. Peter Timmer sets out the case for greater research into public stockholdings as a food security tool; in Chapter 6 Ramon L. Clarete assesses the impact of self-sufficiency policies in ASEAN and proposes policy solutions to the threat of pricing volatility; and in Chapter 7 James McVitty of Fonterra provides a private sector perspective and sets out the case for market-based risk management tools.

The third section focuses on the most significant challenges the current system is likely to face in future, including climate change and resource shortages. The final section then assesses the role which international law can play in addressing these challenges. In Chapter 8 Lee Ann Jackson focuses on the potential supply side constraints that could impact food security and highlights the advantages of a resilience-focused approach to agricultural investment and its critical importance to the effectiveness national food security policies. In Chapter 9 J. Jackson Ewing focuses on the environmental challenges facing Southeast Asia and their likely impact on food security in order to assess the effectiveness of various food security policy options. In Chapter 10 Melanie Vilarasau Slade will examine whether reform of international law is required in order to support collaborative efforts to address future food security challenges.

Finally, this book will look towards the future and assesses the potential for improvement of the current international trade system from a food security perspective. In doing so it will seek to explore whether solutions are possible within the current system and what initiatives are required to create the conditions under which collective food security can be achieved. In Chapter 11 Clemens Boonekamp looks in particular at how international trade rules can be improved to give greater priority and effect to the WTO's stated aim to contribute to global food security through trade liberalization. In this book's Conclusion, the Editors will seek to address the lessons learned and map out the path towards collective food security.

PART I

1. Food security issues and the role of the multilateral trading system

Evan Rogerson and Diwakar Dixit*

1. BACKGROUND

Addressing food insecurity and malnutrition is one of the most pressing challenges that the global community faces. The Global Strategic Framework[1] adopted by the Committee on World Food Security has outlined some of the structural and underlying causes of food insecurity and malnutrition which, inter alia, include broader 'governance' issues, 'economic and production issues', 'demographic and social issues' and issues related to 'climate and environment'. A holistic consideration of this complex matrix of issues is needed. This is the approach taken by the UN High Level Task Force[2] on Food Security in its comprehensive framework of action (UCFA).

While both demand and supply side factors were responsible for triggering the 2008 food crisis, overall food supply or *availability* has not presented a threat to global food security. Global food production/supply has consistently kept pace with demand that has been rising as a result of population and income increases. That is why Amartya Sen considered that food *access* (rather than *availability*) matters most: 'Starvation is the characteristic of some people not having enough food to eat. It is not the characteristic of there being not enough food to eat.'[3]

This should not, however, belittle the scale of the challenge to increase global food production posed by the rising food demand that in turn results from growth in world population and income. According to FAO

---

* The views expressed in this chapter are solely the authors' responsibility and do not purport to be an official position of the WTO.

[1] Accessible at: http://www.fao.org/cfs/cfs-home/global-strategic-framework/en/.

[2] Since 2008, a UN Secretary General-led High-Level Task Force (UN HLTF) has been in action involving 23 UN agencies and international organizations (including the WTO) towards an enhanced coordination and an effective food security response.

[3] Amartya Sen, *Poverty and Famines: An Essay on Entitlement and Deprivation* (Clarendon Press 1981).

estimates, world population is expected to reach more than nine billion by 2050 and feeding that population would necessitate raising overall food production by more than 60 per cent between 2005/07 and 2050.[4] This is seen as achievable subject to, inter alia, strengthened efforts towards increasing agricultural productivity and investment, more favourable domestic agricultural policy frameworks, enhanced global policy cooperation and free and functioning food markets. This chapter will focus on the role of trade and the multilateral trade framework of the WTO towards contributing to the food security objectives.

2.   THE MULTILATERAL TRADING SYSTEM AND FOOD SECURITY

The majority of hungry and food insecure people in the world are directly or indirectly dependent on the agriculture sector for their livelihood and for improving their food security status. Governments principally focus on their agricultural policies in achieving national food security goals. The examination of the multilateral trade rules in this chapter will naturally focus on such rules as applicable to agricultural trade.

There is significant potential for enhancing agricultural production and productivity in many parts of the world. Countries should strive to harness this potential, which would significantly contribute to meeting food security goals. At times, the objective of augmenting agricultural productivity is stretched to make it appear equivalent to the attainment of food self-sufficiency. The notion of food self-sufficiency is often attractive from a political perspective; but the realization of such an objective would necessitate self-sufficiency in natural endowments (land, water, etc.) and supportive climatic conditions in order to produce everything that is demanded by consumers in a country. Natural resources are, however, not evenly distributed and neither are they proportionally aligned to the demographic situation of individual countries.

For almost all countries, national food self-sufficiency would be impractical, environmentally unsustainable and excessively costly.[5] As the Director-General of the FAO has noted, in a globalized world, it is not

---

[4] This implies an additional annual consumption of 940 million tons of cereal and 200 million tons of meat by 2050.

[5] Some activists even go further and advocate the so-called 'food sovereignty'. This notion conveys, inter alia, a sense that States must be allowed to intervene towards achieving food security goals even if those interventions conflict with their international commitments.

possible to achieve food security in only one country.[6] The notion of food self-sufficiency gained ground during the 2008 food crisis when many importing countries found themselves precariously exposed to an extreme price volatility originating in the international food market. Food self-sufficiency was then argued so as to insulate the domestic market and domestic consumers from highly volatile international food prices. These insular tendencies in turn expose the concerned countries to domestic food price volatility resulting from the local supply shocks that have recently become more frequent due, inter alia, to climatic aberrations.

Trade is an essential component of any food security strategy and acts as an engine to the transfer of products from surplus to deficit areas. The WTO system can contribute to global food security through reduction or elimination of trade-distorting measures and by providing a binding and predictable framework to guide intervention by governments in their agriculture sectors. The international commitments that governments have negotiated under the WTO help, not hinder, their achievement of food security goals. There are four specific aspects related to the multilateral trading system that should be highlighted in the context of the food security debate.

(i) Reducing Trade Barriers Towards Open and Functioning Food Markets

One of the most fundamental ways in which the WTO could contribute to global food security is through open, non-distorting and efficient agricultural trade. International trade offers an opportunity for income growth through improved access to external markets, thereby encouraging expansion of agricultural production. By way of encouraging competitiveness, international trade also assists in an efficient allocation of resources, thereby improving agricultural productivity. Food insecurity resulting from inhibited *access* to food is generally caused by a lack of income, and international trade through its income-enhancing potential could be an effective tool to enhance food access.

International trade also plays a balancing role by evening out supply fluctuations across the globe and thus containing food market *price volatility*. With climatic variations becoming more frequent and significant, resulting in frequent production shortfalls, the balancing and stabilizing role of trade will become increasingly important over time. Another factor which often aggravates pricing volatility is the fact that food markets

---

[6] See, by way of example, the statement made by the Director General on the occasion of World Food Day 2012 available at: http://www.fao.org/news/story/en/item/162391/icode/.

are '*thin*' (i.e. a small share of production is traded internationally). The agricultural reform process that was launched in 1995 under the Uruguay Round Agreement on Agriculture[7] (AoA) and being furthered through the Doha Round (DDA) agriculture negotiations would lead to 'fuller' food markets, thus dampening the global price volatility risks.

Import barriers

Tariff reductions under the WTO framework are pursued through commitments on tariff bindings. This contributes to open and predictable international food markets, increased trade volumes, and the ability to diversify sources of supply for food imports, and thus to enhanced food *availability*. Trade liberalization of agricultural products began after the entry into force of the AoA in 1995, which allows the use of tariffs for domestic producers against agricultural imports, but prohibits the application of agriculture-specific non-tariff border measures.

The existing agricultural tariff levels that WTO Members committed to after the conclusion of the Uruguay Round continue to be high. Achieving a substantial reduction of the existing tariff commitments, particularly high tariffs, is one of the important objectives of the DDA negotiations. In that endeavour, special attention is also paid to achieving enhanced market access for products that are of increasing export interest to developing countries. This effort would enable a greater contribution by the agriculture sector to income generation and food security outcomes in developing countries.

One developmental aspect that is often raised in the context of discussions regarding the contribution of the agriculture sector in developing countries is the level of enhanced value addition or product transformation that these countries should achieve domestically. A trade policy aspect that also invariably informs that discussion is tariffs on processed agricultural products and the escalation of those tariffs with increasing value addition. In the DDA agriculture negotiations, there is an emphasis on addressing this tariff escalation especially where it affects developing countries' exports.

Export barriers

During the 2008 food crisis, there was criticism that WTO rules do not discipline agricultural export restrictions.[8] At the peak of the crisis, a number of countries were found to be adopting various measures limiting

---

[7] Agreement on Agriculture (15 April 1994) LT/UR/A-1A/2.

[8] The asymmetry in WTO rules on exports and imports become acute and more exposed when one considers *tariff* commitments on imports and exports, i.e. extensive tariff

exports in order to retain their domestic production locally. Such restrictions raised concerns as to the reliability of the international market as a source of food supplies.[9]

While it is true that the import side is highly disciplined under the WTO rules in order to contain protectionism, the prohibition on maintaining quantitative restrictions (QRs) under GATT Article XI applies to both imports and exports. Members are therefore not generally permitted to maintain export quotas and bans on foodstuffs. Article XI:2(a) of GATT 1994 permits Members to temporarily restrict or prohibit exports of foodstuffs in order to prevent or relieve critical shortage of those foodstuffs. This provision allows Members to apply these, otherwise prohibited, measures temporarily to address critical situations concerning their food security.

Article 12 of the AoA attempts to balance the equation by addressing the concerns of importing Members whose food security may equally be threatened by such measures. Members instituting an export prohibition or restriction on foodstuffs shall give due consideration to the effects of such measures on importing Members' food security. To this end, the Members, before instituting such export limiting measures, shall make a notification to the Committee on Agriculture presenting the details of the measure including its proposed duration, and shall consult, upon request, with interested importing Members.[10]

Timely notifications in the area of export prohibitions and restrictions are seen as very important. These notifications not only ensure a proper review of such measures (i.e. to see that prescribed rules are followed) but they also provide a concrete opportunity to importing Members to seek consultations with the notifying Member in order to address their potential food security concerns. There has been an active discussion in the WTO Committee on Agriculture (CoA) aimed at improving the application of the existing rules. Additionally, in the DDA agriculture negotiations, rules on agricultural export restrictions are a part of the negotiating dossier and there are various negotiating proposals on the table on that issue.

---

bindings on imports and virtually non-existing export tariff bindings (except for some recently acceded Members).

[9] One of the policy advisory proposed by a number of global collaborations on food security activated during the 2008 food crisis was to minimize the use of export restrictions on foodstuffs. The UN HLTF in its Framework, for example, recommended that governments 'ensure that local purchases of food and food components for humanitarian purposes are exempt from restrictions'. A similar declaration was agreed within the G20 framework.

[10] Developing country Members are exempted from these additional conditions prescribed in the AoA unless the developing country Member concerned is a net-exporter of the specific foodstuff concerned.

(ii) Multilateral Rules on Agricultural Subsidization

Trade-distorting subsidy interventions in the agriculture sector by governments have for many years contributed to distorting international food markets and depressing agricultural production in poorer developing countries. These countries, despite their competitive advantage in the sector, faced adverse terms of trade for many decades in the post-war period. Such a negative scenario was also deemed responsible for contributing to under-investment in the agriculture sector and delayed agriculture policy reforms in a number of developing countries.

Domestic subsidization

One of the fundamental changes introduced by the multilateral agriculture rules negotiated in the Uruguay Round was the conclusion of binding rules on domestic agricultural subsidization. The aim is to ensure that the location and quantum of agricultural production is determined by competitive advantage rather than by the magnitude of financial interventions by governments. The rules under the 'domestic support' pillar of the AoA limit trade-distorting support by governments through the so-called *reduction commitments* and simultaneously leave ample scope for governments (and especially developing country governments) to design domestic agricultural policies in response to the specific circumstances of their agricultural sectors. For example, policies to create rural infrastructure, enhanced investment towards agricultural research, provision of training and extension services to farmers, etc., are explicitly encouraged under the Green Box[11] by exempting them from any ceiling on support expenditures.

The multilateral framework on agricultural subsidization has helped to create a more enabling global policy environment to carry out much needed agricultural reforms and thus also contribute to food security objectives. However, trade distorting subsidy amounts that Members (and especially developed country Members) can spend under the existing commitments are still high. This is one of the important issues in the DDA agriculture negotiations that Members seek to address by means of a successful DDA outcome.

Export subsidization

Export subsidies are deemed as highly distorting in terms of their negative spillover effect as subsidization is targeted at production for export to the

---

[11] Annex 2 of the AoA sets out the basic and policy-specific implementation criteria, which, if followed, allow the relevant domestic support measures to be placed in the Green Box. The support measures covered under the Green Box are not subject to any financial limitation under the WTO (i.e. exempt from *reduction commitments*).

international market. Export subsidies on industrial goods have been prohibited under the GATT rules whereas in the case of agricultural primary products they remained permissible subject to a limited multilateral discipline. The proliferation of such subsidies was one of the reasons for disarray in the international food markets in the years prior to the launch of the Uruguay Round negotiations. These subsidies were also deemed responsible for a long-term depression in world prices of subsidized agri-food products, a phenomenon that acted as a deterrent to agricultural investment in many developing countries and prevented them from exploiting the full developmental potential of the agriculture sector.

The rules with regard to export subsidies agreed under the AoA prohibited the introduction of new export subsidies and reduced existing export subsidies. In the Doha negotiations, WTO Members, especially the developing country Members, demanded an end to export subsidies due to their negative effect on world prices and thus on domestic production and exports. In 2005, WTO Members agreed to the final objective of eliminating all types of export subsidies in the agriculture sector. At the 2013 Bali ministerial meeting, Members reaffirmed the importance of reaching this final objective as soon as possible.

One of the areas of focus of the DDA agriculture negotiations under the export competition pillar ensures that WTO Members do not circumvent their export subsidy commitments through the operation of agricultural exporting State trading enterprises (STEs). To this end, one of the decisions foreseen under the negotiations is the elimination of the use of export monopoly powers of exporting STEs. However, the food security aspect informs this negotiating discussion as it is proposed that agricultural exporting State trading enterprises in developing country Members be permitted to use or maintain their export monopoly powers in cases where such STEs aim to preserve domestic consumer price stability and to ensure food security.

(iii) Issues Related to Net Food-importing Developing Countries

At the time of the adoption of the Uruguay Round agricultural reform programme under the AoA, the Uruguay Round package also included a Decision concerning the possible negative effects of the reform programme on least-developed and net-food importing developing countries (NFIDCs). The decision fully recognizes the positive effect of the Uruguay Round outcome as a whole to the benefit of all WTO Members. Simultaneously, there is an acknowledgement that in pursuing liberalization of agricultural trade under to the Uruguay Round reform programme, least-developed and NFIDCs might face difficulties accessing food from the international market at reasonable terms and conditions.

The underlying assumption was that the reform process may result in an upward move in those international food prices that remained depressed due to distorting subsidies in place prior to the launch of the reform programme. Those price movements might entail temporary adjustment costs for such food-importing developing countries.

In order to minimize the potential negative impact of the reform process, the Marrakesh Decision includes a number of mechanisms to ensure that the reform process does not adversely affect the availability of food aid at a level that would enable developing countries to meet their food needs. The CoA is mandated to monitor the Decision's follow-up. The CoA has established a WTO list of NFIDCs and carries out an annual monitoring of the follow-up to the Decision in its November sessions. The relevant international organizations are also invited to contribute to the annual monitoring exercise. The review of the levels of food aid established under the Food Aid Convention[12] and the level of concessions of food aid are specifically considered during the CoA's annual monitoring exercise.

International food aid is also one of the issues considered in the DDA agriculture negotiations under the export competition pillar. The fundamental thrust of WTO negotiations on this topic is to ensure that the WTO Members do not use food aid operations to circumvent their export subsidy commitments and cause market displacement. Simultaneously, there is a recognition of the interest of food aid recipients in the negotiations: that the WTO disciplines to be agreed in the negotiations should not unintentionally impede the delivery of food aid provided to deal with emergency situations.

The AoA[13] contains an undertaking on the part of WTO Members to work toward the development of multilateral disciplines on export credits and similar measures in recognition of the fact that such export financing measures could be used to circumvent export subsidy commitments. This task is now pursued as a part of the DDA agriculture negotiations. The Marrakesh Decision looks at the development of such multilateral disciplines on export credits and similar measures from an 'access to food' perspective and provides that the disciplines relating to such measures make appropriate provisions for differential treatment in favour of least-

---

[12] The Food Aid Convention was a multilateral cooperation instrument that remained in operation from 1967 to 2012. Its aim was to contribute to world food security and to improve the ability of the international community to respond to emergency food situations and the food needs of developing countries. The Food Aid Convention has been succeeded by the Food Assistance Convention, which entered into force on 1 January 2013.

[13] Article 10.2 of the AoA.

developed and net food-importing developing countries. This aspect relating to net food importing countries contemplated in the Decision has been fully taken on board in the DDA agriculture negotiations.

(iv) Multilateral Rules on Food Safety

Food safety is intricately linked to food security. First, and most directly, safety and quality of food is critical from a nutritional perspective. Additionally, countries with proper food safety infrastructures in place can produce food that will have greater market demand and market access, and will thus be able to enhance their agricultural production and productivity. This in turn contributes to food security objectives. Food that is not safe cannot normally be consumed or traded and will thus potentially be wasted. Concerns related to food safety are one of the important reasons for food wastage at 'consumption' stage. In the food security debate,[14] there is an enhanced focus on containing food losses and food waste towards augmenting the global *availability* of food.

The WTO has a rich set of rules in the areas of food safety and quality. WTO rules encourage a science-based approach and recourse to international standards for harmonization purposes. These rules are included under the two separate agreements on sanitary and phyto-sanitary issues (SPS) and technical barriers to trade (TBT). These agreements contain binding rules aimed at ensuring safety and quality of traded food and simultaneously preventing the use of these standards or measures in a discriminatory manner or for protectionist purposes. The WTO also houses and administers the Standards and Trade Development Facility (STDF), a global partnership that supports developing countries in building their capacity to implement international SPS standards and ability to gain or maintain access to markets.

3. MINISTERIAL MEETING AT BALI

On 3–7 December 2013, the WTO held its Ninth Ministerial Conference in Bali, Indonesia. Ministers adopted a series of decisions aimed at strengthening the effectiveness of the multilateral trading system. Specific mention is made of three decisions strongly linked to food security.

---

[14] Zero food loss/waste is one of the five themes identified in the UN SG's Zero Hunger Challenge (ZHC).

(i) Decision on Public Stockholding for Food Security Purposes

One of the most politically visible issues that the Bali ministerial meeting considered, based on a proposal by the G-33 group of developing countries, concerned developing country programmes on public stockholding for food security purposes. The existing WTO AoA rules under the Green Box[15] permit governments to incur expenditures in relation to accumulation and holding of food stocks without any monetary limitation, provided the acquisition and the release of stocks is carried out under market conditions.

The specific issue under consideration at the Bali meeting concerned situations where public stockholding programmes in developing countries intersect with market price support (MPS) policies during the acquisition stage of stockholding. In such cases, under the existing AoA rules the developing country Members might still exempt their public stockholding programmes under the Green Box, provided the price support component is accounted for in the aggregate measurement of support (AMS) calculations. Considering the trade-distorting potential of market price support[16] programmes, the existing rules on AMS calculations provide for a specific methodology to quantify such support. Some developing countries argued that the annual AMS amount calculated as per the prescribed methodology for their public stockholding programmes would lead them to breach their domestic support commitment.

As per the decision[17] agreed at the Bali meeting, the developing country Members were granted interim protection against legal challenge under the AoA with regard to their existing public stockholding programmes in cases where support provided to traditional staple food crops in pursuance of such stockholding programmes conflict with AoA commitments.[18] The beneficiary developing country Members will be subject to transparency, monitoring and consultation requirements. The Bali decision also provides that a fuller discussion on this topic will take place in the framework of a work programme on food security, to be conducted over the next four years, with the objective of finding a lasting solution. Later in November 2014, the General Council of the WTO adopted a decision[19] clarifying that

---

[15] Paragraph 3 of Annex 2 refers.

[16] In the lead-up to the Uruguay Round negotiations which finally created the rules on domestic subsidization under the AoA, market price support was the most prevalent category of trade-distorting support, often practiced by developed countries, and that was deemed responsible for the then existing disarray in agriculture markets.

[17] WT/L/913 accessible at: http://wto.org/english/thewto_e/minist_e/mc9_e/desci38_e.htm.

[18] Articles 6.3 and 7.2(b) of AoA refer.

[19] WT/L/939 refers.

the interim mechanism will continue to be in place if a permanent solution were not to be agreed and adopted within the originally conceived four-year time-frame and simultaneously agreed to make all concerted efforts to negotiate a permanent solution in a dedicated negotiating track by 31 December 2015.

(ii) Decision on General Services

One of the issues considered in the DDA agriculture negotiations has been towards encouraging an increasing recourse to Green Box programmes by developing countries. In this context, and recognizing the contribution that General Services programmes of the Green Box can make to rural development, food security and poverty alleviation, particularly in developing countries, the Ministers at Bali agreed[20] to expand the illustrative list of General Services programmes to include various policies that are grounded on rural livelihood security and poverty alleviation objectives.

(iii) Agreement on Trade Facilitation

Specific mention should be made of the agreement[21] that the WTO members adopted at Bali on Trade Facilitation (TF) towards expediting the movement, release and clearance of goods, including goods in transit. It is widely expected that the new trade facilitation agreement will reduce the transaction cost of trade through streamlined customs procedures, and will improve the predictability and transparency of market access opportunities in global markets, including food markets.

From a food security perspective, special mention may be made of provisions in the TF Agreement dealing with a speedy release of perishable goods. These rules will contribute to limiting food wastage especially in respect of perishable food products (such as fruits and vegetables) and thus contribute to food security through enhanced food availability.

---

[20] WT/L/912 accessible at http://wto.org/english/thewto_e/minist_e/mc9_e/desci37_e.htm.
[21] WT/L/911 accessible at http://wto.org/english/thewto_e/minist_e/mc9_e/desci36_e.htm. Later, in November 2014, the General Council adopted the Protocol (WT/L/940) amending the WTO Agreement so as to legally include the Agreement on Trade Facilitation among the multilateral agreements on trade in under Annex 1A of the WTO Agreement.

4.   CONCLUSION

Ensuring food security is primarily a national responsibility, but it is increasingly becoming a shared endeavour. National governments implement the policies they deem necessary to ensure food security for their people, but they are expected to pay due attention to their international obligations. In the area of agriculture, government policy behaviour was subject to a minimal set of multilateral trade obligations until the conclusion of the Uruguay Round and entry into force of the AoA. The agreed multilateral trade rules and disciplines under the AoA are good examples of how international cooperation can address issues that may not be effectively handled at the national level. Food security is a key case in point. These rules are an outcome of the decision by sovereign States to exercise their sovereignty in a more effective manner, which provides the greatest scope for effecting food security outcomes both nationally and globally.

The wide range of factors influencing food security means that the international effort must be similarly inclusive. No one agency or policy set has all the answers. As discussed above, trade policies and multilateral disciplines have an important contribution to make, but this will be more effective if is part of a coherent and mutually supportive approach shared by all the relevant actors.

The 2008 food crisis led governments and the international community to devote more attention to food and agricultural systems and especially to look deeper into the root causes of such a crisis. Serious remedial efforts to address agricultural under-investment, implement social safety-net programmes and address agricultural productivity, are but a few important manifestations of such endeavours by national governments and intergovernmental organizations. Simultaneously, the topic of agriculture and food systems has attracted global attention, as evidenced by numerous on-going international collaborations. Cooperative undertakings such as the UN High Level Task Force on Food Security and the Agricultural Markets Information System are making a difference to the overall governance food security, both in terms of early warning systems and of coherent messaging and action.

The WTO's participation in various food security discussions has been and continues to be an active one, outlining, inter alia, the important contributory role of the multilateral trading system towards achieving agricultural development and food security goals. The objective of our participation is to facilitate an informed consideration of the contribution trade and trade rules make to food security and to enhance that contribution by working with other agencies and with national governments to improve global responsiveness to food security challenges.

2. Global value chains in the food sector

Julia Tijaja[1]

INTRODUCTION

The emergence of global value chains (GVCs) has gathered pace over the last two decades. The interconnected nature of these GVCs, which span multiple countries, regions and market actors, has implications in many policy areas, including trade, investment and development. However, detailed data on how these GVCs really operate remains limited, particularly for the agri-food sector.

The last few years have witnessed a growing number of case studies on the globally integrated value chains at the product and aggregate level[2] but research into these agri-food GVCs, particularly at the macro level, is still in its early stages. The challenges are numerous: reliable data is often not available at national level, nor easily compared across states, and in the case of some of the most globally integrated value chains, is proprietary to multinational companies.

This chapter will provide an overview of GVCs, with a particular focus on the agri-food sector. The data available paints a picture of increasing interconnectedness. The objective of the chapter is to provide an early snapshot from the emerging data and suggest how we should think about this picture. If much of food production is now increasingly integrated, the implications for policymakers seeking to implement lasting food security policies could be significant as a pure self-sufficiency model would have to be modified in light of the need for more collective and holistic action plans. Despite this, more extensive research will be required in order to better understand the implications of GVCs in the agri-food sector for food security.

---

[1] The views expressed in this chapter are solely the authors' responsibility and do not necessarily reflect those of any institution she was or is affiliated with.

[2] K. De Backer and S. Miroudot, 'Mapping Global Value Chains' (OECD Trade Policy Papers, No. 159, 2013).

GLOBAL VALUE CHAINS

GVCs are increasingly dominating trade, production and investment. Value chains are defined as the full range of activities that firms undertake to bring a product (goods or services) to its market, from conception to its final use and beyond and they are becoming increasingly global. In a world of GVCs, the dispersion and fragmentation of economic activities is enhanced, not only across firms, but also countries. Today, more than half of manufacturing imports are intermediate goods, while for services the share is even higher at 70 per cent. As a result, imported value added accounts for an increasing share of export value.[3] Globalization of production and consumption continues to proliferate, and the food sector is no exception. As food value chains become globalized, spanning more countries, crossing more borders, and involving more participants through different coordination mechanisms, the link between the food value chains and food security becomes increasingly complex.

Conventionally, the term 'food chain' is described as 'the various transformations a food commodity goes through from the point at which seed is planted by the farmer to the last stage when it is acquired by the final consumer'.[4] In practice however, the beginning and end of a 'food value chain' goes far beyond these production and consumption stages, to include the production and sourcing of various inputs such as fertilizers and seeds, and spans post-consumption activities such as waste management.

The GVC approach allows for an assessment of food sector activities beyond production, to include input sourcing; financing; processing; distribution (wholesale and retail); and waste management. It allows for deeper analysis of value chain participation and inter-actor dynamics, efficiency level and technological content, factor intensity, and returns to production factors, as well as the degree of competition and distribution of surplus/risks across production activities. The objective of using this approach is to better our understanding of the drivers and implications of the way in which food is produced, processed, distributed and consumed, as well as to more effectively assess their impact on food security.

Despite advances in agricultural technology and expansion in agricultural trade, the risk of food insecurity still looms as supply struggles to

---

[3] OECD, 'Interconnected economies: Benefiting from global value chains', (Synthesis Report, 2013) http://www.oecd.org/sti/ind/interconnected-economies-GVCs-synthesis.pdf.

[4] FAO, 'Implications of economic policy for food security: A training manual', (FAO, 1998).

match rising and rapidly changing demand. Supply capacity also continues to face manifold disruptions and constraints, man-made and otherwise. This takes place in the context of the industrialization of traditional food producing economies, reallocation of scarce resources away from food production, and growing demand for more resource-intensive food from the emerging middle class and urban population.

As incomes rise and markets globalize, the world population is estimated to shift from a largely grain- and vegetable-based diet to a more varied one with a growing proportion of meat, dairy, and animal protein in general – including fish. China's per capita meat consumption has doubled since 1992, and is expected to continue to increase as it currently stands at just half of the current US average.[5] Over the past 50 years, there had been a 1.5 fold increase in the global number of cattle, sheep and goats, and a 2.5 and 4.5 fold increase for pigs and chickens respectively. The strain on scarce resources will be enormous as an animal-based diet is up to ten times less efficient than a plant-based one in terms of calorific conversion.[6]

The developing world will continue to be a significant driver of the growth in food demand. At the same time, consumers in the developed world, as well as the emerging markets with their growing middle classes, are also becoming increasingly demanding in terms of health and safety, traceability, sustainability considerations along the food chain, as well as variety and cosmetic standards.[7] All these will require changes to the way food is currently produced, processed and distributed. At the same time natural and climatic disasters, volatility in energy prices and other external shocks will add to the challenges faced by global food chain (GFC) operators.

The chapter will continue with an overview of GFCs, before focusing on the three main types of GFCs, the staple crop food chains, the traditional export crop chains, and the non-traditional export crop chains. It follows with a discussion on the impact of globalization of food chains on food security, focusing on the key value chain activities of production, value addition and distribution. It then looks at a number of common trends before concluding.

---

[5] D. Pierson, 'China dumps grain policy to boost meat production', *Los Angeles Times* (18 February 2014): http://www.latimes.com/business/money/la-fi-mo-china-meat-20140218,0,5991417.story#axzz2u7mbjYk4.

[6] H. C. J. Godfray *et al* 'Food security: The challenge of feeding 9 billion people' [2010] *Science*, 327(56967): 812–18.

[7] Deloitte, *The Food Value Chains: A challenge for the next century* (Deloitte, 2013): https://www2.deloitte.com/content/dam/Deloitte/global/Documents/Consumer-Business/dttl_cb_Food%20Value%20Chain_Global%20POV.pdf.

GLOBAL FOOD CHAINS: AN OVERVIEW

Trade in food is not a new phenomenon, but what is new is the way GFC activities are currently organized. In the past, technological constraints resulted in high costs of transportation and food preservation, which in turn restricted cross-border agricultural trade to high-value, less perishable cash crops that could not be grown in a temperate climate. In general, cash crops were produced in the developing world for the developed world, as domestic demand was minimal. In return, cash crop producing economies imported industrial goods and, increasingly, food crops such as grains and cereals from their trading partners.

Within this general pattern there is significant variation. A useful typology of GFCs involves disaggregation into staple crop food chains, traditional export crop chains and non-traditional export crop chains. Governance patterns vary across these three GFC types. Gereffi defines governance as 'authority and power relationships that determine how financial, material and human resources are allocated and flow within a chain'.[8] Governance patterns include the level of State or private governance and the incidence of interlinking. Interlinking happens when market transactions go beyond the exchange of primary produce, to also include inputs, credits and extension services as part of the contract.[9] Swinnen et al. looked into the governance patterns of different types of GFCs and how they have evolved over time. In many cases, the authors found it positively related to productivity/efficiency and, for some, equity. The authors also found that the degree of market competition and the ease of contract enforcement, as well as product characteristics such as perishability and perceived impact on national security, influence the patterns of food chain governance.[10]

Market concentration is uneven along the GFC. For example, North America controls up to 80 per cent of global cereal exports, while cereals accounted for 40 per cent of developing countries food imports, a drastic change from when these economies were largely self-sufficient in cereals in the 1930s.[11] The intensity of trade between countries also varies across

---

[8] G. Gereffi, 'The organization of buyer-driven global commodity chains: How US retailers shape overseas production networks' in G. Gereffi and M. Korzeniewicz (eds), *Commodity Chains and Global Capitalism* (Praeger Publishers 1994) at p. 97.

[9] J. Swinnen, A. Vandeplas and M. Maertens, 'Governance and surplus distribution in commodity value chains in Africa', paper presented at the 106th seminar of the EAAE 'Pro-poor development in low-income countries: Food, agriculture, trade and the Environment', 25–27 October 2007: France.

[10] Ibid.

[11] FAO *supra* fn 3.

commodities and crops. The share of cereal production that is traded is relatively low at 12 per cent, varying from just 4 per cent for rice to 22 per cent for wheat. The share is much higher for traditional cash crops. For example, 99 per cent of global coffee production was traded.[12]

STAPLE CROP FOOD CHAINS

High volume and often at low-value, staple crop food chains are generally more localized, with the exception of the less-perishable cereals. Staple crop food chains have a direct impact on food security, not only for producers and those involved further downstream, but also for low-income urban workers and population in food-deficit areas. Their critical importance to national food security makes them more likely to come under greater State governance and heavier domestic political economy interference. Examples of such State interference are rife throughout Asia: China, for example, had in place a 95 per cent grain self-sufficiency policy, which was only very recently scrapped as it realized the need to boost its meat production to meet demand.[13] In Japan, the effective rate of protection for rice is as high as 700 per cent.[14]

Private sector actors involved in the staple food chains generally have limited capacity to innovate, poor access to credit and other resources, and limited storage capacity. As a result, private sector involvement tends to be in simple spot market transactions with no interlinking.[15] In some cases, governments remain an importance source of inputs, such as subsidized fertilizers, and extension services. Nevertheless, private sector involvement in staple crop food chains has considerably increased of late, particularly downstream of the value chains.

The perceived inability to add value to staple crops can now be challenged by product and market innovation. As income increases, people may demand less staple food in terms of quantity, but the demand for higher quality and variety will continue to increase, as well as for other premium characteristics such as vitamin-enriched and organic

---

[12] Ibid.

[13] See, inter alia, L. Hornby, 'China scythes grain self sufficiency policy' *Financial Times* (11 February 2014): http://www.ft.com/cms/s/0/6025b7c8-92ff-11e3-8ea7-00144feab7de. html#axzz2u7mvIWRP and D. Pierson, 'China dumps grain policy to boost meat production' *Los Angeles Times* (18 February 2014): http://www.latimes.com/business/money/la-fi-mo-china-meat-20140218,0,5991417.story#axzz2u7mbjYk4.

[14] While this tariff level may not appear to be economically rational, it has real implications even in industrialized advanced economies.

[15] Swinnen, Vandeplas and Maertens *supra* fn 8.

certification. Value addition may occur in many areas along the chain from research and development, through to the cultivation process and post-harvest treatment, and to distribution and marketing.

TRADITIONAL EXPORT CROP CHAINS

Traditional export crop chains have also undergone changes, with a strong shift towards private sector governance.[16] In the past, traditional export crops were often, and in some cases still are, treated as a revenue-generating sector, and hence commonly subjected to taxation. Post-harvest treatment, such as grading, storage and exportation is often undertaken by the State or other related authorities. Greater private sector involvement has since led to more interlinking of markets, more competition in the input and product markets and a subsequent improvement in innovation and productivity. It has also led to the shortening of the value chains, with fewer intermediaries and more direct and customized sales from producers to processors and from processors to wholesalers/ retailers. These, in many cases, have led to an increase in producers' prices. Traditional export crops indirectly affect food entitlements, as they are an important source of income for the agriculture community, and are often one of their few options to participate in the market economy with ready market access. The scale requirements often lead to consolidation of buying power; where there are few buyers, contracts become easier to enforce, giving rise to the incentive for interlinking. The benefits of inter-linking in the traditional export crop chains may also have spillover effects to the staple food chains.

Greater private sector governance in the traditional export crop chains has also led to increased product differentiation. Product differentiation has been facilitated by more sophisticated standardization and grading systems, and market innovation. While this implies greater scope for value addition, additional value does not always 'trickle down' to producers; and there is high variation across crops and markets.

There is a near universal striving towards greater domestic value addition the world over. Economies seek to do so, among others, by having more value chain activities done within their borders, from post-harvest treatment, other primary processing (grading, washing, fermenting and drying) to packaging. Domestic value can also be increased by creating and bringing consumer value attributes closer to the products' origin or

---

[16] Ibid.

production processes. This could be a timely strategy in light of growing requirement for product and process traceability, and is reflected in initiatives such as single origin coffee, geographical indicators, freedom food and the rainforest alliance. Less attention, however, has to be given to the input markets, with some exceptions, at least in the developing countries.

NON-TRADITIONAL EXPORT CROP CHAINS

Non-traditional export crop chains are a relatively new phenomenon made feasible by advancements in agriculture technology, transportation and logistics. These chains are almost entirely controlled by private companies with high interlinking. They are characterized by very short lead times, high standard specifications and traceability requirements, and complex coordination; an example of which is the fresh fruit and vegetables value chains. Interlinking is crucial in this type of value chain as production requires very specific inputs and processes to achieve international standards. Further, the high requirement for skills, equipment and knowledge means support and training of suppliers is often necessary both before and during production. Marketing and distribution channels for such complex value chains are often underdeveloped in the developing world, and domestic markets are unwilling to pay the high price for their products. These products are often highly perishable, rendering it difficult for suppliers to look for alternative buyers in time. Contract enforcement is hence less of an issue, as opportunistic behaviour is less likely.

Participation in non-traditional export crop value chains often yields satisfactory financial returns along the chain. However, gaining and maintaining participation in the first place is no easy task, particularly for smallholders. This is because there are economies of scale on a significant portion of value chain activities, such as standard certification. Further, the risks of compliance failure, including private standard compliance, may not be evenly distributed, with producers and primary processors often having to bear a disproportionate share of the costs. The highly demanding production process of high-quality food for advanced economies may be viewed with unease in the less developed part of the world, where having a sufficient quantity of basic food is more often the priority.

Despite significant variation between typologies it is possible to identify common emerging trends including the increasing importance of the private sector; the consequential impact of market forces and the drive towards standards (safety standards; private standards; etc.).

Further pre- and post-production activities warrant more attention as they often form a significant part of the value chain, and are at least as important as cultivation itself in terms of value addition. As the food production process spans borders, competition for inputs and markets will intensify, as will interdependencies between countries, firms and value chains. Pressures from consumer demand, the drive to maximize margins through product differentiation, and the advancement of biotechnology moves food production away from commodity production to niche markets. Closer integration between producers, processors and retailers is increasingly required to enable the production, processing and distribution of food following strict guidelines.

GLOBALIZATION OF FOOD CHAINS AND THEIR LINK TO FOOD SECURITY

While for most countries domestic food production is a key contributor to national food security, food security is not just a matter of food availability. The process of food production also provides cash income to farmers and farm labourers when a surplus is sold in the market. This will in turn provide them with better economic access to the food basket of their households (i.e. their food entitlements). This is the most common mechanism for achieving food security these days, where food self-sufficient households are the exception rather than the norm.

Prices relating to the operation of the food value chains, or any value chain for that matter, will influence resource allocation in the longer term. As price signals current comparative advantage, this may lead to increased specialization in food production, and consequently to commercialization and intensification of production as producers seek to benefit from economies of scale. Allocation of resources may be altered between crops as well as between agriculture and other sectors. Production margins will influence farmers' decisions on what and how much to plant. As farming households have become more integrated to the market, their household food entitlements have become less dependent on direct consumption of own produce and more on the income earned from selling of crops. Food entitlements therefore very much depend on the retail price of food as well as the level of their disposable income. This means that to effectively promote food security, the focus of policy must go beyond food production to a broader approach that covers the entire food value chains, as well as horizontal issues such as market competition, infrastructure and job-creating growth.[17]

---

[17] FAO *supra* fn 3.

At the aggregate level, globalization of food value chains has the potential to reduce the risk of food insecurity by balancing the effect of any regional or local shocks through trade. Better access to larger markets, capital, technology and resources will also increase global efficiency. Countries engaged in GFCs are likely to have better infrastructure, which lowers transportation costs and consequently food prices. Food production will be enhanced through regional specialization where production is focused on locally most appropriate food, although concerns also arise over greenhouse gas emission from the intensification and scaling up that accompanies specialized production, as well as transportation of food. The debate is ongoing.

Yet the globalization process also entails risks, particularly for individual participants: higher returns from external markets may not be evenly distributed along the value chains; hence producers may not gain their fair share. International markets are not necessarily more stable than domestic markets. Producers with a high degree of specialization may not be agile enough to switch crops or activities in the face of commodity shocks. Some grain producers, for example, will have their working capital tied to their crops for 18 months before they can reap the benefits from harvesting. This requires them to internalize the risks of price, exchange rates and interest rates movements.[18] For crops where traded stocks are thin, even a small movement in supply or demand may result in significant price volatility. Increased interdependencies between economies also mean that any volatility in input costs or selling prices will be propagated along the chains.[19]

Another form of risks faced by GFC operators are policy risks. As food value chains span countries, their interface with different policy regimes will be heightened. While in general tariff levels have been in decline the world over, global agriculture trade remains highly distorted. It could be argued that this is partly done in pursuant of public policy objectives, but it also means less transparency and certainty in global food trade with adverse implications for costs. Further, even as tariffs fall, non-tariff barriers have been on the rise. All these add to the costs along the food chain with consequent impact on food security.

Analyzing the impact of globalization of food chains on food security requires considerations of other dimensions, which will be discussed more extensively in other chapters in this volume. Like international trade, impact analysis of these phenomena needs further disaggregation to meaningfully assess their implications.

---

[18] Deloitte *supra* fn 6.
[19] Godfray *et al supra* fn 5.

The next sections look into the three key value chain activities: production, value addition and distribution. While this does not exhaust the range of activities along global food chains, it aims to analyze how globalization of food chains play out in these main activities.

PRODUCTION

The availability of food for human consumption in any locality is determined by a number of factors, including returns from food crop production vis-à-vis other crops, export price vis-à-vis domestic price, any price distortions including taxes or subsidies, and sustainability of the value chain; that is the ability of the chain to produce reasonable return on labour and capital in different stages of the process.[20]

GFCs would allow the available capital to be allocated in most efficient places for food production. Efficiency of production is crucial in the face of resource scarcity and the same goes for pre- and post-production efficiency. Production level will also depend on the incentive regime. Price incentives in agriculture have not always been left free to market mechanism. Distortions may be introduced externally such as by protection in the external markets, or internally such as by bad policies. They prevent price smoothing and correct signalling; locating production in the wrong place and reducing supply capacity in the long term.

GFCs could help close the 'yield gap', defined as 'the difference between realized productivity and the best that can be achieved using current genetic material and the available technologies and management'.[21] As access to input and product markets is broadened, farmers would have better access to hard and soft inputs from fertilizers and crop varieties to management skills and market information. However, farmers may still underinvest in productivity improvement if returns to production factors are too low, either due to distorted incentive regimes, or underdeveloped or costly post-harvest solutions such as storage or infrastructure to markets.[22] From the policy perspectives the challenge will be to balance the appropriate incentive regimes.

Ensuring market competitiveness may be a challenge as increasing return to scale in farming often leads to market power concentration. Farming can be a capital-intensive business, and independent operators often struggle with achieving the required economies of scale. Competitiveness

---

[20] FAO *supra* fn 3.
[21] Godfray *et al supra* fn 5.
[22] Ibid.

and efficiency along other parts of the value chains are also crucial. A good harvest will be wasted if there is poor access to markets, leading to weak bargaining power on the part of the farmers and quality deterioration of the crops. Marketing channels are also more difficult to access for smaller producers.[23]

More attention is warranted on the input markets as farm-level external inputs, along with labour, often form a high share of the value chain costs. The share is as high as one-third in India and Bangladesh rice value chains.[24] Hired farm labour also forms an increasingly high share of total costs, as urbanization and the development of non-farm labour options in rural areas add to the pressure on farm labour availability. This calls for technological upgrading and, in appropriate cases, mechanization of certain farm activities so that farm labour can be freed for more productive activities, increasing their earnings hence food entitlements. There is room to improve efficiency and competitiveness in the input markets, from how they are delivered to how better to target subsidies to achieve optimum results. In fact, addressing imperfections in input markets should be made a priority, including developing and enhancing rural credit schemes, rural transportation infrastructure, and so on.[25]

Waste management is another prevalent issue along the food chains, and production and primary processing stage is no exception. Waste level is higher at the production stage in the developing world. GFCs can help by bringing in better technology; however imported technology and research should be customized to better fit the local economic, environment and social needs. Waste at the production stage can also be found in the developed world, though this is more often due to incentives rather than infrastructure.

VALUE ADDITION

Value addition occurs along the GFCs. This section focuses on value addition during and after production, which includes processing, packaging and branding. In GFCs, value-adding activities could take place in locations other than where food is produced and consumed.

Different ways of value addition will result in different distribution of

---

[23] Deloitte *supra* fn 6.

[24] T. Reardon, B. Minten, K. Chen and L. Adriano, 'The transformation of rice value chains in Bangladesh and India: Implications for food security', (ADB Economics Working Paper Series No. 375, 2013).

[25] Swinnen, Vandeplas and Maertens *supra* fn 8.

returns among value chain participants. When value addition is located close to cultivation, or where a premium is placed based on specific characteristics of the crops or ways of cultivating the crops, there is a higher likelihood that surplus would be closer to the producers. Where surplus can be captured by producers, this would provide them with the right incentives to undertake product and process upgrading.

Value addition is also done post-production, for example through primary processing such as cleaning, washing, grading, sorting, packing and transporting. In fact, a significant share of value in the value chain comes from the post-harvest segment. In the rice value chains in India and Bangladesh, the share is as high as 40 per cent. Therefore these segments are as important as the farm sector in forming food price and in its impact on food security. An efficient post-harvest segment will reduce wastage, prolong product shelf life, and add to job creation and linkages to the domestic economy. It has the potential to increase food entitlements for those inside and outside the food production segment. Yet, its productivity and development has not received sufficient attention.[26]

Distribution of margins from value addition, however, depends on the governance of value chains. Often value capture is highest post-production in processing technology, branding, and retail or marketing; activities controlled by the relatively powerful market actors. Unless surplus is passed on to producers in the form of higher purchasing price, or to consumers in the form of lower retail prices, the link to improvement in food security is likely to be weak.

DISTRIBUTION

From the consumer perspective and for food-deficit countries and households, GFCs allow them to rely on the global market to improve their food security. GFCs allow the fulfilment of food demand in locations where production is not feasible. It also enables economic actors to reduce the risks of domestic shocks. Advancement in information technology and better market intelligence, as well as improvements in transportation and logistics have all contributed to the more efficient distribution of food. On the other hand, GFCs may lead to a reduction in the domestic availability of food should there be arbitrage between international and domestic prices. In theory, the higher income earned from food or non-food exports can then be used to purchase food from the international

---

[26] Reardon, Minten, Chen and Adriano *supra* fn 23.

markets. However, manifold factors come into play in practice, and one might be faced with the ironic situation where hunger, undernourishment and under-nutrition can be found side-by-side with food production for export.

Another implication of GFCs is the proliferation of retail channels and formats, and the move away from commodity-based marketing to one that is more consumer-driven. One specific retail format that has been gaining popularity in more mature markets is convenience over price, where consumers' food shopping behaviour have shifted from pantry-loading visits to ready-meal visits. Unfortunately convenience costs, may not be the best way to address food insecurity. One often-overlooked area is consumer education. Where income, hence food entitlement, is limited, consumers may be unaware of the costs of inefficiently spending their scarce resources on low-nutrition, high-additive, high-fat and sugar-processed food. The problem is exacerbated in the developed world where food retailing is increasingly controlled by corporate giants and fresh food grocers lose out to competition. This is also increasingly a growing problem in the developing world, as dispensable incomes rise and consumers seek to emulate the tastes of those in the developed world.

COMMON TRENDS IN GFCs

Even though as already noted, research into agri-food GVCs is limited, it is possible to identify common trends that are likely to have an impact on food security policies and which on this basis merit both further research and greater attention from policymakers.

Multi-actor and Multi-country Production

As the production process becomes increasingly fragmented, GFCs involve the participation of multiple economic actors across multiple countries. The production process is further complicated by the relationships among value chain participants and discrepancies in policy regimes in different locations of the value chain activities.

When multiple economic actors are involved, contract enforcement becomes a key issue. In an environment of weak enforcement capacity, parties may settle for suboptimal contract terms leading to lower efficiency in the longer term. Parties may also be less willing to invest to improve the overall productivity of the value chain for fear of opportunistic behaviour by others reducing the returns to their investment.

In GVCs (and GFCs), parts and components pass through different countries before they are assembled into final products. The impact of cross-border measures on total costs and hence overall competitiveness of the value chains is thus amplified. Such measures include both tariffs and non tariffs.

The general trend of falling tariffs may not be observed uniformly across crops. Further agriculture trade remains among the most distorted sector, and is often carved out from multilateral and preferential commitments. Tariff peaks and escalations also feature more prominently in agriculture trade.

In addition to tariffs, non-tariff measures also affect the GFC process. With the globalization of food chains, the risks of contamination along the supply chain rises[27] and sanitary and phytosanitary (SPS) measures will play a more prominent role. Consumers are no longer solely concerned about basic food safety issues such as bacteria contamination, animal diseases and poor handling of food, but also with what happens during the production process including farming practices, the use of antibiotics and growth hormones, additives and preservatives. Greater efforts are needed for harmonization and mutual recognition of measures to better facilitate cross-border trade. The same is true with customs procedures, where clearance delays would have disastrous consequences for trade in perishable crops or food products.

One non-tariff measure worth highlighting is standards. The use of standards has become more prevalent with globalization of food value chains. Aside from the public policy objective to protect public health and safety, standards also act as a coordination tool in the food value chain process by serving as a common language between buyers and suppliers on the quality specifications of the products. In this way, standards help address information asymmetry. Standards may also be used by suppliers to signal the quality of their products to buyers and consumers.[28] Standards compliance capacity is increasingly demanded from suppliers who seek to participate in the GFCs.

The lengthening of the food value chains also increases the points of vulnerability along the chains to changes in market conditions, which could be policy driven. Changes may affect the input markets from fertilizers and seeds to labour and energy; or the output markets such as subsidies or export restrictions.

---

[27] Deloitte *supra* fn 6.
[28] J. Tijaja, 'Standards in global value chains: Rationales, role and implications,' (FGI Working Paper, 2013): http://www.fungglobalinstitute.org/sites/default/files/u1913/WP_Standards_0.pdf.

Intensified Competition

Globalized food production means greater competition for inputs: from land to water, between crop choices, and crop uses. Food production is a resource-intensive activity; water and energy – both scarce resources – are in heavy demand in its production and distribution.[29] The limits to the environment mean that food producers also face pressures to curb the many negative effects of food production on the environment.[30]

As food production is very water intensive, trade in food is essentially an indirect trade in water. Water is not a very mobile resource, and moving it requires enormous effort and cost. Moving food production or stages of food production to where water is located is thus a more common practice. Modernization of agriculture also intensifies energy use in the sector. Carbon-based fuel is used not only for production at the farm gate, but also for the processing of food, and the distribution of raw and processed food.[31] There is, however, now an increase in the move to more sustainable energy sources, including the use of waste from agriculture activities (biomass).

Agriculture expansion faces the challenge of competition for land from other human activities. Agricultural land that was formerly productive has been lost to urbanization and other human uses, and also to desertification, salinization, soil erosion and other unsustainable land management practices;[32] food has to be produced on the same amount or even less land. Adding to the pressure on land availability is the cultivation of first-generation biofuel on fertile lands. Any significant expansion of agricultural land is unlikely and costly, and any increase in production is more likely to result from an increase in productivity. Fortunately land expansion is not the only way to increase production. In the last decade grain production has doubled, while agriculture land only expanded by 9 per cent.

Even after production, competition between crop uses is becoming more intense. Populations in emerging economies experience an increase in their spending power that alters their food preferences; the rise of the middle class and growing urbanization all lead to a greater demand for meat, dairy and aquaculture products, and consequently for feed. There is evidence that GFCs are increasingly ending in these markets where the shifts are most significant. As a result food crop production is increasingly

---

[29] Deloitte *supra* fn 6.
[30] Godfray *et al supra* fn 5.
[31] Deloitte *supra* fn 6.
[32] Godfray *et al supra* fn. 5.

utilized as feed. In 2011, China used approximately 70 per cent of its total domestic corn production for feed, 20 per cent for industrial use and only 5 per cent for food. The total global trade in corn is much less than China's entire corn feed demand.[33] Food crops might also be demanded by other value chains such as biofuels and industries. This has given rise to the food, feed or fuel debate.

Managing Waste

The greatest irony in GFCs is that concerns over inability to meet growing food demand sit side-by-side with concerns over the high wastage level of food. The level has been quoted from 10 to 40 per cent of production to as high as 50 per cent.

There has been extensive research on the different levels of wastage in developed and developing countries, with a general pattern that a significant level of wastage occurs at the production stage in developing countries and at the consumption stage in developed countries. Total losses in the value chain in the developed world are estimated between 40–50 per cent, and 30–50 per cent in the developing world.[34]

In developing countries food waste mainly occurs at production stage, due to primitive farming and harvesting methods, and the lack of infrastructure – including storage, technology, transportation, knowledge and managerial skills. In India 35–40 per cent of fresh produce is lost because neither wholesale nor retail outlets have cold storage.[35] Meanwhile 45 per cent of rice in China and up to 80 per cent in Vietnam is lost at the production stage. Waste at the production stage, however, is not exclusive to the developing countries; in the UK 30 per cent of vegetable crops are not harvested because there is an unfavourable price for them.

In developed countries, food waste mostly takes place post-consumer (i.e. after purchase by consumers). In the US 14–26 per cent of food purchased goes to waste, while one-quarter of the food purchased in the UK is thrown away, most of which is still fit for human consumption.[36] Post-consumer waste happens because in these economies food expenditure is relatively low compared to disposable income, while consumers have exceptionally high expectations of the appearance of food and

---

[33] S. Sharma, 'The need for feed: China's demand for industrialized meat and its impacts', (Institute for Agriculture and Trade Policy Report, 2014): http://www.iatp.org/files/2014_02_17_FeedReport_f.pdf.

[34] Deloitte *supra* fn. 6.

[35] Godfray *et al. supra* fn. 5.

[36] Ibid.

there is an increasing disconnect between people and food production.[37] Retailers often discard or reject edible products with only slight blemishes. Consumers often discard food because they have bought too much, have bought inappropriate portions or because of suboptimal expiration labelling policy (the use of 'use by' as opposed to 'best before'). The latter is exacerbated where a fear of litigation and the lack of education on food safety leads to food still edible being thrown away.[38] As waste occurs along the value chains, attention should also be given to the processing state; the total processing waste stands at more than 30 per cent – this calls for an improvement in supply chain capability and efficiency.[39]

The alarming situation on food waste gives rise to a number of policy implications. First, more effort is needed to improve post-harvest treatment, which is often neglected when the focus is on closing the yield gap. Developing countries the world over require large-scale investment in agriculture, including infrastructure, storage, transportation and distribution, knowledge development and dissemination. To prevent post-harvest loss, small-scale storage technology suitable for use in a poorer context needs to be developed. Public incentives may be required for these innovations to be realized. For developed countries, changes are needed at the retail front, including food processors, retailers and consumers.[40] In the future, climate and resource limitations are likely to push the value of food up. This will discourage food waste, and lead to higher investment in more efficient food supply processes. Industrialized food supply chains will also be likely to respond by increasing efficiency through shared logistics to achieve economies of scale and a better demand forecasting or retail strategy.

Increased Vertical Coordination

Globalization of food chains changes the nature of governance, defined as 'the means by which products move through the value chains from producers to consumers'.[41] An increase in vertical coordination has been observed.

The trend towards increased vertical coordination has been driven by a

[37] J. Parfitt, M. Barthel and S. Machaughton, Food waste within food supply chains, [2010] *Philosophical Transactions of the Royal Society*, 365: 3065–81.

[38] Godfray *et al supra* fn. 5.

[39] Deloitte *supra* fn. 6.

[40] See Parfitt, Barthel and Machaughton *supra* fn. 36 and Godfray *et al. supra* fn. 5.

[41] L. M. Young and J. E. Hobbs, 'Vertical linkages in agri-food supply chains: Changing roles for producers, commodity groups and government policy', (2002) *Review of Agricultural Economics*, 24(2): 428–41.

number of factors. Changing consumer preferences for more differentiated products and a greater preference for traceability call for closer coordination along production activities, as do environmental pressures for more responsible products and production processes. Advances in biotechnology also contribute to the trend as production involves specific inputs and more sophisticated processes, giving rise to the need to preserve product identity to capture the premium over intangible characteristics. From the supply perspective, a major impulse propagating vertical coordination arises from food safety and reputation concerns. Big multinational brands have a lot at stake if anything goes wrong in their value chains, hence the increasing preference for them to control, or even own, as much as possible of their value chains. This trend increases the relative searching and monitoring costs related to spot market transactions compared to that of coordinated production, and has been facilitated by developments in information technology and standards.

Increased vertical coordination is observed as the spot market declines, and production and marketing contracts, alliances, joint ventures and full vertical integration become more prevalent. In close vertical coordination the importance of supply chain relationships are also heightened.[42] The rise in contracting has a number of implications. First, is the decline in the relevance of spot market price, particularly for differentiated commodities and products with thin supply. Second, it may also lead to more restricted access to the global market for certain economic actors due to the requirement for skills, equipment and capital. Third, it leads to consolidation of power at the supply level as processors seek to deal with bigger suppliers in order to keep transaction costs low. Fourth, it increases the importance of contract negotiations and enforcement – which will be discussed later. Fifth, is the inevitable need for effective dispute settlement mechanisms when more than one party is involved in the value chain process.

In vertically coordinated value chains, the relationship between suppliers, processors and buyers is governed by contract. Distribution of gains and risks along the chain depends on how the contract is drafted and applied. Contract transparency, completeness, negotiation processes and verification mechanisms for compliance, all play important roles. Large contractors might use their market power to suppress input prices or get disadvantageous contract terms agreed to by the suppliers. As a response, there has been an observed rise of commodity groups or collective bargaining among producers, which aims to mitigate the risk of abuse

---

[42] Ibid.

by facilitating the development of standardized industry practices. Such initiatives may also stimulate buy-in from other producers, which would in turn reduce the costs of allocating suppliers.[43]

Increased vertical coordination helps facilitate product differentiation. Coordinated production allows for more specific processes, quality measurement and verification, which lead to differentiated products beyond simple grading and sorting. Governments can support this through measures that reduce quality measurement costs, such as providing support to research and development for such technology, and ensuring competitiveness in the conformity assessment markets.

In such value chain governance, the importance of inter-actor relationships is highlighted. Sophisticated production processes often require the education of suppliers to acquire the demanded level of skills and technology. However, when a patron-client relationship is established, it raises a new risk of abuse of market power. More assessment, therefore, is also needed on the impact of the growing disappearance of independent farm producers on prices and product availability for consumers.

Growing Concentration

Globalization of the food industry has led to greater consolidation in the processing community across sub sectors in the industry, particularly in the past 30 years. The food processing industry has recently observed global mergers and acquisitions, as large multinational corporations aim to achieve economies of scale, and find new avenues of growth.[44] The same trend, however, has not been observed – at least to the same extent – at the production level. Aside from some large-scale farmers, food production is still mostly undertaken by small farming business. Enterprises involved in food production are of relatively small scale when compared to farm input suppliers (seeds, fertilizers, machinery). As a result, farmers are at risk of being squeezed from both ends of input supplies and product markets.

For example, coffee is produced by 25 million producers throughout the world and consumed by 500 million consumers, but with four roasters controlling 45 per cent of production, and four traders controlling 40 per cent of production. Three companies control 80 per cent of trade in tea, while four hold a 40 per cent stake in cocoa trading. From a national perspective, Brazil has 200,000 soya bean farmers competing to sell to just

---

[43] Ibid.
[44] Deloitte *supra* fn. 6.

five commodity traders, while three-quarters of the UK grocery market is controlled by four retailers.[45]

Dominant buyer power may be abused to extract more surpluses from suppliers or consumers. Buyers may pass on only a disproportionate share of any market price increase to suppliers, while suppliers have to bear more than their fair share of any fall in price. When the producer price is suppressed, the incentive to invest and innovate to improve agricultural productivity and upgrading will be removed. For consumers, this may mean a reduction in quality or choices of products, and receiving less than their fair share in any production price reduction. An effective competition infrastructure can help reduce such risk; but a competition policy that is focused only on consumer protection, as it commonly is, may not be able to address anti-competitive behaviour outside the State (the anti-competitive behaviour of a foreign buyer towards domestic suppliers); this could be a problem as food value chains become more globalized. The abuse of the buyers' position to suppress producer price will affect the long-term availability of food supply.

PARTICIPATING IN GLOBAL FOOD CHAINS: POLICY CONSIDERATIONS FOR FOOD SECURITY AND COMPARATIVE ADVANTAGE

In the face of a world of GFCs, policymakers need to recalibrate their way of thinking on matters often perceived to be strictly in the welfare/social domain e.g. food security, as well as new opportunities and challenge vis-à-vis their current comparative advantages.

Food self-sufficiency is not a feasible means to achieving food security for every economy (or every household for that matter). Qatar and Bahrain, for example, import as much as 90 per cent of their food.[46] A similar situation can be found in city States like Singapore and Hong Kong. The economic and technical feasibility of food crop cultivation or farming depends on a number of factors, some of which are given. In this regard, international trade and the development of GFCs can improve food security either by balancing out any domestic shocks or by addressing local food deficit through imports.

---

[45] O. De Schutter, 'Addressing concentration in food supply chains: The role of competition law in tackling the abuse of buyer power', (Briefing Note 03-UN Special Rapporteur on the Right to Food, 2010).

[46] 'Food security in the Gulf: How to keep stomachs full' *The Economist*, 22–28 February, at p.41.

Second, food security depends not only on food production, but also on a range of other food chain activities including processing, storage, transportation, distribution and access (physical, social and economic). Different inputs, direct and indirect, are involved in the process, some of which are limited or increasingly scarce, including water, arable land, energy and environmental limitations, and not evenly distributed among economies. The formation of GFCs help address the problem of uneven distribution of resources through the reallocation of production activities to the most efficient locations.

A further question in this debate is whether the specialization of food production based on comparative advantage actually works. Specialization in agriculture has the benefits of improving producers' income and reducing consumer price, hence contributing to the food security of producers and non-producers. Even when farmers are engaged in cash crop production, the income earned can be used to improve their access to staple and other food. At the same time, however, there have been studies and evidence of the downside of monoculture and the benefit of diversification to spread risks.[47]

To an extent comparative advantage in crop production will depend on given advantages such as climate and soil situation. However, it also depends on decades of investment and research, and thus is dynamic. An economy without current comparative advantage in growing its own food may have the option to increase cash crop production in exchange for manufactured inputs and food crops, but this does not exclude the option of trying to improve its food production capacity over the longer term.

CONCLUSION

Globalization of production and consumption has had profound effects on the food sector. As food value chains become globalized, a deeper assessment on how this affects different value chain activities will contribute to a better understanding of the impact on food security.

The increasing prevalence of GFCs raises a number of issues that deserve further consideration. The involvement of multiple actors and multiple countries in food production requires greater awareness from the policymakers of how the impact of policy design and administration is propagated along the value chains. It also highlights the importance of

---

[47] T. Wise, 'Malawi's paradox: Filled with both corns and hunger', *The Global Post*, (25 February 2014): http://us5.campaign-archive2.com/?u=74907371d448da77287940e4d &id=a93bce4d15&e=743b2d0b54.

well-functioning competition and contract enforcement infrastructure for value chain efficiency.

Also highlighted in this chapter are the changing dynamics of relationships among value chain participants. As food value chains become globalized, value chain governance has continued to shift to increased vertical coordination, which changes the dynamics in the relationship from the spot market transactions of the past. The consolidation of market power in certain parts of GFCs also warrants more attention. All these factors have real implications for the distribution of surpluses and of risks, and consequently on food entitlements.

Addressing food security issues in a GFC context requires a holistic and collaborative approach to policy. The focus needs to go beyond increasing food production to covering the whole length of the value chains. Consideration should also be given to issues beyond the food sector such as infrastructure, competition, contract enforcement and energy policy, which are just some of the factors that have direct and indirect implications for food security.

3. Food security initiatives in Asia and the impact of WTO Regulation

Roehlano M. Briones

INTRODUCTION

In many developing countries, 'food security' policies are typically associated with public sector action based on the exercise of State sovereignty: there is an emphasis on direct command by the State over markets, and 'food sovereignty' over reliance on international trade, particularly for sensitive commodities. In Southeast Asia, this contrasts with the push for an ASEAN single market and production base, as described in the ASEAN Economic Community Blueprint. Most countries in Asia have furthermore already acceded to the WTO.

Food reserves, both private and public, command a renewed level of attention in today's era of pricing volatility. In addition to various national initiatives, ASEAN, together with the Plus Three countries, namely China, Japan, and Republic of Korea, have recently established a regional emergency rice reserve. This chapter provides an overview of current practice of public stockholding in the case of Southeast Asian countries and explores association of food security with market-distorting schemes. It then goes on to examine the countervailing forces for trade liberalization and their likely impact by focusing on their effect on food security policies in the Philippines.

APPROACHES TO PUBLIC STOCKS IN SELECTED SOUTHEAST ASIAN COUNTRIES

The structure of the rice market varies greatly across ASEAN. By way of illustrative example, the markets in the two largest ASEAN exporters, Thailand and Vietnam, contrast sharply.

Thailand's rice exports are mostly carried out by the private sector, with the top 25 companies accounting for 90 per cent of these.[1] In contrast, in Vietnam the government maintains a highly interventionist stance. Only 10 per cent of exports are from the private sector; the remaining 90 per cent are contributed by public sector companies, the most prominent being VINAFOOD1 (exports from northern Vietnam) and VINAFOOD2 (exports from southern Vietnam). The latter accounts for half of the country's rice exports and is responsible for most public procurement of rice. Exports are tightly regulated through the Vietnam Food Association (VFA), a government-controlled body, primarily to deflect rice supplies from the foreign to the domestic market. The VFA sets a discretionary minimum export price, which discourages private traders owing to its unpredictability. All export contracts need to be registered with VFA, hence the simple expedient of not recognizing these contracts can prohibit exportation. This transpired in early 2008 when Vietnam stopped private rice exports; in the meantime, VINAFOODS2 continued to export under government-to-government arrangement (with the Philippines), effectively turning it into a trade monopoly.[2]

It is within this highly differentiated context that the national stockholding schemes described below coexist.

Thailand

Historically, Thailand has not kept a food security reserve for rice, citing its status as a surplus country. Since the 1970s, the government has been implementing a price-hedging scheme under a paddy-pledging programme. Farmers took out a loan, pledging their harvest as collateral; the loan could be settled at the government price, which was normally on par with the market price. But if the market price turned out to be higher, the farmer could then sell to the market and settle the loan on favourable terms.

In 2011, the newly elected government under the Pheu Thai Party (PTP) raised the settlement price to about $500 per ton of paddy, about $770 per ton of milled equivalent. This was far above the prevailing Free on Board (FOB) prices, even disregarding processing and marketing costs. The pledging programme was transformed into an expensive produce price support scheme.

Naturally, public stockholding was deployed in service of this scheme. Government stockpiles ballooned, reaching 16.7 million tons in milled

---

[1] Hamid R. Alavi, Aira Htenas, Ron Kopicki, Andrew W. Shepherd, and Ramon Clarete, *Trusting Trade and the Private Sector for Food Security in Southeast Asia* (World Bank 2012).

[2] Ibid.

equivalent by the end of 2013, compared to 7.2 million tons at the end of 2011, the start of the new pledging scheme. The programme was successful in raising the paddy price; however Thai rice exports have fallen, with the country now ceding the top position to India.[3] The programme has furthermore imposed an enormous fiscal burden on the country; from 2011 to 2014, government spent THB 680 billion, purchasing 44 million tons of paddy, but managing to sell only THB 200 billion.[4]

The programme has been roundly criticized for its cost, distortionary effect on the rice market, and vulnerability to corruption, although it was defended at the time as being important for food security.

The PTP and its key officials were removed from power in early 2014; followed by military rule. The military government discontinued the paddy pledging scheme on April 2014 due to lack of funding. It has not announced officially its own programme for supporting rice production, focusing rather on paying the current arrears to farmers under the defunct programme.

Indonesia

In contrast to Thailand, Indonesia has formulated an explicit State policy on food reserves based on national law. The Food Law of 2012 enacts a system of public food reserves, based on a hierarchy from a government food reserve, down to provincial, regency/city, and to village food reserves. The Law furthermore mandates food self-sufficiency, (i.e., ensuring domestic production and reserves are adequate to meet food demand). Imports are prohibited except when necessary in case of a shortfall of domestic production and reserves.

Unfortunately self-sufficiency provisions in Indonesia (and similar regulations in other countries) suffer from vagueness; when domestic supplies are low (relatively say to past harvest or to trend growth), the domestic demand can be fitted to that supply simply by making domestic price sufficiently high. The Food Law does provide for food affordability, but assumes that imports can be eliminated without compromising it; presumably this can be achieved by promoting domestic production and reserves.

In fact, the Perum BULOG – a state trading enterprise – stockpiled two million tons of rice by the end of 2013, following government

---

[3] FAO, *Rice Market Monitor November 2013*, (vol. XVI No. 4. 2013).
[4] Phusadee Arunmas, 'Seeking a grain of truth', *Bangkok Post* (3 January 2014): http://www.bangkokpost.com/business/news/387566/seeking-a-grain-of-truth.

instruction.[5] Total stocks in the country are estimated at 6.5 million, up from 3.6 million tons for the period 2008–10. Clearly this is to ensure that the country need not resort to imports in the event of a domestic production shortfall.

Meanwhile on the production side, since 2002 the government has been implementing a massive fertilizer subsidy scheme.[6]

Malaysia

The food security argument in favour of stockholding does not necessitate public ownership of stocks; the desired level can be reached by some incentive or regulation scheme (or both) on private stocks.

Malaysia is an example of deployment of private stocks, in this case owned by BERNAS, for national food security. The company is under contract with the government to maintain a national rice stockpile, currently at 292,000 tons, up from 92,000 tons before 2008. The contract confers exclusive import rights to BERNAS, effectively making it a monopoly (although the right can be assigned by BERNAS to other traders). BERNAS views the national rice stockpile not only as a guarantor of food security but also a method of price stabilization. Such treatment of the stockpile is understandable in the context of the overall distortion caused by the import monopoly and producer support schemes of the national government. One may therefore regard the Malaysian policy, despite private sector participation, as falling well within the traditional mould of buffer stocking.

Singapore

In contrast to Malaysia, Singapore exemplifies the case of full private sector engagement for the food security requirement of the State. Such engagement is enforced by a minimalist regime of market regulation. Singapore imports all its rice requirement; by law, the government implements a rice stockpile scheme, which compels importers to store two months' worth of imports in a private warehouse designated by the government. The importers continue to own the stocks; however the

---

[5] USDA FAS 2013, 'Indonesia grain and feed Annual Report 2013'. GAIN Report No. ID 1318.

[6] By 2009 the subsidy reached IRP 16.3 trillion (approx. $1.63 billion); in 2012 the subsidy was adjusted downward to hold down costs, but was still at IRP 13.9 trillion, compared to the IRP 19.5 trillion of the budget of the Ministry of Agriculture World Trade Organization, 2013. Indonesia Trade Policy Review, WTO, Geneva.

government can acquire the stocks subject to compensation. Importers are also responsible for rotating stocks; any batch of stock may be stored for a maximum of one year.[7]

Philippines

Among the Southeast Asian countries, the Philippines presents a timely case of the effectiveness of public stockholding for price stabilization. In mid-2013, the retail price of regular milled rice jumped by 13 per cent over a span of four months, catching many consumers by surprise, especially since rice prices had remained stable over the previous two years. As the rice price hike made headlines, the Senate Committee on Food and Agriculture called a series of hearings on, among other things, the true supply situation for rice in the country.[8] The Secretary of the Department of Agriculture (DA) blamed the spike on an 'artificial shortage' caused by some unscrupulous traders or possibly even smugglers.[9] Likewise a nationwide farmer's organization has blamed the machinations of a nefarious cartel.[10]

Empirically however collusion in the rice market has been difficult to establish; all the available evidence points rather to a competitive rice market along the supply chain.[11] The answer proposed here is that the mid-2013 price hike was due to the government clampdown on imports, not matched by either increased domestic production, nor accelerated releases from the buffer stock.

The distortionary regime (based on import restrictions and delayed response from the buffer stock) is supportive of domestic farmers; however for consumers the adverse effect is amplified with ever-tightening restrictions.

Regional Cooperation

The ASEAN Plus Three Emergency Rice Reserve (APTERR) is a system of earmarked and stockpiled emergency rice reserves. Earmarking is

---

[7] R. Briones, 'Complementing regional rice reserves with novel domestic reserve mechanisms', Technical Assistance Consultant's Report (ADB 2013).

[8] The author testified as a resource person at the hearing held on 24 February 2014 on the very subject matter of this section.

[9] 'DA building cases vs rice smugglers, hoarders', says Alcala', *Philippine Daily Inquirer* (9 September 2013).

[10] 'Rice price hike blamed on cartels', *The Philippine Star* (1 September 2013).

[11] R. Briones and B. de la Pena, 'Diagnostic country report: Food staples sector' Report submitted to CUTS Jaipur, India. (Philippine Institute for Development Studies 2014).

understood to be a permanent commitment, (i.e., a country that releases its earmarked stocks is obligated to replenish it). Earmarked stocks are owned or controlled by a member country government, but are pledged to be available for use during an emergency in another member country. A demanding country (i.e., the country in an emergency) may avail itself of earmarked rice based on market price (under a pre-arranged forward contract); it can also avail itself on concessional terms, or even as a grant.

In 2012 the APTERR Agreement came into force; in 2013, APTERR was launched formally during the first Council Meeting, which adopted the rules and procedures for establishment and release of APTERR stocks, as well as other internal administrative procedures. The host country of the APTERR Secretariat is Thailand, housed in the facilities of the Office of Agricultural Economics, under the Ministry of Agriculture and Cooperatives. Financing, negotiated under the APTERR Agreement, is provided by the 13 member countries.

Under this new approach, public stocks are held as emergency reserves. Releases from public stocks can be triggered by a severe supply contraction and/or price increase. Price stabilization is not a goal of emergency reserves, although sizeable and well-timed releases may exert a calming effect on markets and thereby stave off even worse price increases.

Such a rationale for public stocks contrasts sharply with traditional public buffer stock schemes that usually aim at price stabilization, as seen above. In such schemes, stocks are usually owned and procured by parastatal agencies, often as part of a domestic producer support scheme. Releases are supposedly made during periods of rising prices to protect consumers, in some countries at below market rates. The aim is to maintain a target price for producers and consumers, or at least to keep prices within a band.

The resurgent interest in food reserves can be justified in response to market failure in assuring short-term food security. In particular, private storage cannot be expected to address extremes of supply shocks or market instability. The new approach to public stocks rationalizes these as emergency reserves, in contrast to traditional buffer stock approaches for price stabilization and in service of price support schemes.

In contrast to national stocking policies in ASEAN (with the exception of Singapore), the design of the regional cooperation scheme for public stocks does adhere to the new approach to emergency food reserves. The regional reserve is not to be deployed to achieve a target price or even price band, but only to meet food requirements of a member country *in extremis*. The release mechanism is designed to implement a cross-border release of rice in a timely fashion.

However, whereas national stocking policies tend to be conducted under dedicated enforcement and generous financial support, the regional reserve is weakened by the tepid commitment of the participating member countries. The terms of the agreement place caution above rapid response: Council decisions (including release of the reserve) require a consensus; clauses in the APTERR Agreement allow a country to unilaterally suspend its obligation or even withdraw from APTERR, without penalties.

Ultimately the reason for such caution is political: each APTERR Party is reluctant to acknowledge the inadequacy of its domestic response to an emergency and need for external assistance. Nor are the parties willing to risk the political fallout from deploying the national food security reserve for non-domestic purpose, especially in case of a worldwide crisis in the rice market (as in 2008).

The experience of the region may serve to illuminate the potential as well as pitfalls of relying on a public stockholding approach to short-term food security. At its worst, the new rationale for public stocks for food security may unfortunately end up promoting public stock schemes in the traditional mould, where price stability is narrowly equated to food security and the considerable powers of the State placed at the service of the traditional stabilization programme.

Two liberalizing forces are likely to curb such tendencies: the ASEAN AEC 2015 and WTO membership.

Legal issues

Over the course of negotiations of the APTERR Agreement, a proposal was made regarding the origin of rice by a rice exporting country. Analogous to rules of origin in preferential trading agreements, the proposed provision required that rice pledged for APTERR must be harvested from within the ASEAN Plus Three countries. Rice being a sensitive commodity, the proponent saw the provision as a way to protect the region's rice producers from undue competition with external rice stocks being released under the APTERR mechanism.

Several of rice importing APTERR Parties did not support the proposal. Food security stocks of some of the importing countries were augmented by imports; in the case say of Singapore or Brunei, imports comprised the bulk or even the whole of the food security stock. Japan is a special case: minimum access commitments made by Japan to the WTO permit imported rice to be released for food consumption within the country. This has led to huge stockpiles of rice imported from WTO member countries; these are simply being carried over to succeeding years (at great cost to the Japanese government), or intermittently released for industrial use (e.g., glue and paper manufacture), for feed, or (under tight regulation) for foreign aid.

In principle, earmarked stocks could be sourced from among ASEAN Plus Three countries, as rice stocks to be earmarked can be imported from one of the ASEAN Plus Three countries. As a practical matter there is actually no problem with the proposed restriction (Brunei for instance sources most of its imports from Thailand).

A bigger problem however is the potential legal challenge, (i.e., the possible conflict with the most-favoured nation (MFN) rule under the WTO Agreements). All APTERR Parties are members of the WTO. The restriction on the origin of rice may be seen by WTO members outside ASEAN Plus Three as conferring an advantage to the rice producers in the region. The proponent maintained there was no inconsistency with the WTO Agreement. An impasse ensued with several rounds of negotiations unable to reconcile the positions.

Resolution

During these negotiations, an Asian Development Bank Technical Assistance (TA) grant was supporting the ASEAN Integrated Food Security Framework. One of the TA components was technical support for the APTERR. Under the TA, a WTO legal expert was engaged to render an opinion on the issue.

The resulting opinion found the proposed restriction on the origin of rice to be inconsistent with WTO rules. The first major inconsistency is, as mentioned previously, with the MFN principle as enshrined in the General Agreement on Tariffs and Trade (GATT). The opinion found a related inconsistency, this time with the Agreement on Government Procurement, to which several APTERR Parties were also signatories. The origin of rice restriction could be construed as distorting government procurement decisions when supplying rice stocks for APTERR, possibly deploying public funds to extend an undue advantage to the region's rice producers.

The opinion conceded that exceptions to WTO principles were permitted. However the scope of the exception is narrow, namely, exceptions should qualify as necessary to maintain safety of humans and/or that of the environment. Unfortunately the origin of rice restriction does not seem to meet this criterion. Rice imported from outside the region could equally comply with plant, animal, and human safety standards as rice obtained from within the region. In fact by providing flexibility to the country which is earmarking or donating the rice, one may argue that allowing an APTERR Party to source earmarked stocks from any other WTO member will facilitate fulfillment of its commitment to release rice to meet an emergency in ASEAN Plus Three countries.

The opinion was presented during the negotiations and discussed at length. Ultimately the proponent withdrew the proposal. Drafting of the APTERR Agreement proceeded, with the final version being signed on October 2011 *sans* the provision on origin of rice.

ASEAN AEC 2015, WTO AND TARIFFICATION – THE PHILIPPINES CASE STUDY

The WTO Agreement on Agriculture (AoA) requires WTO members to convert import restrictions, except for restrictions required to safeguard safety of humans and the environment, into customs duties, these are mainly quantitative restrictions (QRs): Conversion of QRs to customs duties is called tariffication.

Under the AoA, WTO members may invoke a special treatment provision for their primary agricultural product. Special treatment allows a country to temporarily suspend tariffication for the staple. Upon expiration, QRs must be converted to tariffs based on a formula for computing the tariff equivalent. Moreover, upon expiration, the tariff must be bound at rates that would have applied had the country been on a tariff reduction programme (involving a minimum of 15 per cent reduction spread annually over five years beginning from its accession).[12]

In compliance with the AoA, the Philippines passed the Agricultural Tariffication Act (RA 8178, 1996), which repealed section 23 par. 10 of the Magna Carta of Small Farmers. RA 8178 converted trade barriers into tariffs, to meet the country's WTO obligations. However RA 8178 specifically exempted rice; rather, it conferred on the National Food Authority (NFA) the authority to undertake direct importation of rice, or to allocate the import quota among licensed importers.[13] Nevertheless the country conceded a minimum market access, ranging from 30,000 tons in 1995 up to 224,000 tons in 2004. Volumes within the market access charged a maximum tariff of 50 per cent. Upon expiration in 2005, the country negotiated and obtained an extension of its special treatment for rice up to 2012. In exchange the country raised its minimum access to 350,000 tons, of which 163,000 were in the form of country-specific quotas (CSQs) to Thailand, China, India, and Australia. In practice, the high prices of rice produced in these countries tend to limit the usage of CSQs by private

---

[12] The Philippines was one of four countries that obtained special treatment for rice (the others were Japan, Republic of Korea, and Taiwan). Special treatment was set to expire in 2004 – and has done so for Japan; Taiwan; and Republic of Korea – however the Philippines has negotiated further extensions, see below.

[13] Currently equal to 350,000 tons per year.

traders. One positive development though was the shift to private sector importation beginning in 2008, which intensified from 2010 onwards.

In 2008 the allocation to private importers was only 200,000 tons, of which only 76,000 was actually imported; total imports that year totalled 2.2 million tons. Private sector availment was low due to very high world prices prevailing at the time; moreover as explained above, the CSQ scheme prevented importers from selecting their least cost supplier.

By 2011 the private sector (inclusive of farmer organizations) was allowed to import 660,000 tons, 77 per cent of that year's import quota of 860,000 tons. However the annual import quota is now restricted to the minimum market access owing to the self-sufficiency target of 100 per cent by 2013, to be sustained up to 2016. In 2013 the import quota is 350,000 tons, of which 163,000 is to assigned to the private sector under the CSQs.

Given the significance of intra-ASEAN rice trade, the implementation of trade agreements geared towards the creation of an ASEAN Economic Community by 2015 are also highly relevant to the future shape of rice markets.

In 1992, ASEAN member states established the ASEAN Free Trade Area (AFTA), which implements a comprehensive program of tariff reduction under the Common Effective Preferential Tariff (CEPT). Tariff lines within the CEPT are restricted to a 0–5 per cent band within a time-table. Tariff lines under the Inclusion List fall under fast-track reduction, while lines under the Sensitive List provides a longer timetable. Lines under the Highly Sensitive List are given a higher tariff by the end of the timetable.

Tariff reduction was further accelerated under the ASEAN Trade in Goods Agreement (ATIGA). Under ATIGA, 99 per cent of tariff lines under the Inclusion List would fall to zero-duty. The ATIGA retains the Sensitive and Highly Sensitive Lists; in the case of the Philippines for example, rice tariffs are expected to be reduced to 35 per cent while sugar tariffs should fall to 5 per cent by 2015 (Bureau of International Trade Relations, 2012).

ASEAN is moving towards a single economic community based on an ASEAN Economic Community (AEC) Blueprint, which calls for a single market and production base. A priority focus for integration is enhancement of trade among ASEAN member countries and long-term competitiveness of food and agriculture products produced within ASEAN. By harmonizing their standards and quality and by standardizing their trade certifications, ASEAN agricultural products are expected to become more competitive in the global market.

Effect of Tariffication

Tariffication in 2017 will serve as the vanguard of market reform against the decades-old interventionist policy in the country's rice sector, which was founded on the country's misguided policy of rice self-sufficiency. Tariffication will erode NFA control over the domestic rice market. It can still intervene by way of procurement, price support, and consumer subsidy. However, these would entail financing from government, which is increasingly becoming difficult to obtain, whether by way of Congressional appropriation, or sovereign guarantee over NFA debts.

Efforts at rice sector reform are not new. The last major reform initiative happened in the 2000s under the Grains Sector Development Program. Unfortunately the opposition of special interest groups scuttled the House bills on import liberalization. Currently a number of bills are pending before Congress to reform the NFA, essentially divesting it of its commercial function, leaving only a regulatory function. In some versions, the commercial function will still be carried out by a government corporation with no oversight power – a reform known as 'decoupling'. The corporation would have a narrow mandate to acquire, maintain, and release rice stocks for the purpose of food security, emergency relief, and perhaps for welfare of indigents.

The current push for self-sufficiency by the DA is politically expedient. However in the presence of huge benefits from quota allocation – due to the large wedge between domestic and world prices of rice – a system of quota allocation that is efficient and credible to all participants has yet to emerge. Rice importation policies need to be rationalized, to protect the interests not only of producers but also of consumers and other market participants. Huge differences in the cost of bringing in imports and moving domestic supplies to consumers makes smuggling lucrative. Complaints of rice smuggling now abound, with the Senate Committee on Agriculture and Food currently conducting hearings 'in aid of legislation' to deal with the problem.

Quantitative restrictions on imports as exemplified by NFA's regulations raise the domestic price of rice and allow the concentration of legally imported supplies in the hands of a few. Tariffication – involving liberalized importation of rice subject to payment of import duty – can still confer some protection for producers while reducing the price of rice, stabilizing domestic supplies and prices, and deterring any attempt to control supplies to manipulate market prices.

There is no need to negotiate a further extension of the special treatment for rice. A simple way to implement this is to delete the provision in the Agricultural Tariffication Act that exempts rice from tariffication.

This at once eliminates the problem of setting up a fair, efficient, and credible allocation of the import quota. This of course assumes an open and reasonable regime of import licensing, as mandated under WTO rules.

Yet opposition to the above-mentioned reforms remains strong. As set out by Toletino and de la Pena.[14]

> the NFA provides access to a favoured few to its stock of imported rice, which is likely to have been imported at the low border price, and which may be sold in the domestic market at the relatively high domestic retail price. Many of those favoured with access are the local political elites.

There are countervailing forces – including the country's economic managers and its WTO commitments which obligate it to undergo tariffication by 2017. Tariffication will likely create an unstoppable momentum of reform of the NFA. Post-reform, the NFA may continue to operate, but within the context of decoupling. Its functions may be limited to regulation and managing the food security reserve. NFA storage and marketing facilities may be transferred to a different, perhaps new government corporation with no regulatory powers; thus NFA may outsource procurement of the food security reserve to this marketing entity. Lower prices of rice will improve affordability of food to poor rice consumers and boost domestic food security; further concerns (e.g., a volatile world rice market) can be allayed by targeted safety nets, (e.g. conditional cash transfers). Unlike past reform efforts, which have ended in failure, the next few years may well be the turning point in staple food competition policy in the country.

CONCLUSION

WTO sceptics have pointed out the ineffectiveness of the organization in addressing agricultural development and food security needs of developing countries. Stalled negotiations under the Doha round, together with failure to invoke disciplines on grain exporting countries during recent episodes of world price volatility, do justify some of this criticism. Regional approaches to trade liberalization can fill some of the gap, as they grapple with the challenge of domestic trade barriers. Such reforms

---

[14] J. Tolentino, Bruce and B. Dela Pena. 'Stymied reforms in rice marketing in the Philippines, 1980–2009'. In: R. Fabella, J. Faustino, M. Mirandilla-Santos, P. Catiang and R. Paras, eds. *Build on Dreams, Grounded in Reality: Economic Policy Reforms in the Philippines* (The Asia Foundation, 2011).

towards regional market integration are useful, but may themselves introduce distortions. For instance a preferential trade agreement may set up a cumbersome verification system to implement rules of origin; preferential tariffs may cause trade diversion, artificially inducing imports from a high-cost supplier simply due to an uneven tariff structure.

The WTO is a potent force for food security, when properly harnessed. This chapter has presented two illustrative cases. The first relates to a regional emergency reserve scheme in which member countries faced a choice of a restricted or flexible approach to rice stocks in the reserve; the second is a country-specific policy choice between open and restricted rice trade. In the former, WTO principles broke an impasse in favour of flexibility. In the latter, WTO treaty obligations are gradually eroding an archaic regime of government controls over the rice sector. For all its faults, the WTO remains an indispensable instrument in the pursuit of trade-based solutions to the food security challenge.

4. A case study of regional food security: APTERR

Michael Ewing-Chow and Melanie Vilarasau Slade

1. INTRODUCTION

As this book will further explore, climate change and environmental degradation pose a critical challenge to food security policies. When the significant increase in human population growth is also taken into account, a Malthusian scenario where global supply of food fails to keep up with demand, once held at bay by faith in scientific advancement in agricultural techniques, becomes alarmingly possible if not probable. Unilateral policies by individual States to address this dystopian future will not be sufficient. Collective action at the international level either by multilateral agreements, joint action within existing international institutional structures or specific regional approaches will have to be explored as a set of responses for enhancing global food security.

One of the authors of this chapter was fortunate enough to be involved in the creation of a regional initiative to address the problem. While regional arrangements are only one of several options available, they often represent the low hanging fruit for collective food security initiatives. First, they often deal with the same staple food – in the case of Asia, it would be rice. Second, States in the relevant region often have common experiences with the production of this staple resulting in a greater sense of enlightened shared interest when faced with climate change and environmental degradation. Finally, as these regional States often meet and negotiate on other issues, the familiarity with the culture and interests of the regional players tends to shorten the time needed to develop an understanding of the various sensitivities and any intractable issues.

Regional agreements and initiatives – by their very nature involving parties that are closer in geographical and often cultural terms than is the case under international initiatives – are able to provide a safety net which is not as vulnerable to the natural or economic circumstances which may cause a national food emergency, and which would render many unilateral national food security initiatives ineffective.

They thus represent one solution – albeit an important one – and the ASEAN Plus Three Emergency Rice Reserve (APTERR) is one example of such a regional agreement.[1] Significantly, from a trade and food security perspective, in addition to emergency reserves it provides:

- Disciplines on agricultural export restrictions including a *de facto* partial prohibition of export restrictions up to a certain threshold;
- Greater market transparency; and
- Regional cooperation on pricing information.

By assessing the experience of APTERR in addressing its compatibility with current WTO rules, we aim to provide one regional answer to a crucial, wider question: can the present food security challenges be tackled within the current WTO framework?

We choose to start with this part of the answer to the wider question because regional stockpiles are a critical safeguard in the event of a food security emergency. Perhaps most importantly, they are also an essential first step towards building confidence between countries in a politically sensitive sector, in which the cost of choosing to 'go it alone' is often paid by the most vulnerable.

2. APTERR: A CASE STUDY IN REGIONAL FOOD SECURITY POLICY

2.1 The Creation of APTERR

Prior to the 2008 crisis, the Member States of the Association of Southeast Asian Nations[2] (ASEAN) had already been collaborating with the Plus Three (+3) countries[3] on an emergency rice reserve system in the ASEAN+3 region. The collaboration took the form of a project called the East Asia Emergency Rice Reserve (EAERR), which the government of Japan funded for a total period of four years until March 2010.

---

[1] The ASEAN Plus Three Emergency Rice Reserve Agreement was signed during the 11th Meeting of the ASEAN Ministers of Agriculture and Forestry and the Ministers of Plus Three Countries (AMAF+3) held in Jakarta, Indonesia in October 2011.

[2] Brunei, Cambodia, Indonesia, Lao PDR, Malaysia, Myanmar, Philippines, Singapore, Thailand and Vietnam.

[3] China, Japan and South Korea.

Unfortunately, the processes and triggers of the EAERR were limited and vaguely formulated, and the EAERR was not triggered by any of the food crises which occurred during the period it was in force, including Cyclone Nargis.

As a result, the parties concerned decided to improve food security in the region by developing APTERR as a permanent institution created for the purpose of maintaining and distributing rice in times of emergency for the benefit of the populations of the parties concerned.

Under the Agreement signed in 2011, APTERR members are to pledge specific volumes of rice per year for the regional stockpile by way of 'earmarked emergency rice reserves' for a virtual stockpile, and to provide a capital fund to convert APTERR into a working body coordinating the implementation of the rice reserve system. Each member has the responsibility of maintaining that earmarked reserve and upon a request from another APTERR member pursuant to a trigger event occurring,[4] will provide that member with rice from the earmark reserve according to the terms of the APTERR Agreement.

The current price mechanism proposed for APTERR is in the form of a forward contract based on an average price over a pre-agreed period. As such, the mechanism does not discriminate between APTERR producers and non-APTERR producers on the basis of price. Furthermore, this avoids affecting market prices for rice, thus allowing for prices to rise while smoothening out rice price spikes.[5]

The regional model embodied in APTERR also has the advantage of ensuring that at least 1.75 million metric tons[6] of regional rice will not be subject to export restraints, at least amongst the APTERR members. This will also help reduce the rice price spikes as it limits the opportunity for speculators to take advantage of panic buying by ensuring that there will be enough rice to meet short-term needs.[7] While a special report by *The*

---

[4] The proposed mechanism by which a rice trade would be triggered under APTERR is still pending approval. It is proposed that in order to trigger a release the country in need would need to make a request of the APTERR Secretariat which would then find an appropriate trading match. The price for the trade would be calculated by the APTERR Secretariat based on a monthly average formula rather than market price.

[5] Crucially, price hikes as a market signal would not be disrupted as APTERR – as an emergency reserve – would only be triggered in case of need, defined in accordance with the different Tiers under which the APTERR rice may be triggered (for more details see below section on the Release and Distribution of Rice).

[6] This is the target set by the APTERR. At the initial stages the amount is more likely to be around 800,000 metric tonnes.

[7] C. Peter Timmer cited in David Dawe and Tom Slayton, 'The World Rice Market Crisis of 2007–2008' in David Dawe (ed.), *The Rice Crisis: Markets, Policies and Food Security* (The Food and Agriculture Organization of the United Nations and Earthscan 2010). Timmer argues that market structure has both short-run and long-run significance in the

Economist suggested that '[a]n agreement to limit trade bans might make exporters think twice before disrupting world markets',[8] considering the political sensitivities, it is unlikely that a multilateral agreement entirely prohibiting export bans will be forthcoming.[9]

Instead, arrangements like APTERR may be the solution particularly for politically sensitive staples like rice in emergency situations. Further and deeper cooperation is required if a long-term sustainable collective food security solution is to be found.

2.2 WTO Compliance of APTERR[10]

It is accepted that the creation of a regional rice reserve, which works to coordinate rice supply in the ASEAN+3 region, could, without careful structuring, clash with WTO rules. This was a concern of the negotiators when designing the architecture of APTERR and its regulations. The APTERR Agreement includes in its preamble the statement '[a]ffirming the need for the implementation of APTERR to be consistent with relevant internationally recognised rules such as those under the World Trade Organization (WTO)' and the Rules and Procedures for APTERR make clear that '[n]othing in this APTERR Agreement nor these Rules and Procedures shall derogate from the obligations of the APTERR Party pursuant to its membership of the World Trade Organisation (WTO)'.[11] Far more relevant however to this chapter is the question of whether the WTO rules are an obstacle to APTERR's establishment and effective functioning.

In practice, at no time in the discussions which determined the shape of APTERR did the WTO rules prevent the development of a useful policy and effective rice reserve. Rather, international trade law's focus on the

---

downward trend for rice, since the world's rice economy is highly decentralised. It is therefore subject to changes in price expectations on the part of participants all along the supply chain, which translate into panic buying, subsequent destocking and sharp destabilization of actual prices.

[8] *The Economist*, 24 Feb 2011 Special Report 'Feeding the World'.

[9] The failure of the WTO December 2011 Ministerial Conference to agree on even a limited restraint according to which WTO members were to 'agree to remove food export restrictions or extraordinary taxes for food purchased for non-commercial humanitarian purposes by the World Food Programme (WFP) and [. . .] agree not to impose them in the future' is indicative of this.

[10] This section is based on the legal opinion given to APTERR by Michael Ewing-Chow, and also features in a chapter of the upcoming publication of the Centre for International and Public Law (ANU) and Cambridge University Press entitled 'Rethinking Security Institutions at the Intersection of International and Public Law'.

[11] Annex 8: Revised Rules and Procedures of Release and Replenishment of Rice Reserves as of 10 September 2012.

systemic implications of APTERR's design meant that these were central to negotiations of APTERR. Indeed, this chapter provides examples of how the WTO Rules provided a virtuous discipline which forced clarity as to the parameters employed in the design of the proposed mechanisms of the rice reserve from an early stage.[12]

To illustrate this, we will now explore the impact of WTO trade obligations such as non-discrimination, the prohibition of subsidies and the limits of the WTO Agreements exception clauses on APTERR's design. The setting up of a rice reserve – and an assessment of its WTO compatibility – requires the answering of three questions. Where will the rice come from? Where will it be stored? Finally, how should it be released? These questions raise legal issues regarding the origin of the rice; and the release and distribution of the rice; as well as the potential for export subsidies.

2.2.1 The origin of the rice

During the negotiations which the first author of this article was privy to, there was considerable debate as to where the rice for stockpiling (whether virtual or physical) should come from, with some APTERR members proposing that the rice for the emergency reserve comes from APTERR member countries, and others envisaging imports exclusively from non-APTERR member countries.

Ultimately it was determined during the discussions that the emergency reserve would be origin neutral.[13] WTO rules were a factor in this debate as any restriction on the origin of the rice for the emergency rice reserve has the potential to violate the non-discrimination principle under WTO rules.

(a) The principle of non-discrimination   Article I of the General Agreement on Tariffs and Trade (GATT), the famous Most-favoured Nation (MFN) clause, requires that 'with respect to all rules and formalities in connection with importation and exportation', all advantages granted to products originating from any other country shall be accorded immediately and unconditionally to the like product originating from all the other WTO members.[14] Non-discrimination as a principle reflected in the MFN

---

[12] This statement is based on eyewitness accounts by Michael Ewing-Chow, legal counsel to APTERR.

[13] ASEAN internal discussions to which the author was privy.

[14] See *General Agreement on Tariffs and Trade* 1867 UNTS 190, Article 1. For the original version of the GATT, see *General Agreement on Tariffs and Trade*, opened for signature 30 October 1947, 55 UNTS 187 (entered into force 29 July 1948) (*GATT 1947*). Note, that *GATT 1947* has been subsumed into the latest 1994 version of *GATT* (*Marrakesh Agreement Establishing the World Trade Organization*, Annex 1A).

and National Treatment (NT) obligations may well be regarded as the fundamental principle of the WTO trade regime.[15]

Therefore if APTERR were to specify the origin of the rice in the stockpile, this would result in discrimination, either in favour of rice produced in APTERR member countries or non-APTERR countries. This has two effects: it imposes certain obligations on the APTERR members to discriminate; and it gives certain benefits or advantages to the rice exporting countries, as a set amount of rice export is practically guaranteed due to APTERR members being obliged to import that amount of rice to satisfy the APTERR Agreement.

In the *Canada-Auto* case, the WTO Appellate Body (AB) confirmed that Article I:1 covers both *de facto* as well as *de jure* discrimination.[16] Thus, a measure, 'origin-neutral' on its face, will violate Article I:1 if it in effect discriminates. The proposed origin-specific measure of restricting the origin of rice to certain countries will produce discrimination both 'in law' and 'in effect'.

Thus, the advantage of a certain amount of guaranteed rice export volumes to some WTO Members would be a prima facie violation of GATT Article I, unless it could be justified under one of the GATT exceptions.

On a practical level, if the origin of rice is restricted to non-APTERR members, since the agreement for the establishment of APTERR is agreed and signed by APTERR countries, it would hardly be seemly for them to file a complaint with the WTO. However, if the origin of rice is restricted to APTERR members, non-APTERR countries who are WTO members may file a complaint that the MFN obligation has been violated. If so, APTERR would have to rely on one of the exceptions found in GATT Article XX to justify the continued existence of a non-compliant measure.

---

[15] The Preamble of the Marrakesh Agreement Establishing the World Trade Organization proclaims 'the elimination of discriminatory treatment in international trade relations' as one of the chief objectives of the World Trade Organization (WTO). See *Marrakesh Agreement Establishing the World Trade Organization*, opened for signature 15 April 1994, 1867 UNTS 3 (entered into force 1 January 1995) pmbl., cl.3, Apr. 15.

[16] *Canada – Certain Measures Affecting the Automotive Industry*, WTO Doc WT/DS139/ AB/R WT/DS142/AB/R, (2000), (Appellate Body Report), para 78. Further, the Appellate Body emphasized that:

> the words of Article I:1 refer not to some advantages granted 'with respect to' the subjects that fall within the defined scope of the Article, but to 'any advantage'; not to some products, but to 'any product'; and not to like products from some other Members, but to like products originating in or destined for 'all other' Members (para. 79).

GATT Article XX(b) allows for an exception if the measure was necessary to protect human, animal or plant life or health and GATT Article XX(j) allows WTO members to adopt measures which deviate from their WTO obligations when the measures are 'essential to the acquisition or distribution of products in general or local short supply' provided that such deviation be temporary and that 'all contracting parties are entitled to an equitable share of the international supply of such products'.

If the origin of rice for the rice reserve is restricted only to APTERR member countries, in the situations where APTERR is triggered because of local short supply (for example, during natural disasters) the member countries may argue that by giving preferences to rice from APTERR members, it may reduce the time of transportation in emergencies. In the event of an emergency, time is of the essence and regional supply chains would be the most effective way for providing such a supply especially since Thailand and Vietnam, both APTERR members, when not imposing export restrictions, are the biggest rice exporters in the world and in 2008, 91 per cent of the rice imports in ASEAN are sourced from the region.[17]

It is less clear how the other condition of Article XX(j) – 'all contracting parties are entitled to an equitable share of the international supply of such products' – should be interpreted. It has been suggested that this requirement should be understood in three elements, first, it applies to WTO Members only; second, if a country is 'entitled to' a product, it has a just claim to that product; third, each individual member may not be entitled to a strictly equal share of a product just an equitable one.[18]

Non-discrimination is a fundamental principle of the WTO regime. However, Article XX was designed to give some policy space to WTO members while being carefully drafted to avoid abuse.[19] The drafting of Article XX would suggest that the requirement under Article XX(j) is arguably not to guarantee each individual member an actual equal share of the international supply, but to prevent the Member States from implementing certain measures on the basis of a shortage of supply which would prevent specific WTO Members from getting access to product in question.

---

[17] Riza Bernabe, 'The need for a rice reserve mechanism in Southeast Asia', Presentation for The Asian Farmers' Association, online: http://www.iatp.org/files/451_2_107542.pdf.

[18] Ben Sharp, 'Responding internationally to a resource crisis interpreting the GATT Article XX(j) short supply exception', (2010), *Drake Journal of Agricultural Law*, 15(2), 259.

[19] Article XX sets out general exceptions to the WTO members' obligations, yet, it is a close list which does not allow the members to expand the exceptions and impact the multilateral trading system.

In the *US-Gasoline* case,[20] the AB set a two-tiered test for the application of Article XX.[21] As such, all exceptions found in GATT Article XX are subject to the proviso of the 'chapeau' that 'such measures are not applied in a manner which would constitute a means of arbitrary or unjustifiable discrimination between states where the same conditions prevail or a disguised restriction on international trade'.

Applying the two-tiered test to APTERR, given the relatively small size of APTERR, which initially will have an earmarked quantity of rice of less than 800,000 tons,[22] it would be hard to argue that, relative to total rice production and consumption figures,[23] APTERR would impact on other members' right to an equitable share of that trade in rice.

The question would therefore be whether the APTERR measure would meet the general *chapeau* requirements. This is where the origin of rice issue faces its biggest challenge. Article XX sets forth limited and conditional exceptions from the obligations of the substantive provisions of the GATT. The chapeau prohibits arbitrary or unjustifiable discrimination between countries where the same conditions prevail. APTERR members may argue that the conditions in APTERR members and non-APTERR members are not the same, in terms of distance; the rice that they grow; and the variety of rice that the people usually consume. However, it may still be difficult to argue that the discrimination would be indispensible for general or local short supply as in most cases, food security and emergency crises would not necessitate policies requiring choices about the origin of a foodstuff.

The effect of Article XX on APTERR is therefore not to restrict the options available to it, but rather to oblige its creators to ensure that any potential discrimination is justified (in accordance with Article XX) and that it is not arbitrary, or a disguised restriction on trade.

(b) Specific rules on government procurement   In addition to the GATT, the restriction on the origin of rice may also violate the Government

---

[20] *United States – Standards for Reformulated and Conventional Gasoline (US-Gasoline)*, WTO Doc WT/DS2/AB/R, (1996), (Appellate Body Report).

[21] The AB examined the Panel's findings that the United States' ostensibly environmental regulation concerning the quality of gasoline (known as the 'Clean Air Act') was inconsistent with GATT Article III:4 and not justified under either paragraph (b), (d) or (g) of Article XX. The AB then suggested two-tiered test for Article XX.

[22] Roehlano Briones, Alvaro Durand-Morat, Eric J. Wailes and Eddie C. Chavez, 'Climate change and price volatility: Can we count on the ASEAN Plus Three Emergency Rice Reserve?', (2012), *ADB Sustainable Development Working Paper Series*, No. 24.

[23] See the statistics on http://worldfood.apionet.or.jp/alias.pdf.

Purchase Agreement (GPA).[24] The GPA is to date the only legally binding agreement in the WTO focusing on the subject of government procurement. It is a plurilateral treaty and not an agreement that is mandatory for all WTO members. It applies to contracting parties' government procurement regimes and is based on the principles of openness, transparency and non-discrimination. In the ASEAN+3 region, Japan, South Korea and Singapore are members of the GPA whereas China is in the process of acceding to the GPA.[25]

GPA members are required to publish a procurement notice and treat the bidders on a non-discriminatory basis. GPA Article III requires that any favourable treatment accorded to the products, services and suppliers of any contracting party to the GPA shall be 'immediately and unconditionally' accorded to the other contracting parties. Therefore, if Japan, South Korea and Singapore are required to purchase physical stocks of rice pursuant to APTERR, the non-discrimination rule in the GPA would require them to purchase those stocks on an origin-neutral basis.

As the GPA is a plurilateral agreement among contracting parties it only binds parties to the GPA to obligations owed to other parties of the GPA. If there is discrimination in APTERR in favour of rice produced in APTERR States only, it would be discriminatory against other States outside APTERR who are GPA contracting parties. Thus, other parties to the GPA could challenge any such governmental purchases made by Japan, South Korea and Singapore. Conversely, if the discrimination is against rice produced in APTERR States then APTERR GPA members namely Japan, South Korea and Singapore would be entitled to complain against such purchases.

However, GPA Article XXIII, which is similar to GATT Article XX, may allow for an exception if the discrimination was indispensable for national security reasons or was necessary to protect human, animal or plant life or health provided that 'such measures are not applied in a manner which would constitute a means of arbitrary or unjustifiable discrimination between States where the same conditions prevail or a disguised restriction on international trade'. However, it is hard to envisage a scenario in which this form of origin-specific discriminatory measure

---

[24] *Agreement on Government Procurement*, 1915 UNTS 103 (being Annex 4(b) of the Marrakesh Agreement establishing the World Trade Organization, see above Note 15, Ann. 1. For a more detailed introduction to the GPA, please refer to the WTO website, online: http://www.wto.org/english/tratop_e/gproc_e/gproc_e.htm.

[25] While GPA only affects certain APTERR members the structure of APTERR must take into account the obligations imposed on all of its members.

would be indispensable for national security reasons or necessary to protect human, animal or plant life or health.[26]

The GPA therefore also imposes certain constraints on APTERR members from specifying the origin of the rice.

Instead, the combination of the non-discrimination rules, GATT Article XX and the GPA, resulted in APTERR using non-discriminatory criteria based on the type and quality of the rice instead of using the origin of rice. This was an example of the virtuous discipline provided by current WTO rules.

2.2.2 Release and distribution of the rice

There are three types of triggers for the distribution of rice pursuant to APTERR:

(a)   Tier 1 – A release from the earmarked rice reserves under commercial terms;

(b)   Tier 2 – A release from earmarked rice reserves under long-term loan or grant; and

(c)   Tier 3 – A release from the stockpiled rice reserves (in the case of acute and urgent emergency; or under the circumstance that stockpiled rice is not utilized within at least 12 months, a release as food aid for poverty alleviation or malnourishment eradication programs).

While there is no enforcement mechanism or dispute settlement mechanism coercing APTERR members to respond to a demand trigger, it is understood that – at least for the time being – the parties have decided that the political constraints would be sufficient to ensure that such trigger events elicit an appropriate response from producing members.

It is important to clarify how the release of the rice is triggered. If the release particularly for Tier 1 and Tier 2 is triggered and the distribution is

---

[26] There are not many cases concerning GPA under the WTO dispute settlement mechanism, and the only one panel report issued on the GPA matters is *Korea – Measures Affecting Government Procurement* (DS163), WTO Doc WT/DS163/7, (2000), (Panel Report). On 16 February 1999, the US requested consultations with Korea in respect of certain procurement practices of the Korean Airport Construction Authority (KOACA), and other entities concerned with the procurement of airport construction in Korea. The US claimed that such practices were inconsistent with Korea's obligations under GPA. The panel found that the entities conducting procurement for the project at issue were not covered entities under Korea's Appendix I of the GPA and were not otherwise covered by Korea's obligations under the GPA.

not carefully managed, the release and distribution may be prohibited by the existing trade obligations of APTERR members.

In addition, a failure to properly establish and manage the pricing mechanisms under these tiers might render transactions vulnerable to interest capture. This would be contrary to the aim of constructing an effective rice reserve capable of acting as a buffer to price fluctuations and could itself contribute to pricing instability. The priority therefore was to establish mechanisms through which the market price is transparently set and triggers are activated based on carefully defined 'needs'.

This requires a balancing act between granting APTERR scope to establish working practices, and defining the parameters for the working practices. For example, if the concept of 'need' required to trigger Tier 3 is defined in terms that are deemed too restrictive, meaning that the rice reserve may only be tapped in extreme emergency situations, the whole rice reserve mechanism may never be put into actual use, because a government may not publicly admit that it is experiencing an emergency so as to avoid exacerbating an already bad situation, causing domestic panic buying, and undermining its standing in the region.

As it stands, the triggers and mechanisms have yet to be formally approved. They will be guided by the Rules of Procedure[27] and the task of implementing these has been left to the APTERR Council and soon to be established Secretariat. However, certain aspects of APTERR's functioning were established as part of the assessment as to its WTO compatibility. We will proceed to highlight the parameters and constraints that the trade obligations impose in this regard. In particular, three areas may be constrained being: (a) selective purchase of rice by governments; (b) preferential customs treatment; and (c) subsidized pricing.

(a) Selective purchase of rice by governments   As explained above, Japan, South Korea and Singapore are subject to GPA disciplines. National Treatment in the GPA requires contracting parties to accord 'no less favorable' treatment to the 'products, services and suppliers' of the contracting parties of the GPA. GPA Article VIII provides that '[i]n the process of qualifying suppliers, entities shall not discriminate among suppliers of other Parties or between domestic suppliers and suppliers of other Parties.' Thus rice purchases by these three APTERR members must be done on a non-discriminatory basis regardless of whether they are facing an event that would trigger Tier 1, 2 or 3 interventions.

---

[27] Annex 8: Revised Rules and Procedures of Release and Replenishment of Rice Reserves as of 10 September 2012.

There are however some exceptions in the GPA. GPA Article XV provides an exception for limited tendering which is not used with a view to avoiding maximum possible competition or in a manner which would constitute a means of discrimination among suppliers of other parties or protection to domestic producers or supplier in so far as is strictly necessary when, for reasons of extreme urgency brought about by events unforeseeable by the entity, the products or services could not be obtained in time by means of open or selective tendering procedures. If the rice reserve mechanism can be justified in accordance with the Article XV exceptions, the contracting parties to the GPA could avoid public tendering, but only limit tendering to the APTERR States. But the conditions for the exceptions are strict; it requires 'strictly necessary', 'extreme urgency', 'events unforeseeable', and time pressure. Therefore, subject to how Tier 1 and 2 are defined, only Tier 3 may be said to clearly fall within this exception.

As mentioned above, GPA Article XXIII provides that:

> [s]ubject to the requirement that such measures are not applied in a manner which would constitute a means of arbitrary or unjustifiable discrimination between states where the same conditions prevail or a disguised restriction on international trade, nothing in this Agreement shall be construed to prevent any Party from imposing or enforcing measures: necessary to protect. . . human, animal or plant life or health.

Under this general GPA exception, two criteria need to be met. First, the measure must be one taken to protect human life. Second, the measure should not be a means of arbitrary or unjustifiable discrimination between States where the same conditions prevail or a disguised restriction on international trade. While, all three Tiers can be interpreted as seeking to protect human life, proving that the measure is not arbitrary or unjustifiable discrimination may be more difficult. An argument may be made that it is necessary to implement Tier 3 to ensure a quick response to an emergency or disaster. Depending on the triggers for Tiers 1 and 2, it may be less easy to justify their implementation.

There is a common practice of tied food aid such that cash grants may be tied up with certain requirements of purchasing from its home producers only. Such officially supported export credits tied to preferential purchasing may have a similar effect to export subsidies, if the total costs for financing the purchase of the exported goods are lower than would otherwise occur. Officially supported export credits as described above give a supplementary commercial advantage to an exporter, which is nominally exporting at the prevailing world market price but is in effect getting a complete subsidy.

The ASCM prohibits 'subsidies contingent, in law or fact, whether solely or as one of several conditions, upon export performance'. This blanket prohibition on export subsidies is stricter than the treatment of most other domestic measures such as domestic subsidies (subsidies that are not contingent on export performance), taxes or regulations.[28]

Indeed, the EU highlighted the potential abuses for food aid in the subsidy context in a submission to the Committee on Agriculture. The EU highlights Article 10.4 of the AoA, which provides that:

> [m]embers donors of international food aid shall ensure: (a) that the provision of international food aid is not tied directly or indirectly to commercial exports of agricultural products to recipient countries, (b) that international food aid transactions, including bilateral food aid which is monetized, shall be carried out in accordance with the FAO 'Principles of Surplus Disposal and Consultative Obligations', including, where appropriate, the system of Usual Marketing Requirements (UMRs); and (c) that such aid shall be provided to the extent possible in fully grant form or on terms no less concessional than those provided for in Article IV of the Food Aid Convention 1986.

While Article 16 of the AoA does provide for some flexibility in regard to the implementation of the Marrakesh Decision on Measures Concerning the Possible Negative Effects of the Reform Programme on Least-Developed and Net Food-Importing Developing Countries,[29] the specific rules and modalities have yet to be agreed. Furthermore, few of the APTERR countries would qualify as Least-developed Countries (LDC) or Net Food-importing Developing Countries (NFIDC) with only Cambodia, Lao PDR and Myanmar currently listed as LDCs and none of the APTERR countries currently notified as a NFIDC.[30] As a result, it was recommended that when considering the modality of food aid, the obligation to comply with the prohibition on subsidies under the WTO Agreements should be taken into account and food aid in grant form would be the preferred APTERR method.[31]

---

[28] Andrew Green and Michael Trebilcock, 'Enforcing WTO obligations: What can we learn from export subsidies?', (2007), *Journal of International Economic Law* 10(3), 653–683.

[29] Decision on Measures Concerning the Possible Negative Effects of the Reform Programme on Least-Developed and Net Food-Importing Developing Countries, Apr. 15, 1994, Marrakesh Agreement Establishing the World Trade Organization, Decisions adopted by the Trade Negotiations committee–Results of the Uruguay Round, 1867 UNTS 60 (1994).

[30] LDCs are defined as 'least developed countries as recognised by the Economic and Social Council of the United Nations.' Under the first criterion, 48 least-developed countries defined as such by the UN are automatically contained in the list (available at http://www.un.org/en/development/desa/policy/cdp/ldc/ldc_list.pdf). See also Decision by WTO Committee on Agriculture G/AG/5/Rev. 10 of 23 March 2012.

[31] It was also felt that the choice of grants limited the opportunities for rent-seeking behaviour.

(b) Preferential customs treatment Under GATT Article I, customs duties and charges of any kind on products are required to be applied on a MFN basis. Therefore, the rice imported from the rice reserve must be subject to the same tariffs as rice from non-APTERR States.

It may be that in emergency situations that require a quick response, rules regarding pre-agreed procedures for accelerated custom clearances for rice need to be created to facilitate a faster response to the emergency. While such rules may be prima facie discriminatory against rice not part of the rice reserve mechanism, it is likely, depending on the severity of the emergency and the viability of other options available to address that emergency, that it could be justified as being 'necessary for the protection of human life' pursuant to the exception found in GATT Article XX(b).

The necessity test included in GATT Article XX(b) has been recently addressed in the Appellate Body (AB) Report on *Brazil Tyres* in which the AB suggested that WTO Members have the right 'to determine the level of protection that they consider appropriate in a given context' and if a measure is apt to produce a material 'contribution to the achievement of its objective'[32] and it was the least trade restrictive to reach that level of protection, it would be justified if it was shown to be done in good faith.

In addition, should a dispute occur, a WTO Panel is obliged to consider the importance of a State's regulation.

> In order to determine whether a measure is 'necessary' within the meaning of Article XX(b) of the GATT 1994, a panel must assess all the relevant factors, particularly the extent of the contribution to the achievement of a measure's objective and its trade restrictiveness, in the light of the importance of the interests or values at stake. If this analysis yields a preliminary conclusion that the measure is necessary, this result must be confirmed by comparing the measure with its possible alternatives, which may be less trade restrictive while providing an equivalent contribution to the achievement of the objective pursued.[33]

(c) Subsidized pricing As APTERR is a new measure that was not contemplated at the time of the AoA negotiations, the APTERR mechanism is not a subsidy that has been carved out pursuant to Article 13 of the AoA. As such, the basic obligations of the AoA and the other WTO Agreement specifically for subsidies, the ASCM, will apply to APTERR.

The AoA at Article 9.1(b) provides that the following export subsidies are subject to reduction commitments: 'the sale or disposal for export by

---

[32] *Brazil – Measures Affecting Imports of Retreaded Tyres*, WTO Doc WT/DS332/AB/R, (2007), (Appellate Body Report), para 210.
[33] Ibid., para 156.

governments or their agencies of non-commercial stocks of agricultural products at a price lower than the comparable price charged for the like product to buyers in the domestic market'.

'Export subsidies' are defined in Article 1(e) of the AoA as 'subsidies contingent upon export performance, including the export subsidies listed in Article 9 of this Agreement'. Thus, for a measure to be an export subsidy for the purposes of Article 9 of the AoA, it must be a subsidy contingent upon export performance.

The AoA does not define a 'subsidy contingent upon export performance' but Article 3.1(a) of the ASCM provides that 'subsidies contingent, in law or in fact, whether solely or as one of several other conditions, upon export performance' are prohibited. Footnote 4 of the ASCM explains that a subsidy 'in fact' is one where 'the facts demonstrate that the granting of a subsidy, without having been made legally contingent upon export performance, is in fact tied to actual or anticipated exportation or export earnings'. The footnote goes on to explain that '[t]he mere fact that a subsidy is granted to enterprises which export shall not for that reason alone be considered to be an export subsidy within the meaning of this provision'.

The APTERR sale of rice at the international price is not a subsidy per se that is contingent in law or in fact upon export performance making it a prohibited subsidy pursuant to Article 3.1(a) of the ASCM. This is because the domestic purchase of the rice by the APTERR member, which may be higher than the international market price, is not dependent on any export of the rice. The subsidy (if any) is provided to the rice farmer who is not involved in the decision to sell on the rice through APTERR and therefore is not contingent per se on export performance. The only reason that the domestic purchase price is higher than the international market price is the specific country's trade barriers on rice. This may or may not be WTO compliant depending on the agriculture commitments of individual countries but the WTO compliance of APTERR is not dependent on that.

If it is not a subsidy contingent on export performance, it is not an export subsidy as defined by the AoA. This is because the scheme is not specifically targeted for export but rather may result in an export only when the APTERR triggers are activated. At the time of the purchase of the rice, there is no guarantee of export. This delinks the high domestic purchase price from the contingent (and not guaranteed) export.

However, Article 10.1 of the AoA further provides that '[e]xport subsidies not listed in paragraph 1 of Article 9 shall not be applied in a manner which results in, or which threatens to lead to, circumvention of export subsidy commitments; nor shall non-commercial transactions be used to circumvent such commitments'. In the *US – FSC* case,[34] the Appellate Body interpreted the term 'export subsidy commitments' to have 'a wider reach [than the reduction commitments alluded to in Article 9] that covers commitments and obligations relating to both scheduled and unscheduled agricultural products'. The Appellate Body made a number of observations relevant to the interpretation of the phrase 'applied in a manner which results in, or which threatens to lead to, circumvention': '[t]he verb 'circumvent' means, inter alia, 'find a way round, evade . . .'. Article 10.1 is designed to prevent Members from circumventing or 'evading' their 'export subsidy commitments'. This may arise in many different ways. We note, moreover, that, under Article 10.1, it is not necessary to demonstrate actual 'circumvention' of 'export subsidy commitments'. It suffices that 'export subsidies' are 'applied in a manner which . . . threatens to lead to circumvention of export subsidy commitments'.'

Thus, apart from strict export subsidies restrictions, there is a restriction on transactions that are used to circumvent commitments on export subsidies. Again, so long as the purchase of the rice is not made contingent on exports whether in law or in fact, it will be difficult to argue that a transaction pursuant to APTERR is meant to circumvent existing commitments.

While APTERR is likely not to be a Prohibited Subsidy, it could be an Actionable Subsidy under Article 5 of the ASCM. An Actionable Subsidy is one that causes 'adverse effects to the interests of other [WTO] Members'. While the same article provides that this does not apply to subsidies maintained on agricultural products as provided in Article 13 of the AoA, as stated above, since APTERR was not carved out pursuant to Article 13 of the AoA, this does not apply although it may apply to existing subsidies that APTERR members carved out for their own domestic agricultural policies.

'Adverse effects' is defined as injury to the domestic industry, nullification or impairment of benefits or serious prejudice to the interest of another WTO member. Injury to the domestic industry and nullification or impairment is an evidential issue which requires an econometric analysis of the injury or nullification. However, 'serious prejudice' is defined in Article 6.3(c) of the ASCM as 'the effect of the subsidy is to displace or impede the exports of a like product of another [WTO Member] from a third country market'. In accordance with Article 6.4 of the ASCM, this

---

[34] WTO Appellate Body Report, *United States – Tax Treatment for 'Foreign Sales Corporations' (US-FSC)* WT/DS108/AB/R, 14 January 2002, paras 144 and 147.

can be evidenced simply by showing a 'change in the relative share of the market to the disadvantage of the non-subsidized product'.

With that said, while injury may be evidenced, it will be difficult to attribute that injury to an APTERR transaction. APTERR transactions are intended to be not in the usual course of business but export trade based on emergency triggers. Further, the pricing mechanism of the transaction is based on the international market price. This will make it difficult to link the APTERR transaction to any adverse effect as all like products would compete at those prices.

Unless the APTERR members in fact use the APTERR mechanism as a loop hole to regularly export rice at a price lower than their domestic purchase price and at a competitive advantage other than price, such as pursuant to a preferential mandatory purchase agreement, this is unlikely to be seen as an actionable subsidy if the international market price mechanism referred to early is adhered to as such a price mechanism reduces discrimination and thereby potential adverse effects.

2.3   WTO Compliance of APTERR

The experience of APTERR overall in grappling with WTO rules has been a positive one. Though resistance to the restrictions imposed by the WTO was initially voiced by some negotiators; all eventually came to accept that the WTO rules applied. While a significant amount of creative thinking was required to design an appropriate architecture in compliance with the rules, the WTO rules were eventually proven to be flexible enough to allow for a regional rice reserve to be set up to the satisfaction of the members. In addition, the rules forced the negotiators to articulate their concerns more precisely, limited opportunities for interest capture and prevented politics from unduly influencing trade and food security policies arbitrarily.

PART II

5. Managing food price volatility in Asia: Why, what and how?

C. Peter Timmer

INTRODUCTION: WHY

What does price instability have to do with food security? It is widely agreed in the development community that, in general:

1) Price *spikes* hurt poor consumers;
2) Price *collapses* hurt farmers; and
3) Price *risks* reduce investments, including by smallholder farmers for agricultural modernization.

But food price instability also has a deeper and more insidious impact: it slows down economic growth and the structural transformation that is the pathway out of rural poverty. Thus food price instability really hurts the poor in both the short run and the long run.

Consider a very simple model of food security that focuses on the short run versus the long run, and on the macro level (of policymakers) versus the micro level (of household decisionmakers) (see Figure 5.1 below). When the global economy is reasonably stable, and when food prices are well behaved, policymakers can concentrate their political and financial capital on the process of long-run, inclusive growth. Keeping the poor from falling into irreversible poverty traps is easier and less costly in a world of stable food prices, and the poor are able to use their own resources and entrepreneurial abilities to connect (via the small horizontal arrow) to long-run, sustainable food security for themselves.

If the food economy is highly unstable, constantly in crisis, policymakers spend all of their time and budget resources in the 'upper left' box, trying to stabilize food prices and provide safety nets for the poor. During food crises, vulnerable households often deplete their human and financial capital just to stay alive. This is the world of poverty traps and enduring food insecurity. We are also trapped in short-run— macro and humanitarian—crisis management.

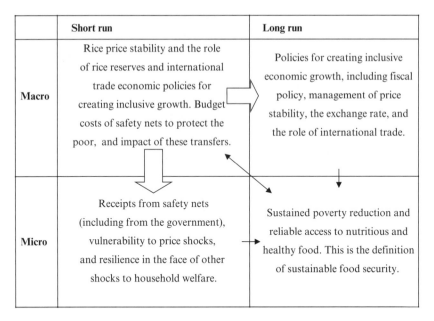

	Short run	**Long run**
Macro	Rice price stability and the role of rice reserves and international trade economic policies for creating inclusive growth. Budget costs of safety nets to protect the poor, and impact of these transfers.	Policies for creating inclusive economic growth, including fiscal policy, management of price stability, the exchange rate, and the role of international trade.
Micro	Receipts from safety nets (including from the government), vulnerability to price shocks, and resilience in the face of other shocks to household welfare.	Sustained poverty reduction and reliable access to nutritious and healthy food. This is the definition of sustainable food security.

Figure 5.1   Basic framework for understanding food security issues in Asia

With success in achieving the objectives in the upper right and lower left boxes, market forces gradually—over decades—bring the poor above a threshold of vulnerability and into sustained food security (connecting macro to micro and short-run to long run). The goal is to get to the 'lower right' box where households have sustainable access to food in the long run. That is, they are food secure.

How do we break out of these traps? Franck Galtier and his colleagues at CIRAD in France have designed a simple framework to think about managing food price instability. It builds on two critical distinctions: first, between preventing food price instability and coping with the consequences of unstable food prices; and second, between the role of the private sector in each domain and the public sector. Thus there is a 2x2 matrix with four cells – A, B, C and D (see Figure 5.2).

With the rise of market fundamentalism since the mid-1980s, most donor efforts have concentrated on A and B measures, and on D measures when food crises still erupted (which they did, despite efforts in the A and B arenas). In view of the relative lack of success with the A B D approach, the issue is whether approaches to 'C' might work, especially to complement investments in the A B D arenas. Are there public interventions that could stabilize food prices?

	Prevent	Cope
Private	'A' storage and transportation	'B' insurance hedging & futures markets
Public	'C' buffer stocks import/export controls	'D' safety nets

Figure 5.2 Approaches to managing food price volatility

The answer depends on the level of action: Local, national, regional and/ or international. Although most analytical attention focuses mainly on the distinction between national and international actions, examples exist where farmer organizations at the local level and regional bodies such as ASEAN+3, for instance, have engaged in price stabilization initiatives.

GENERAL ISSUES FACING PRICE STABILIZATION EFFORTS: THE WHAT AND HOW?

Within these four levels of action, five main issues are relevant.

1. *Where* is Price Instability a Problem?

At the local level, highly unstable farm gate prices are a significant burden to small farmers seeking to invest in modern agricultural techniques and raise their productivity. Consuming households (and many smallholder farm households are net consumers) are obviously the locus of burdens from high food prices and especially from price spikes.

At the national level, the concern is for price stability in major urban markets and is often the focus of action by macro policymakers.

At the international level, the concern is for the level and stability of food prices from the major exporters, and the possibility that export barriers might prevent access to food by importing countries in times of rising prices.

2.   *Which* Commodities Need More Stable Prices?

Three categories of agricultural commodities might be considered for stabilization activities: food staples, cash crops and perennial tree crops. Prices of cash crops are a real concern to farmers but have relatively little impact on consumers—perhaps onions in India and red chili peppers in Indonesia are exceptions. Perennial tree crops present special financing problems because of the long time horizon for the investment to start to pay off, and there is a very sharp distinction between short-run marginal costs and long-run average costs. But price variability has little impact on consumers—perhaps coffee in Brazil and the U.S. are a minor exception.

Accordingly, recent emphasis has been on price stabilization techniques for the major staple food grains, especially rice, wheat and maize. Although these commodities have much in common because they often form a large share of energy input among the poor, the world rice market behaves very differently from the world markets for wheat and maize. There are other food grain markets with their own unusual trading regimes: cassava, millet and white maize, for example, often behave more like 'non-tradable' commodities than the tradable commodities with large, liquid international markets. Any efforts to stabilize food grain prices will need to recognize the special characteristics of individual commodities.

3.   *What* Instruments are Available to Stabilize Food Prices?

In general, there are three main categories of stabilization instruments: border (trade) controls, buffer (reserve) stocks, and regulation of financial markets involving agricultural commodities.

Border controls are a national issue because nations are defined by their borders. Economists do not like political borders very much because they impede the free flow of goods and services (and hence reduce the 'gains to trade'), but the nation state is the main modern actor in many areas of economic, political and diplomatic initiatives. Borders, and border controls over trade, are a reality. The WTO seeks to impose disciplines on what border controls are legitimate, and agriculture has been included in those disciplines since the Uruguay Round, but the food crisis in 2007/08 revealed a serious asymmetry in how the WTO approaches border controls for food grains. Virtually all of the trade disciplines, and all of the current negotiations under the Doha Round, refer to import barriers rather than export controls. There is now wide agreement that export controls on food grains have been a significant source of price instability. The asymmetry of trade discussions should be rectified, but it is difficult to imagine grain-exporting countries agreeing to significant restrictions on their ability to control exports as a means of stabilizing their domestic food prices. Food security is simply too important as a political mandate for national leaders to forgo this policy instrument. Only significantly more stable world grain markets are likely to change this reality—an obvious challenge in the face of export barriers.

Large reserves of grain, at whatever level, have the obvious advantage that they can be drawn on when harvests are damaged or there are surges in demand. Large reserves tend to hold price levels down as well, although there is a clear endogenous relationship, explained by the theory of supply of storage, between expectations of price changes and levels of stocks held by the private sector. The issue is whether the public sector should be holding reserve stocks of grain above and beyond the willingness of the private sector to hold stocks (and the subsequent willingness of the private sector to hold these stocks in the presence of public stocks).

Holding public reserve stocks faces three key issues: their costs (and who should pay), monitoring the level and quality of stocks (and who should manage them), and enforcement of agreements to buy and release stocks according to some transparent rules. Each of these issues has been difficult to resolve even in the case of national stocks. There is virtually no experience at the international level of procuring, managing and releasing reserve stocks on behalf of an agreed protocol to stabilize grain prices. The experience of using Japanese 'WTO' rice stocks in 2008 as an external supply source to prick the rapidly rising spike in world rice prices was clearly a unique episode (and even then the stocks were never actually released). Very serious doubts exist that any internationally viable scheme of holding reserve stocks of grain for stabilization purposes could be agreed and implemented (but see the specific discussion below).

Regulation of financial markets for agricultural commodities was vigorously discussed within the context of the French chairmanship of the G-20 in 2011. Attention focused on two possibilities: re-imposition of position limits on speculative positions for important food commodities traded on futures markets (such as existed before the financial deregulations in the 1990s), and a 'Tobin-tax' on each financial transaction to slow the emergence of speculative bubbles. The difficulties with either approach are clear—many of the financial transactions in commodity markets do not actually take place on organized exchanges where regulators can see what is happening, no single market could initiate such regulations unless others around the world did as well, and there is no experience with taxing financial transactions of this sort. Still, it is recognized that the 'financialization of food commodities' is a relatively recent and rapidly growing phenomenon and urgently needs more research and understanding.

4. *How* Can Stabilization Interventions be Governed?

The issue is important at three different levels (four, if the regional level is somehow distinct from the international level because of greater commonality of interests).

At the local level, especially for farm or community organizations, governance would seem to depend on active participation and 'voice'. The great advantage of local initiatives, of course, is precisely their ability to be responsive to local conditions and aspirations. General guidelines on how to manage them are probably not very useful.

At the national level, democratic processes are widely thought to be the basis of good governance generally, and should provide appropriate feedback to national leaders on how well they are doing in managing the country's food security. Still, it is important for outside analysts, donors and the private sector to realize that food security is inherently a political issue subject to political decisionmaking. It is certainly desirable that good technical analysis, especially economic analysis, be brought to bear on these decisions, but history has shown how difficult it is to make such analyses relevant and implemented.

At the international (and regional) level, negotiations informed by transparent technical rules would seem to be the best way forward. But there is deep skepticism that such negotiations can be successful. Even within ASEAN, for example, the interests of Vietnam and Thailand diverge sharply from those of the Philippines and Indonesia.

5. *How* do we Evaluate Success or Failure in Stabilizing Food Prices?

At the local level, the basic issue is whether sustained gains are seen in agricultural productivity on smallholder farms. Of course, many other ingredients are needed for 'getting agriculture moving', but a major rationale for stabilizing commodity prices at the farm gate is to enhance the profitability of these other investments. The feedback from success at this level is also critical: nothing would improve the outlook for food security more effectively than rapid increases in farm productivity, especially for staple food crops grown by smallholders.

At the national level, success in stabilizing food prices is likely to be seen primarily in greater political support for the government that gets credit, and ultimately in a more stable investment climate that should stimulate economic growth. Although the political payoff is likely to be primarily in the short run, the contribution to economic growth will be apparent to economic historians, and to the country's consumers as they gradually escape from poverty.

At the international level, if a price stabilization accord can be agreed and implemented, success will almost certainly have to be measured using technically sophisticated but transparent methodologies that are part of the initial framework. Cost-benefit analysis is a powerful tool when stakeholders agree on the methodology and the result.

MOVING THE AGENDA FORWARD

Reducing food price volatility is likely to be a highly specific process—depending on commodity, country, and global market conditions—but countries should be encouraged to engage in this process, not discouraged. It is also important to recognize the unique characteristics of the world rice market. Rice has not been 'financialized' to a significant extent, but there continue to be speculative hoarding episodes driven by widespread expectations of scarcity and surplus. Still, history demonstrates that rice prices within many Asian countries *can* be kept reasonably stable with respect to world prices. There are often spillovers from the actions under-taken by countries to stabilize their domestic prices, and these spillovers increase price instability in world markets. A little-researched topic is how to minimize the impact of these spillovers, or cope with them on a country-by-country basis, rather than to follow the standard policy advice, which is to avoid the actions altogether, and thus avoid the spillovers in the first place. The standard policy advice turns out to be politically impossible in times of turbulent markets. Is there a better alternative?

Three things would move this agenda forward:

First, we need a serious new research program on the benefits and costs of stabilizing food prices within domestic economies, including a focus on implementation of policy, management of food logistics agencies, and instruments to control corruption in these agencies. We would know a lot more about these topics if we had spent the same resources answering these questions as we have spent over the past three decades in estimating the gains from free trade in agriculture.

Second, we need to keep up the confidence-building measures that have helped renew trust in the world rice market. Very severe damage to this trust was inflicted during the 2008 food crisis, mostly because of the Indian ban on exports, the on-again, off-again ban on Vietnamese rice exports, and open talk in Thailand of withholding stocks from the market and creating an 'OREC', or Organization of Rice Exporting Countries, to boost prices in the world market. Still, there is plenty of blame to go around in explain-ing the political distrust of the world market for rice. Important importing countries, such as Indonesia and the Philippines, speak publically of their desire to end 'dependence' on supplies from the world market. Such rhetoric does not make them a market that exporting countries can trust (although this rhetoric also has little short-run impact on rice traders, who tend to judge market impact from actions rather than political statements).

This retreat into autarky comes at a very high price to economic efficiency and the welfare of poor consumers. It makes the world market even more unstable and less reliable. Is there anything we can do to re-build confidence and trust in international trade in general and in the world rice market in particular? Any confidence-building measures will need to involve both exporting and importing countries, acting in their own self-interest. One possibility—already underway—is a country-by-country investment in greater rice reserves to cope with shocks to rice supplies, while gradually increasing the use of trade to lower costs of rice consumption. A higher level of stocks does not alter the requisite flow of rice from producers to consumers, but it does create a buffer against interruptions to that flow. Thus:

Third, we need larger rice reserves at four different levels of the global rice economy—those held by the private sector; in small importing countries by the public sector; in large rice producing and consuming countries held publicly; and internationally.

Most of the rice stocks in the global economy are held by the private sector—farmers, traders, processors, retailers and consumers—to even out seasonal production patterns and to keep trade pipelines flowing smoothly. Few private stocks are held to even out inter-annual price fluctuations, but the pipeline stocks carried across crop-years are probably equal to a month or two of consumption, a considerable quantity. With greater price instability expected in the future, and greater uncertainty about the reliability of supplies in world markets, optimal (profit-maximizing) levels of privately held rice stocks have increased (although there are no data to prove this). We know little about the actual levels of these stocks, or the behavioral parameters that affect them, but even the most basic models of supply of storage suggest there has been a significant increase in privately held rice stocks since 2008. Of course, if publicly held stocks succeed in stabilizing world rice prices, privately held stocks will then gradually be drawn down.

A completely overlooked potential for the private sector to provide greater stability of rice prices through stock management comes from the 'supermarket revolution' in Asia. Before the turn of the Millennium, supermarkets in the region were niche players catering mostly to the urban middle and upper classes. Now they provide—via modern supply chains—perhaps one-third to as much as one-half of the rice consumed in East and Southeast Asia, with the share growing rapidly (although even the rough numbers are not really known).

The potential of modern supermarkets to stabilize rice prices comes from the large market share of individual companies under central management control. If consumers desire stable food prices, astute supermarket managers can supply it. This potential of supermarkets to stabilize prices contrasts with traditional small, competitive, retail rice markets, where prices change regularly on the basis of daily supply and demand. Historically, 'food price stability' has been a public good because no private entity found it profitable to provide it. The rise of supermarkets may mean that stable food prices could become primarily a private good. This would truly be a revolution in the food industry.

Next, for similar reasons, small countries that rely heavily on imports for their rice supplies, such as Malaysia, Singapore, or Brunei, have found it desirable to increase the level of stocks held publicly, or (as in Singapore) held privately but with levels determined by public regulations. Even a modest increase in rice stocks in these countries will increase confidence that the world market remains their best long-run source of supply (which, of course, it is).

Large countries face a somewhat different situation. Because of the sheer size of their *domestic* rice economies, actions to increase production, reduce consumption, or alter the size of stocks held by public agencies will also have a noticeable impact on the international rice economy. These countries certainly include China and India, probably Indonesia, and possibly the Philippines and Bangladesh.[1] Larger rice reserves in these countries are probably desirable for reasons of domestic food security, but they have also altered the perception of global observers about the adequacy of worldwide stocks. That is, larger rice reserves in these countries—built up since 2008—have had a positive spillover impact on the global rice economy by stabilizing price expectations, and thereby actual rice prices. The stability in global rice prices since 2008, relative to wheat and maize prices, is largely attributable to more attention in the large Asian countries to their own domestic food security, including holding larger rice stocks.

A ROLE FOR THE INTERNATIONAL COMMUNITY?

Finally, the hardest question is whether there is any role for international ownership and control of rice stocks as a means to stabilize rice prices on global markets. Ever since the publication of the classic Newbery and

---

[1] Thailand and Vietnam, as the world's leading rice exporters, carry substantial stocks both seasonally and as part of their normal pipeline for regular deliveries to their customers. They are unlikely to need larger stocks for food security reasons.

Stiglitz volume, *The Theory of Commodity Price Stabilization*, in 1981, the answer has been a clear 'no'. Both history and theory demonstrate that it is impossible to stabilize the price of a commodity in world markets for long periods of time—from cocoa to coffee to copper to tin to wheat to whatever—using internationally managed buffer stocks. Budget constraints and the asymmetry of storage—it can never be negative—mean that stochastic variations in supply or demand will eventually overwhelm the ability of a buffer stock to stabilize prices. No international commodity agreement (ICA) with binding provisions has been negotiated since the Newbery and Stiglitz volume.

Still, it is important to address a more modest question. Would the availability of a limited amount of rice under international control help stabilize expectations about the behavior of world rice prices? If expectations can be stabilized, panicked behavior on the part of multitudinous participants in the world rice economy could be sharply reduced, with self-reinforcing price bubbles and collapses made less frequent and less extreme. The availability of international stocks would not need to keep rice prices within some legally specified band, but could be useful if world rice supplies suddenly tighten and prices threaten to spike. Is this more limited objective possible?

Three Possibilities for Holding International Rice Stocks

There are four levels at which this question can be addressed. First is within Asia: the ASEAN + 3 (which includes China, Japan and South Korea), or possibly a new ASEAN + 6 (to include also India, Bangladesh and Pakistan) would include nearly all of the world's major rice importers and exporters (except the U.S.), not to mention about 90 percent of world production and consumption. An expanded ASEAN rice buffer stock has been under 'active' consideration for years, with little discernible progress. How do we stimulate such progress, beyond the steps underway to improve information flows and policy coordination? Or is this enough, if the large countries actually succeed in stabilizing their domestic rice economies?

Second, by an accident of international trade negotiations and strong protection of domestic rice producers, Japan holds over 1.5 million metric tons of high quality 'foreign' rice that it imports under its WTO accession agreement but which it refuses to sell to domestic consumers. The potential availability of this rice in May of 2008 was sufficient to prick the rapidly exploding rice price bubble at that time, once the stocks were put 'in play' by U.S. policymakers in private negotiations with Japanese officials. Would it be possible to manage these Japanese stocks with a more active concern for movements in international rice prices?

Finally, the question inevitably comes up: can the international community itself commit to publicly managed international rice stocks that would be an effective stabilizer of world rice prices? At the height of the world food crisis, the International Food Policy Research Institute (IFPRI) put forward a proposal to create 'virtual reserves' of grain to dampen financial speculation on world grain markets. Whatever the merits of such grain reserves for wheat, corn and soybeans, they clearly will not work for rice. Without deep futures markets, and with less-than-transparent price discovery in the world market, virtual reserves for rice will not influence real participants in real transactions.

The historical record on managing an international commodity agreement, with fixed price bands and the ownership of physical stocks, is not encouraging, and it was never even tried for rice because of the difficulties of stock deterioration, quality variations and poor information on the prices of actual rice trades. None of those problems has gone away.

The proposals here are incremental. They seek to change the long-run incentives for stockholding behavior, and to use increased stocks to build confidence in the international market for rice, which is clearly the most efficient source of supply for many countries. Because holding larger stocks will turn out to be very expensive, a scenario can be imagined where the larger stocks gradually build renewed confidence in the world rice market, prices become more stable and stocks will then be reduced gradually as the reality of the fiscal burden sinks in.

CONCLUSION

The world rice economy, and the various domestic participants in it, is a dynamic system subject to shocks and self-reinforcing behavior that creates price spikes and collapses. This instability has enormous costs, economically and politically, to farmers and consumers. But Asia is considerably richer now than it was even a decade ago, and rice is no longer the overwhelming determinant of food security for most of Asia's consumers, or of income for its farmers. The new reality of a less rice-dependent Asia in purely economic terms means we should be able to do better for a commodity that still feeds two-thirds of the world's poor.

6. Deepening ASEAN rice trade

Ramon L. Clarete

1. INTRODUCTION

The ASEAN region is important in the global rice market, particularly because the region includes the largest rice exporting and importing countries of the world. In 2011, about half of global rice exports came from the region. The share may increase further with possible gains in productivity and competitiveness of the rice industries of Myanmar and Cambodia. On the other hand, Indonesia and the Philippines are among the largest rice importers, claiming on average two-thirds of rice imports of ASEAN member states. However, both countries actively pursue becoming fully self-sufficient in rice, investing to expand production and restricting imports to increase local prices to encourage production.

The dynamics of rice trading in ASEAN may explain to a great extent why rice trade in the world remains thin, at about 5.9 percent of output in 2011. In the Philippines, the government-owned National Food Authority (NFA) monopolizes rice imports, keeping the volume of rice imports within limits. Indonesia licenses rice imports to control the quantity of rice that comes in. In normal situations, local production may meet local rice demand as influenced by local prices, which in turn are high relative to world prices due to import restrictions. The major rice importing countries up their rice imports substantially in times of extreme climatic situations, when their local rice outputs fall short of expected utilization requirements, or when they perceive a tightening of global rice supply as in 2008.

Because of this off-on market participation of the major rice importing countries in ASEAN, the bulk of the region's rice exports goes outside the region. In 2011, only about 27 percent of the region's rice exports went to ASEAN member states. This share could have been larger if imports of rice were not restricted by ASEAN member states, and more importantly their import demands of rice were more predictable.

This chapter points out that integrating more closely and predictably the respective national rice industries of ASEAN member states tends to deepen not only regional but also global rice trade. The region hosts two of the world's largest rice trading countries in the world. A more steady demand for imported rice from Indonesia, Malaysia and the Philippines elicits corresponding expansions of export supply from Thailand, Vietnam, Myanmar and Cambodia. It presents data indicating a low prospect over a period of ten years for sustained self-sufficiency in rice in Indonesia and the Philippines. Moreover, the chance that rice exporting countries, Thailand and Vietnam, run out of exportable surplus is zero.

The respective efforts of importing countries to attain self-sufficiency may have just trimmed down the size of the region's and thus world's rice exportable surplus, a key reason that drove importing countries to insure themselves from food security risk by producing as much rice as they can and only going to rice markets when they absolutely need to do so. They tend to also raise national rice prices because of import restrictions. Using Philippine data, rice self-sufficiency programs can be costly, and may turn out to be a case of bad politics. The poorest of the rice farmers are more consumers than producers of the commodity. Accordingly, they are penalized by the rice import quantitative restriction that the government has invoked ironically in their behalf. Integrating rice, rather than treating it as a highly politically sensitive commodity, in the ASEAN economic community, makes the region more resilient to extreme rice price volatility, lowers the regional average production cost, and reduces the need for costly self-sufficiency programs.

2.   SELF-SUFFICIENCY AS A FOOD SECURITY POLICY

Rice self-sufficiency programs are implemented to cope with the current risks to food security. One is that of extreme rice price volatility in world markets spilling into a country's domestic rice markets. In 2008, world rice supply was not substantively reduced but the lack of accurate rice market information over the short term triggered market speculation that only caused rice market prices to spike and plunge in just less than a year.

Another concern are the random supply or demand shocks, which are large relative to the relatively shallow level of rice world trade. These disturbances have the potential to push large importing countries cornering available supplies to avoid higher national rice prices. A sharp drop of rice production in Thailand, Vietnam or China can trigger a sharp increase of world rice prices. With limited foreign exchange resources, there is the risk that importing member states may not be able to afford to import rice. Worse, there may not even be enough rice available for sale, if rice exporting countries decide to unilaterally restrict their rice exports for their own national food security, as happened in 2008.

But how appropriate are these programs in keeping rice price volatility in world markets out of national rice markets in importing countries. The chances these countries attain and sustain self-sufficiency are assessed for Philippines and Indonesia below. Typically, governments subsidize irrigation services, seeds, and credit to increase rice farm productivities each year. More importantly, non-tariff barriers are maintained to control the flow of imported rice into the country to increase rice prices above their world market levels. Using Philippine data, the budgetary cost of these programs and the inefficiency cost of high rice prices as a result of import restrictions are examined.[1]

2.1 Likelihood that Importing Countries Become Self-sufficient?

A stochastic multi-year projection for the period from 2013 to 2022 of rice output, consumption, trade, prices, and related variables was done using the Arkansas Global Rice Model (AGRM) for Indonesia and the Philippines.[2] The exercise assembled historical data of rice yields in the region's two largest rice importing countries, and calculated the respective probability distributions of key rice variables over the ten-year period ending in 2022 each year. It subjected the AGRM repeatedly with plausible rice yields randomly generated based on the estimated distribution of the variable. Each time a rice yield variable is introduced into the model as a supply shock, the AGRM's market equilibrium is computed. The exercise was done in order to calculate the probability that Indonesia and the Philippines become fully self-sufficient in rice.

Based on their respective 2013 cumulative density functions of net rice imports, the Philippines had only a 5 percent likelihood of becoming self-sufficient. Indonesia, however, had apparently no chance of becoming one.[3] Both countries have invested to increase rice yields to become self-sufficient. The simulations were done given the scale of these investments recently. If these investments are sustained in the next ten years with

---

[1] The discussion draws heavily from R.L. Clarete, 'Philippine Rice Self-Sufficiency Program: Pitfalls and Remedies' in A. Balisacan, U. Chakravorty, M. Ravago (eds) *Sustainable Economic Development – Resources, Environment and Institutions* (Elsevier 2015), hereafter Clarete (2015).

[2] Distinguished Professor Eric Wailes from the University of Arkansas did the simulations in 2012 under an Asian Development Bank technical assistance program on food security to the ASEAN Food Security Reserve Board. The AGRM is the largest and most widely used partial equilibrium model of the world's rice markets. See Wailes, E.J. et al. (1997).1

[3] See Clarete (2015) *supra* fn 1.

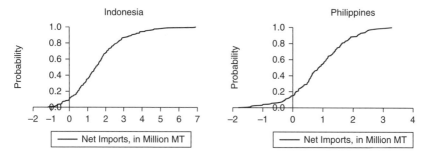

Source: E. Wailes as cited by Clarete (2015).

Figure 6.1   *Cumulative density function of rice net imports, Indonesia and the Philippines*

continued high price policy due to import restrictions, there is likelihood that Indonesia and the Philippines accumulate positive net exports. The prospects, however, are low and considering the high cost of these interventions, these programs may not be worth pursuing.[4]

Figure 6.1 above illustrates the average cumulative density functions of net rice imports over the period from 2013 to 2022 of the two countries. Compared to the estimates for 2013, both countries have higher chances of becoming self-sufficient: Indonesia has about 10 percent chance of becoming one, while the Philippines has roughly 15 percent. The larger rice requirement of the former may explain the difference of the prospects for success between the two. However, both countries are much more likely over the ten-year period not to attain their respective goals of self-sufficiency and thus of insulating their national markets from extreme world rice price volatility.

2.2   Cost of the Program

The relatively large public spending set aside in pursuit of self-sufficiency and the economic cost of import controls on rice cast doubt on the economic desirability of the program as the data from the Philippines indicate.

The Philippine Department of Agriculture (DA) aimed for the country to produce all its rice requirement in 2013. It failed to attain the target. Under the plan, the alternative year is 2016, when the current administration would have completed its term in office. The program managers

---

[4] In the Philippine case, the Philippine government had announced that the country would become fully self-sufficient in 2013. The result showed that in 95 percent of the time, the government would fail in this objective, and indeed it failed.

Table 6.1 *Planned output and budget of the Philippine Rice Self-Sufficiency Program: 2011–2016*

	2011	2012	2013	2014	2015	2016	Total
Incremental output (rice paddy)[a]	1.19	1.5	1.58	1.46	0.63	0.6	6.96
Budgetary cost by intervention[a]							
Improved water management							
NIA	13.59	30	20	15	10	5	93.59
BSWM	0.5	0.72	0.62	0.65	0.68	0.71	3.88
R, D, and extension services							
PalayCheck field schools	1.17	1.86	2.55	2.58	2.86	3.07	14.09
Bureau of plant industry	0.16	0.25	0.18	0.18	0.19	0.19	1.15
PhilRice	0.32	0.52	0.47	0.43	0.38	0.35	2.47
Farm mechanization and postharvest loss reduction							
PhilMech	0.2	5.46	5.99	2.58	2.12	2.18	18.53
Organic farming							
BSWM/NOAB	0.5	0.75	0.75	0.75	0.75	0.75	4.25
Others	1.17	0.57	0.57	0.57	0.57	0.57	4.02
Total budgetary cost	17.61	40.13	31.13	22.74	17.55	12.82	141.98

Notes:
Output in million metric tons and budget in billion pesos.
[a] Clarete (2015) obtained the data from the National Economic Development Authority (NEDA) based on the DA's submission in the 2011–2016 Public Investment Plan. According to the 2011 version of the program, as shown in a DA's PowerPoint presentation on Food Self-Sufficiency Roadmap, 2010–2016, the budgetary cost was originally estimated at PhP 177.44 billion.

Source: Table 19.4 in Clarete (2015).

targeted the growth of rice output at 6 percent per year for the period from 2011 to 2016. To become sufficient, the DA aimed to harvest 20 million tons of rice paddy in 2013, and 22.7 million tons in 2016.

To reach the target, the government increased production support to rice farming, and continued the quantitative restrictions on imported rice. The planned budget of the program from 2011 to 2016 is shown in Table 6.1 above. The total budgetary outlay of the program is PhP 141.98 billion. This is to produce an additional 6.96 million metric tons of rice paddy or 4.524 million tons of milled rice. Figure 6.2 below tracks the program's plan from 2010 to 2016.

The amount exceeds what the country may spend to import the same amount of rice from the region. At the average annual world price of rice

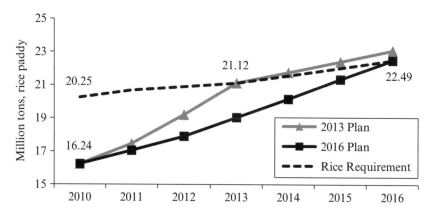

Source: Department of Agriculture.

Figure 6.2   *Target Palay outputs of the food self-sufficiency plan of the Department of Agriculture, 2010–2016*

from Vietnam during the period 2010–12 of PhP 18,362 per metric ton, the equivalent import bill would have been PhP 91.38 billion. It implies that the country is spending an extra PhP 50.6 billion for the expected output of rice of the program.

On top of what taxpayers pay, rice consumers pay 40 percent above the world price because of the quantitative import restrictions, which translates to the extra cost of PhP 33.28 billion. The total program costs PhP 83.83 billion over what the rice consumers and taxpayers would have paid for importing 4.524 million tons without any import restriction.

Part of what consumers pay over and above the world market value of rice goes to rice farmers and importers. Accounting for these income flows to determine who is paying and who is receiving them produces an estimate of the magnitude of the economic inefficiency or deadweight loss of the rice self-sufficiency program.

In Table 6.2, the computation of the cost of both the program and price distortion arising from import restrictions is applied only on the incremental output of 4.525 million tons of the program. Consumers pay PhP 36.55 billion because the local rice price is 40 percent above its border price. What is not considered here is the added cost to consumers on the prevailing rice consumption in 2010 amounting to 13.16 million tons. Rice farmers gain nearly PhP 22 billion due to the higher price. Since it is assumed in this analysis that the country becomes self-sufficient in rice, then no rice imports, and accordingly no transfers to and from importers,

Table 6.2 *Economic cost of the incremental output of the program (in billion pesos)*

	Receipts
Consumers pay 40% above world price on the incremental rice output of the program of 4.524 million tons in 2016 and reduce their consumption on account of the high price due to the quantitative import restriction.[a]	−36.55
Farmers gain producers surplus on the incremental output of the program, assuming country is self-sufficient in 2016 due to the higher rice price.[a]	21.93
No activity as country is self-sufficient and import quantity limit is set to zero.	0.00
Taxpayers pay the added cost of producing the incremental output over what they would have paid if the quantity were imported at world market value.	−50.60
Budgetary cost of program.	−141.98
Value at the border of incremental rice produced by the program.	91.38
Net receipts	−65.22

Note: [a] Supply and demand elasticities are assumed equal to 1.

Source: Clarete (2015).

are recorded. As mentioned above the taxpayers spend the additional PhP 50.6 billion pesos for the incremental rice whose value is 40 percent lower. Altogether, the net receipts amount to negative PhP 65.22 billion.

The policy restricting rice imports is believed to be assisting farmers by raising the price of rice and thus transferring income from rice consumers to rice farmers, particularly the poorest of them. In Table 6.2, the amount is nearly PhP 22 billion just on the incremental output. Clarete (2015) however pointed out that the claim that consumers subsidize the poorest farmers appears unsupported by the data. Only one-third of the producers' income gains from import restrictions accrue to the bottom 60 percent of the farmers. Moreover, as the poorest farmers are also consumers of rice in the rest of the year after the harvest, this greatly offsets the rents they received from import controls. Worse, for the poorest 7 percent of rice farmers in the Philippines, the net benefit of import restrictions is negative (see Figure 6.3).[5]

---

[5] Clarete (2015) used the entire output of rice farmers in estimating the producers' surplus in Figure 6.3, resulting in an estimated amount of income transfer amounting to PhP 96.65 billion.

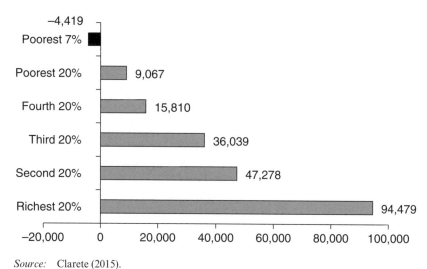

Source: Clarete (2015).

Figure 6.3   *Net benefit of rice farm households (RFH) in the Philippines from rice import restrictions (in PhP per year per RFH)*

3. SELF-PERPETUATING THIN RICE TRADE

Countries implement self-sufficiency programs to protect themselves from being unable to buy rice in world markets at times when they need it the most. The risk stems from the fact that rice trade in proportion to output is low compared to other cereals such as wheat or maize. Figure 6.4 charts the export to output ratio (XOR) as well as the import to output ratio (MOR) of the three cereals from 1961 to 2012.

From 1961 to 2012, the average trade to output ratios of the three cereals indicated that rice is the least traded (see Table 6.3). Its average XOR is 5.23 percent compared with 13.55 percent and 18.79 percent for maize and wheat respectively. There is hardly any difference between these figures and the corresponding import to output ratios (MORs), except that the latter are slightly lower compared to XORs. Since the 1960s, these ratios have increased in multiples of 1.07 for maize, 1.1 for wheat, and 1.2 for rice. The trade to output ratios of wheat and maize rose significantly from the 1960s to the turn of the past century, while that of rice had slightly expanded.

Two changes may be observed in the tradability of these cereals from 2000 onwards. The XOR for rice rose from 4.82 percent in the last two decades of the 1900s to 7.26 percent in the period from 2000 to 2012. Since

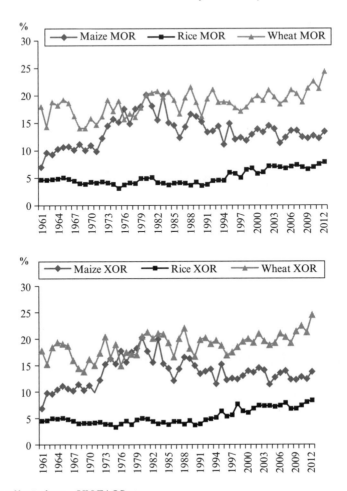

Source of basic data: UN FAOStat.

Figure 6.4   Export to output (XOR) and import to output (MOR) ratios, maize, rice and wheat, 1961–2012

2010, the figure was at least 7.37 percent. These numbers represent a significant increase in the tradability of rice. The other change regards maize. For the same periods of time, the trade to output ratios of maize fell. One possible factor explaining this is the diversion of maize to bio-ethanol particularly in the U.S., which is a major corn exporter.

Indonesia, Malaysia and the Philippines are the largest rice importing countries in Southeast Asia. Figure 6.5 plots their import to output

Table 6.3   *Average annual trade to output ratios, maize, rice and wheat, 1961 to 2012 (%)*

Period	Export to output ratio			Import to output ratio		
	Maize	Rice	Wheat	Maize	Rice	Wheat
1961–1979	12.56	4.28	17.02	12.35	4.28	16.82
1980–1999	14.75	4.82	19.30	14.71	4.64	19.13
2000–2012	13.15	7.26	20.61	13.03	6.94	20.55
1961–2012	13.55	5.23	18.79	13.43	5.08	18.64

Source of basic data: UN FAOStat.

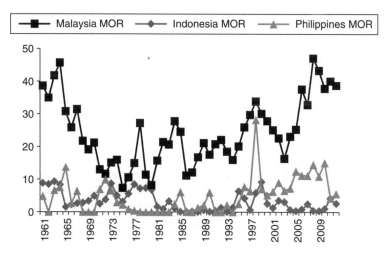

Source of basic data: UN FAOStat.

Figure 6.5   *Rice import to output ratios, Indonesia, Malaysia and the Philippines, 1961–2012*

ratios from 1961 to 2012. The volatility displayed by these ratios is higher compared to that of the world market for rice as shown in Figure 6.4. Malaysia appears to be the most open to trade among the three countries. Indonesia and the Philippines, with lower ratios, appear to be less open. Moreover, the ratios of the two countries are more volatile than those of Malaysia. The two countries appeared to be self-sufficient in selected time periods, i.e. in the second half of the 1970s to first half of the 1980s for the Philippines and in the second half of the 1980s for Indonesia. Occasional

Table 6.4   Average annual import to output ratios, rice, selected ASEAN countries, 1961–2012 (%)

Period	Import to output ratio		
	Indonesia	Malaysia	Philippines
1961–1979	5.47	23.03	3.76
1980–1999	2.21	20.68	3.60
2000–2012	1.80	32.09	9.18
1961–2012	3.30	24.39	5.05

Source of basic data: UN FAOStat.

imports however punctured these self-sufficient periods, indicating low levels of rice surplus. Starting in the middle of the 1990s, the two countries became consistently net rice importers.

Table 6.4 shows the average import to output ratios of the three countries, which confirm Malaysia being the most open to rice trade. Indonesia and the Philippines have substantially lower average ratios, and the latter is more open to rice imports.

The 'stop-and-go' behavior in rice importation of the region's importing countries does not encourage long-term investments to attain higher rice productivity in rice-exporting countries, particularly in Cambodia and Myanmar. Both have the potential of increasing their exportable rice surpluses, particularly the latter, which in the 1960s was the world's largest rice exporter.

The region's thin trade in rice can be self-perpetuating. Large rice-deficit countries in ASEAN – Indonesia and the Philippines – adopt self-sufficiency programs apparently to insure themselves against the risk of relying on thin trade for their rice requirements each year. On the other hand, facing this off-on pattern of import demands, exporting countries do not expand their respective rice production, which in turn maintains the need of rice importing countries to insure themselves with costly self-sufficiency programs.

The recent actions of rice exporting countries, which restricted their exports, do not help in building the trust of importing countries in the rice trade. In 2008, Vietnam restricted rice exports perceiving that the country may run out of rice to sell locally. Subsequent events following its export restrictions failed to validate the perceived risk, but actions like that and that of India just reinforced the need of importing countries to stay away from world markets.

Then in October 2011, Thailand reintroduced its rice-pledging program,

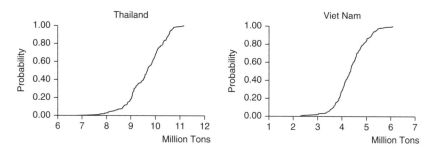

Note: The usage Viet Nam has been retained as in source material.

Source: Wailes, E. (2012) as cited in Clarete (2015).

Figure 6.6   *Cumulative density function of rice net exports, Thailand and Viet Nam, 2013–2022*

under which it procures paddy rice as loan collateral to farmers at about 100 percent subsidy rate. The effect on trade has been enormous: the difference between Thailand's rice exports one year before and one year after the program's implementation is a staggering reduction in volume by 78 percent, or 5 million tons.[6]

3.1   Likelihood of Rice Export Restrictions

These export restrictions may become the norm if the major rice exporting countries in Southeast Asia find themselves vulnerable to the risk of running out of rice to sell to their local markets. But how likely is the depletion of the exportable rice surpluses of Vietnam and Thailand? Figure 6.6 above shows the cumulative frequency distribution of average net exports from 2013 to 2022.

Over the next ten years starting in 2013, the exportable surplus of Thailand ranges from about 7 million tons to a high of 11 million. Similarly, Vietnam's rice surplus ranges from slightly over 2 million tons to about 6 million. In 2022, there is an 80 percent chance that its net exports increase from a minimum of 10.3 million to as high as 12.4 million tons. In 2012, its rice exports reached 7.6 million tons.[7] However, there is an 80 percent chance that Vietnam reduces its marketable surplus from a minimum of 4.6 million to 3.3 million tons in 2022 from its level of 7

---

[6] R.L. Clarete, L. Adriano and A. Esteban (2013).
[7] These numbers are not shown in Figure 6.6.

million tons in 2012. At worst, the projected reduction of rice exports of Vietnam is offset by the minimum forecasted gain of Thailand.

Clarete, Adriano and Esteban (2013) looked at the relationship between the volatility of monthly prices of three cereals (i.e. rice, corn and wheat), and their tradability as indicated by their export to output ratios from the 1960s until 2010. Rice prices were the most volatile with a standard deviation of the month-to-month rates of change equal to 152.28 percent, followed by wheat (139.08 percent) and corn (133.72 percent). In contrast, rice is least tradable with an export to output ratio of 4.98 percent, followed by corn (13.57 percent) and wheat (18.63 percent). The numbers apparently show that price volatility is inversely related to tradability, that is, the cereal that is least integrated in world markets tends to have the highest price volatility.

But is world rice trade low due to high rice price volatility or the other way around? Using the Granger causality test, Clarete, Adriano and Esteban (2013) regressed the quantity of rice exports against one- and two-period lagged quantities of rice exports and extreme rice price volatility variables, in one test, as well as in the other causality direction the extreme rice price volatility against lagged rice price volatility variables and the quantity of rice exports. The empirical test showed that the causality is from extreme rice price volatility to thin trade in rice. The implication of their finding is that rice self-sufficiency programs are implemented to insure themselves of the risk of extreme rice price volatility, rather than primarily to protect rice farmers. In the following section, a menu of actions for moderating rice price fluctuations is taken up.

4. A FRAMEWORK FOR REDUCING PRICE VOLATILITY

4.1 Extreme Rice Price Volatility

Food price crises involve sharp changes of food prices that are largely unexpected by both consumers and producers. Accordingly, they cause substantial adjustment costs in the economy, including reallocations in household spending, financial losses, and hunger. The G20 leaders[8] have

---

[8] The G20 comprises the governments of the world's largest economies, mostly developed. The group includes 19 countries and the European Union. Collectively, the G20 economies account for more than 80% of the gross world product.

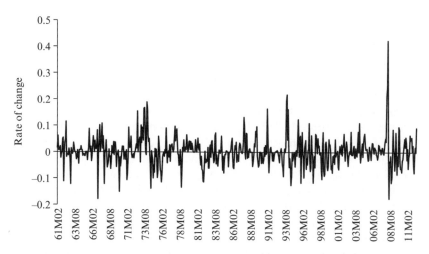

Source: Author's computation using data for 1961–94 from the Rice Committee Board of Trade of Thailand. Market Report. SGS Far East Limited, as provided to author from the World Bank project on Trusting Trade; and for 1995–2012, The Pink Sheet. World Bank.

Figure 6.7 Volatility of monthly rice prices, February 1961–May 2012

referred to this situation as one of extreme food price volatility.[9] They stress that excessive volatility will not only undermine access to food, particularly of the poor in cases of price spikes, but also weaken the incentive of farmers to produce food in times of price slumps. Moreover, every food price crisis tends to undermine the trust of stakeholders of food markets in the international food trade.

Figure 6.7 above shows the volatility of monthly rice prices from January 1961 to May 2012, using Thai 5 percent broken rice as an example.[10] In most of the months, these rates of price changes are low and may be considered by stakeholders to be part of the normal operations of the market. However, there were months in the 1970s, 1990s, and particularly in 2008, when the monthly price increases reached at least 15 percent.

Extreme rice price volatility refers to the set of rates of changes of rice prices with the likelihood of realization equal to no more than some low

---

[9] Interagency Policy Report, 'Price Volatility in Food and Agricultural Markets: Policy Responses' (OECD 2011).

[10] J. Subervie 'The Variable Response of Agricultural Supply to World Price Instability in Developing Countries' [2008] *Journal of Agricultural Economics 59* (1), 72–92 used as benchmark a moving trend of periodic food prices.

level of chance. To consumers averse to price spikes, extreme price volatility refers to high order surges of periodic prices. In the case of farmers, unexpected plunges of food prices may inflict financial losses, perhaps leading to business closures. Both consumers and producers find extreme swings of rice prices to be bad news as these introduce uncertainty in spending and business. In both cases, governments are concerned because of the adjustment costs that their constituencies have to bear.

In either situation, their likelihood of happening is low. In Figure 6.7, most of the rates of change in monthly rice prices since the 1960s are no more than the absolute value of 10 percent. Thus, these rates are very likely to occur. These rates are likely to be expected by the market stakeholders as part of the normal operations of the rice market. However, the high order rates of change, at least equal to the absolute value of 15 percent, are very unlikely to happen. If one assumes that these rates of price changes are distributed normally, then the extreme rice price volatility is located in the upper or lower tail of that frequency distribution. Martins-Filho et al. (2010) suggested a likelihood of no more than 2.5 percent of the time for extreme price volatility. Following this convention, the rice price crises that concern consumers would involve rates of changes of periodic rice prices in the upper tail end of the frequency distribution.[11]

4.2   Menu of Options for Reducing Price Volatility

The 2007–08 rice price spike in the world market had been attributed to several factors, the most immediate contributors being the set of export restrictions by India and Vietnam, and the panic buying in the global rice market by the Philippines. But even before the price bubble developed, global rice prices had gradually increased from a period of stable and low rice prices. The upward drift of prices was due to market fundamentals. On the supply side, these included stagnant to declining rice yields, the deteriorating state of the natural resource base (principally land and water), high petroleum prices and interlinked prices of commodities, climate change, and reduced stocks-to-use ratios for rice. On the demand side, these included increasing population and urbanization, and the rapid growth of per capita income, particularly in China and India.

Following their peak in April 2008, rice prices sharply fell, following

---

[11] C. Martins-Filho, F. Yao, and M. Torero 'High Order Conditional Quantile Estimation Based on Nonparametric Models of Regression' International Food Policy Research Institute (IFPRI 2011) used a non-parametric generalized additive model of commodity price movements estimated using the spline-backfitted kernel (SBK) estimator in computing the higher-order quantiles.

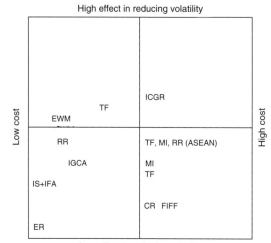

High effect in reducing volatility

Low effect in reducing volatility

Source: Adapted from Torero (2011).

Figure 6.8   Proposals for reducing price volatility

Japan's announcement that it was making available its rice stocks to importing countries like the Philippines to help ease the pressure on the world rice market. The financial crisis in 2007–08 and the ensuing global economic slowdown may have likewise helped in stabilizing the global rice market by reducing demand for the commodity. While floods hit the major rice producing areas in Southeast Asia in the second half of 2011, putting renewed pressure on world rice prices, their impact was however mitigated when India removed its rice export restrictions.

This chapter focuses on policy actions designed to prevent extreme price volatility over those meant to cope with its impact, particularly on the poor. Rice price spikes expose countries to rice insecurity by depriving, particularly their poor, economic access to this food item. Considering that rice is a major spending item of the population of ASEAN countries, the sharp increases of rice prices can also push up inflation.

Torero[12] reviewed several proposed mechanisms to determine their relative implementation cost and contribution to managing volatility. This is shown in Figure 6.8 above, where the administration cost of the

---

[12] M. Torero, Alternative mechanisms to reduce food price volatility and price spikes. Foresight Project on Global Food and Farming Futures (2011). Project website: http://www.bis.gov.uk/Foresight.

mechanism is measured on the east–west axis, while its contribution to reducing volatility is on the south–north axis.

Of several actions recommended by analysts for governments to take to avoid another rice crisis, which have the greater potential of helping them do so? Looking back at past rice crises, three broad categories of actions have the potential of reducing excessive price volatility in rice markets. This chapter focuses on two low-implementation cost but high-impact interventions for reducing volatility, i.e. trade facilitation (combined with productivity potentials) and market information, plus one intervention that is mid-level in terms of implementation costs and low impact on reducing volatility, i.e. reserve stocks. These three major interventions are the key areas of the ASEAN Integrated Food Security Program (AIFS) (Figure 6.8 above).

The ASEAN heads of state had issued the AIFS in 2009. The framework comprises four areas of action, including provision of market information, expansion of conducive food trade, emergency rice reserves, and productivity innovations. A more detailed list of actions in support of the AIFS is found in the ASEAN Strategic Plan of Action for Food Security (SPA-FS). The components identified in the framework for reducing price volatility are all in the AIFS. Of the three, much groundwork has been accomplished in the development of the regional rice reserve and market information and facilitation.

5.   TOWARD FOSTERING TRADE FACILITATION

5.1   Is Rice the Culprit or the Victim?

Rice trade can reduce above normal price volatility by making available the rice surpluses of exporting countries to those experiencing shortages. The rice crisis in 2007–08 and in the 1970s had inflicted significant damage to the confidence of market stakeholders, including their governments, in rice trade. The resurgence of self-sufficiency programs in rice following the recent crisis illustrates what Timmer[13] called the 'retreat to autarchy.' It is unfortunate that rice trade became its casualty.

It is no surprise to observe this inward looking orientation not only of importing countries but exporting countries as well, particularly when global rice trade is thin. The goal of self-sufficiency in rice turns out to be some self-insurance mechanism of governments in rice deficit coun-

---

[13] C. Timmer, 'Reflections on food crises past' [2010] *Food Policy 35* (1), 1–11.

tries against the risk that exporting countries may refuse to supply an adequate volume of rice to them at the right time. This inward orientation is observed among exporting countries as well. The disruptions of rice exports from India and Vietnam in 2007–08 were meant to keep their domestic rice prices within the reach of most of their population.

Trade restrictions exact a higher price for food security from all countries concerned. Headey[14] illustrates the role that rice export restrictions and panic buying by key importing countries such as the Philippines played in the rice price bubble in 2007–08. The total supply shortfall was estimated to be 2.87 million metric tons (mt), which raised world prices by 60.9 percent. However, the accelerated purchases of major rice importers within the first four months of 2008 in reaction to the supply shock added 65.4 percent to the price spike. The combined effect of trade shocks, which amounted to 126.3 percent year to year, contributed significantly to the actual change in world prices from 117 percent to 149 percent.

5.2 Links of Price Volatility and Trade

Excessive price volatility in turn has the effect of reducing trade further. Estimates from a gravity model of trade regression (Table 6.5 below) provide evidence that extreme rice price volatility has a statistically significant negative effect on an already thin rice trade. Extreme rice price volatility is represented in this model by the number of months where the observed monthly price fluctuations exceeded the 97.5 percent higher order quantile. In Table 6.5, three alternative measures of extreme price volatility are reported, and the estimated coefficients of all three are statistically significantly negative,[15] indicating that excessive price volatility tends to dampen rice trade.

Wright[16] called for the strengthening of international trading rules on export restrictions. Stronger disciplines at the multilateral or regional level may provide a counterweight to pressures from the urban population of exporting countries to divert exports toward the domestic market.

---

[14] D. Headey, 'Rethinking the global food crisis: The role of trade shocks' [2011] *Food Policy 36*, 136–46, at Table 2.

[15] One estimator of the 97.5 percent price threshold is based on the assumption that the rates of monthly price changes are normally distributed. The second estimator is from Martins-Filho et al. (2009) who use the generalized additive model of commodity price movements estimated, which also uses the spline-backfitted kernel (SBK) estimator. The third is the generalized autoregressive conditional heteroskedasticity (GARCH) (Bollerslev 1986).

[16] B. Wright, 'International Grain Reserves and Other Instruments to Address Volatility in Grain Markets', Policy Research Working Paper 5028 (August 2009) The World Bank.

Table 6.5   Contribution of extreme rice price volatility to rice export volumes

	Basic model	Alternative Extreme Volatility Measures		
		A[1]	B[2]	C[3]
ln GDP agriculture of exporting country	0.66***	0.76***	0.73***	0.75***
ln GDP per capita of importing country	−0.49*	−0.51*	−0.50*	−0.51*
ln population of exporting country	0.63	0.41	0.51	0.47
ln population of importing country	0.11	0.05	0.08	0.07
time trend	0.03*	0.03*	0.03*	0.03
standard deviation of 24 monthly price fluctuations	−0.08***	0.03	0.01	0
standard deviation of 24 monthly prices one year lag	−0.06*	0.01	0	0.01
extreme volatility A[1]		−0.18***		
extreme volatility A one year lag		−0.26***		
extreme volatility B[2]			−0.18**	
extreme volatility B one year lag			−0.11	
extreme volatility C[3]				−0.16**
extreme volatility C one year lag				−0.21***
F-test: 2 Extreme Var:		0.00***	0.06*	0.01***

Notes:
F-Test results denote P-value that the 2 extreme variables jointly exceed zero.
*** significant at 1%; ** significant at 5%; * significant at 10%.
1   97.5% quantile estimated assuming that the rates of monthly price changes are normally distributed.
2   97.5% quantile estimated using a non-parametric generalized-additive-model of commodity price movements estimated using the spline-backfitted kernel (SBK) estimator (Martins-Filho et al. 2009).
3   97.5% quantile estimated using the generalized autoregressive conditional heteroskedasticity (GARCH) (Bollerslev 1986).

Source: Labao (2012).

Sarris[17] proposed the creation of a food import financing facility and an international grains clearance arrangement. The food import financing facility is a financing facility for net food importing developing countries. Although in place since 1981, the facility has hardly been used because of the policy conditions attached to its access. What is proposed is a facility without the International Monetary Fund conditions to facilitate trade.

[17] A. Sarris. 2009, 'Hedging cereal import price risks and institutions to assure import supplies', FAO working paper.

Wiggins and Keats[18] look at the international grains clearance arrangement as capable of providing guarantees for grain forward trade contracts to reduce counterparty risks.

5.3 Would Rice Trade Help in Reducing Price Volatility?

The ASEAN region is less vulnerable to extreme rice price volatility if it pursues a deeper trade strategy. The point is illustrated using the Riceflow model.[19] The impact of a hypothetical 10 percent decline of the respective outputs of rice in China and India is simulated, using two alternative policy configurations of the ASEAN region.

One is the baseline rice trade policy configuration, which represses rice trade flows. This includes relatively high rice import tariffs of net importing countries such as Indonesia and the Philippines, and off-and-on access to rice imports depending upon the realized domestic outputs of these countries. The other involves a hypothetical scenario that trade is deep, which is represented in the Riceflow model by eliminating tariff and non-tariff restrictions on rice trade, excluding export restrictions.

Table 6.6 below shows the baseline rice import policies of three of the largest importing countries in the region. Malaysia has 40 percent *ad valorem* Most-Favored Nation (MFN) tariff rate on milled rice, while the Philippines has the higher rate at 50 percent. Indonesia has a specific MFN tariff rate of $43/metric ton, which if converted into *ad valorem* rates translates to a variable rate from 9 percent to 11 percent. The Philippines and Indonesia decide on the volume of rice imports that are allowed into the country. On the export side, there are no rice export restrictions in the baseline Riceflow model database.

In Table 6.6, the Philippines has the largest rice import volume at 1.884 million tons in 2009, followed by Malaysia at 0.757 million tons. Indonesia has the lowest volume of rice imports in that year at 0.236 million tons.

---

[18] S. Wiggins and S. Keats. *Volatile World Food Prices and Their Implications: Grain Stocks and Price Spikes* (Overseas Development Institute 2009).

[19] Riceflow is a multi-region, multi-product, spatial equilibrium model that tracks bilateral trade flows and rice value chain adjustments. Developed and maintained by the University of Arkansas Global Rice Economics Program, the latest Riceflow database corresponds to calendar year 2009, and is disaggregated into 60 regions (including all ASEAN countries), three rice types (long grain, medium and short grain, and fragrant rice), and three milling degrees (paddy, brown, and milled), for a total of nine rice commodities. Riceflow has been used extensively to assess different rice market scenarios, such as technological changes, policy changes, consumption changes, and weather-related see A. Durand-Morat and E. Wailes 'Riceflow: A multi-region, multi-product, spatial partial equilibrium model of the world rice economy' Staff Paper SP-03-2010 (Department of Agricultural Economics and Agribusiness, University of Arkansas 2010).

Table 6.6   Baseline rice import most-favored nation (MFN) tariff policies and import flows in the Riceflow model import policies of selected countries in 2009

Country	Policy Type	Paddy	Brown	Milled
Indonesia	Specific import tariff	$43/mt	$43/mt	$43/mt
Malaysia	Ad valorem import tariff	40%	40%	40%
Philippines	Ad valorem import tariff	25%	50%	50%

Import Matrix for Selected Countries (tmt) in 2009

From/To	Indonesia	Malaysia	Philippines
India	0	8	0
Myanmar	0	17	13
Pakistan	0	49	16
Thailand	219	50	147
Viet Nam	17	634	1,708
Total	236	758	1,884

Source: University of Arkansas Riceflow model database in Durand-Morat and Wailes (2010).

The bulk of these imports come from either Thailand or Vietnam. However, Malaysia and the Philippines also source their rice imports from India, Myanmar, and Pakistan.

The results of the two simulations of the impact of a supply shortfall in China or India, are compared with the baseline scenario and the other, the deep trade scenario. These are shown in Table 6.7 below. The production shortfall in China or India moderately increases market import prices in Indonesia, Malaysia, and the Philippines. China's production shortfall increases Indonesia's import price by 9.3 percent, which exceeds the rate of increase for Malaysia and the Philippines by about 5 percentage points. This differential reflects the importance of having more access to imports in mitigating the adverse effects of a supply shock in China, a major rice stakeholder.

In the case of India, a major rice exporter, the pattern is reversed. Indonesia has the lowest increase of import prices. This finding may be explained by the fact that India is not a source of rice for Indonesia, while it is for Malaysia and the Philippines. The decrease of output in India reduces its rice exports, affecting adversely by a relatively larger proportion the two countries in relation to Indonesia. From this result, it appears that trade ties with a country whose output had declined exposes it to the risk of paying a higher import bill. However, given the fact that Malaysia

Table 6.7   Impact of a 10 percent supply shock in China or India with two alternative policy configurations

	Percent Change				
	Baseline	Ben1*	Ben2**	Sce1 – Ben1***	Sce2 – Ben2 ****
Average market price of imports ($/mt)					
Indonesia	445	9.3	0.5	−6	−5
Malaysia	693	4.1	1	−23	−21.6
Philippines	871	4	0.5	−27.7	−26.2
Average retail price of rice ($/mt)					
Indonesia	646	0.9	0	−0.4	−0.4
Malaysia	450	3.6	0.9	−18.7	−17
Philippines	780	3.1	0.4	−17.9	−16
Aggregate demand (tmt)					
Indonesia	41,437	−0.1	0	0	0.1
Malaysia	2,411	−1.1	−0.3	6.1	5.7
Philippines	12,973	−0.8	−0.1	4.9	4.4
Aggregate imports (tmt)					
Indonesia	236	−28.3	−1.8	17.4	20.7
Malaysia	757	−2.9	−0.7	35.7	39.4
Philippines	1,884	−5.2	−0.4	84.9	100
Global trade (tmt)					
World	29,659	4.2	−0.1	5.1	6.2

Notes:
* Benchmark 1: Status quo + 10% production decrease in the PRC ** Benchmark 2: Status quo +10% production decrease in India.
*** Scenario 1: deeper trade by removal of import tariffs in Indonesia, Malaysia, and the Philippines + 10% production decrease in the PRC decrease in India.
**** Scenario 2: deeper trade by removal of import tariffs in Indonesia, Malaysia, and the Philippines + 10% production decrease in India.

Source: Computation by Wailes using the Riceflow model database in Durand-Morat and Wailes (2010).

and the Philippines have access to rice from other countries (e.g. Thailand and Vietnam), the impact of the decrease of output in India is only at no more than 1 percent for Malaysia and 0.5 percent for the Philippines. Thus, it is interesting to note that the larger baseline imports of Malaysia and the Philippines have buffered against the supply shock in one of their export sources.

That trade buffers importing countries from supply shocks is more clearly illustrated with the results from the alternative policy configuration of a deeper trade strategy in the three countries. The last two columns in Table 6.7 show the percentage changes of market import prices of the supply shocks of China and India under the condition that the three countries eliminate their import tariffs.

The same supply shock in China or India reduces, instead of increases, market import prices of rice for the three countries. The strategy aligns the domestic rice prices of these countries to their corresponding world levels. The net fall of rice prices in all three countries indicates that the supply shortfall in China or India is more than offset by the higher exports coming from countries like Thailand or Vietnam, which supports the argument made in this chapter. Resiliency to supply shocks is enhanced with the deeper trade integration of national rice markets within the region. Moreover, it is important to note that the benefit of lower prices is relatively larger for Malaysia and the Philippines.

Domestic retail price movements in all three countries reflect the same pattern in all scenarios as those of the market import prices. However, compared to the latter, the percentage changes of retail prices are lower. This may reflect existing domestic policy distortions in these countries such as rice consumption subsidies.

In response to these price movements, rice domestic demands in the selected countries under the two baseline scenarios fall because of the higher prices induced by the supply shocks. Rice imports fall as market prices of imports rise. Indonesia has the largest percentage decrease in rice imports for the supply shocks in China at 28.3 percent, and in India, at 1.8 percent. However, under the other two deep trade scenarios, where import and local rice prices fall, domestic demands increase except for Indonesia, which has a tenth of a percent decline. Rice imports in all three countries expand as well.

In the case of two counterfactual simulations, the decrease of market import prices encourages more consumption and imports significantly. The Philippines has the largest percentage increase in both local and import demands. In the case of China, its rice imports rise by 84 percent and this is doubled in the case of the supply shock in India. These imports allow higher levels of domestic demands in Malaysia and the Philippines, compared to hardly any impact on consumption in Indonesia.

Global rice trade increases despite the production decline in China, indicating that the higher exports elsewhere in the world more than make up for the loss of production in China. However, global trade slightly falls in the case of the production cut in India. India is one of the top rice exporters in the world. Lastly, global trade in rice and the imports of the three countries rise under a deeper trade scenario.

5.4   Food for Thought: Policy Options for Rice Trade

As noted above, rice export or import to output ratios of the ASEAN region are even lower than their global average of about 7 percent. This reflects the fact that the net importing countries have pursued self-sufficiency in rice that is likely to insure them against the risk of trade disruptions. However, the self-sufficiency strategy raises the cost of rice security in the region.

A more desirable solution is for ASEAN to find a mutually beneficial arrangement to cope with the risk: reduced self-sufficiency targets for guaranteed rice imports. One promising area of cooperation is for importing countries to agree to gradually reduce their respective levels of self-sufficiency targets in rice in exchange for commitments of exporting countries in the region to stay away from unilateral export restrictions. Concretely, in exchange for the commitment of the net importing countries in ASEAN to gradually reduce their self-sufficiency targets, forward contracts in rice in the region, regardless of whether they are between government to government (GtoG), or those involving the private sector (BtoG, GtoB, or BtoB) have to be exempt from export restrictions by the rice exporting countries.

This potential deal is a confidence-building measure for trade, which is particularly important for the net importing countries in the region. It is noted that the retreat to self-sufficiency has been triggered by the loss of confidence of importing countries in an uncertain and already thin rice trade. Exporting countries gain new market access from the commitments of importing countries to source part of their consumption from them. This has the potential of deepening the regional rice trade and makes the region better prepared for supply or demand shocks.

It is worth noting that the level of imports, not exports, constrains rice trade in the region. ASEAN is a net exporter of rice to the world. This export capacity increased with the entry of Vietnam into the league of the world's top five rice exporters. It can still increase further with improvements in both the productivity and processing capacity of Cambodia and Myanmar. The signal to investors to attain this result is that the import demands from the key importing countries such as the Philippines and Indonesia become more predictable, instead of the present pattern of only going to the market as a last resort, i.e. when domestic output and stocks are inadequate.

With adequate and predictable rice demand and investments in the supply chain inside and outside these countries, the rice export supply capacity of the region can increase. In Cambodia, investments to modernize its road infrastructure, logistics, and its rice mills have the potential of increasing the country's marketable surplus to the world. However, if the rice self-sufficiency objective dominates food policy in the region, then rice deficit countries only prove the obvious result that rice trade is thin and unreliable.

Clear set of criteria on the ATIGA waiver
This arrangement for enhancing rice security could be recognized in the ASEAN Trade in Goods Agreement (ATIGA), which entered into force in May 2010. One of the region's landmark economic agreements, ATIGA consolidates all commitments related to trade in goods. ATIGA has two obligations in so far as rice trade is concerned: the reduction of ASEAN Free Trade Area (AFTA) tariffs, and the requirement for member states not to introduce new tariff rate quotas. However, the current obligations in ATIGA as far as rice is concerned continue to reflect the strategy of resorting to trade as a last resort.

Article 24 of ATIGA declares the Protocol to Provide Special Consideration for Rice and Sugar as an integral part. The protocol describes a process by which a member state can waive its obligations under ATIGA as they apply to rice. The process has at most 90 days from the time a member state applies to the AFTA Council. The critical evaluation of the application is done by the Coordinating Committee for the Implementation of the CEPT Scheme for AFTA (CCCA).

A waiver granted is a step away from deepening rice trade in the region. It keeps rice trade thin, and makes the region more vulnerable to extreme rice price volatility. A clear set of criteria by which the CCCA shall evaluate waiver requests for rice is useful. These measures, for example, may draw from those used in general safeguards or the special safeguards in agriculture (e.g. the volume or the price tests). The point is, there has to be objective criteria by which the net importing countries may be allowed to temporarily move away from their respective obligations under ATIGA. Furthermore, the above protocol provides for bilateral consultations between the importing country and the principal suppliers (e.g. Thailand and Vietnam). It is useful to look at putting some structure into these possible consultations.

Decoupling Thailand's pledging program
Unilateral export restrictions need not only come in the form of minimum export prices, export tax, or outright bans. Thailand's rice pledging program provides disincentives to its exporters and reduces rice exports. Based on the official pronouncement about it, the farm price subsidy is about $500 per metric ton of milled rice. Assuming there are adequate fiscal resources to fully implement the pledging program, all rice in Thailand is priced above world market. While Thailand may be able to pass some

of that cost to the consumers overseas, its capacity nonetheless is limited. Other large rice exporters such as Vietnam, India and Pakistan do not need to make world rice consumers pay beyond the production cost of rice. Thus, Thailand is priced out of the market and some of its rice gets diverted to the domestic market or to the warehouses as rice stocks. According to the Thai Rice Exporters Association, Thailand has been continuously losing rice export revenues since late 2011 after the start of the pledging measure. As of 28 May 2012, exports were down by 43.1 percent or 2.86 million tons.

Thailand may consider accompanying its paddy-pledging program with an export subsidy to offset the penalty on its exports. But this would undoubtedly increase the fiscal cost of the program. It may be easier for Thailand to decouple its support to its farmers in order to remove the export restrictive character of the pledging program. The Thai government may use lump sum payments to farmers. These can be administratively difficult to implement considering the number of farmers in Thailand that the program is supposed to reach. However, other countries have shown that cash transfers to a target group of beneficiaries are doable. While the penalty of the pledging program on rice exports remains uncorrected, some Thai exporters are exploring the feasibility of producing and exporting rice in far-flung but trade-friendly African economies.

Expanded coordinated rice policy action
Rice trade can be further deepened if exporting countries such as India and Pakistan become ASEAN partners. India is an off-and-on exporter of non-basmati rice. For instance, it restricted its exports in 2007. However, when its rice stocks ballooned, it dumped them in the world market. Net rice importing countries would be concerned if a large rice exporting country such as India comes and goes in the world rice market. Such disruptions do not build confidence of importing countries in trade. It is suggested that the ASEAN continues to pursue its dialog with both South Asian countries and make them part of the deal, i.e. lower self-sufficiency ratios for exemptions from unilateral export restrictions of all rice forward contracts.

6. MARKET INFORMATION AND MARKET INTELLIGENCE

Wright[20] has pointed out the importance of sharing information about food stocks. Generating and interpreting correctly market information are

---

[20] See *supra* fn 17.

needed to nip in the bud any herding process toward a self-fulfilling crisis. That trade shocks had a very important contribution to explaining the 2007–08 rice crisis[21] may not comprise a fundamental explanation to the crisis. Trade shocks are the outcome of decisions of market stakeholders. Even the policy actions of India, the Philippines, and Vietnam responded to the abnormal market behavior of households in response to developing information of a possible shortage in rice. Timmer[22] argued that speculative behavior destabilized rice price formation in 2007 and in early 2008. Instead of being driven by financial speculation, the price spikes in 2007–08 may be traced to 'the psychology of hoarding behavior. . . by millions of households, farmers, traders and some governments. . . .'

Herd behavior is anchored on the notion of information cascades where succeeding stakeholders ascribe greater weight on the actions taken by their predecessors. It involves a simple follow-the-leader process where followers respond to the signals derived from the action of the leader. If one starts to stock up on rice to avoid future rice prices, the rest of the market buyers follow suit, and as the information sets into a larger group of participants, then the tipping point for a crisis is reached. This typically happens when the followers possess only a 'rough' idea of their own private information, which can easily be overshadowed by previous agents' actions. Accordingly, one would rather be part of a 'consensus,' because it may be more costly for them to gather information about the true state of the market.[23] Banerjee[24] extensively discussed this type of action and established that the resulting equilibrium is normally inefficient.

The G20 policy report[25] sees the importance of investment in information about the food market system. This is only one part of the equation, the other part being the interpretation of such information. The latter may be met by having a regular forum of policymakers that go over the market situation to further share and interpret information as accurately as possible, and to coordinate policies in response to developing events that have the potential of causing excessive volatility in the market.

---

[21] See Heady *supra* fn 15.

[22] C.P. Timmer, 'Did speculation affect world rice prices?' ESA Working Paper No. 09-07 (Agricultural Development Economics Division, FAO 2009).

[23] S. Bikhchandani and S. Sharma, 'Herd behavior in financial markets', *IMF Staff Papers* 47 (3) (2000).

[24] A. Banerjee, 'A simple model of herd behavior' [1992] *Quarterly Journal of Economics 107* (3) 797–817.

[25] G20. 2011. 'Price Volatility in Food and Agricultural Markets: Policy Responses', Policy Report including contributions by FAO, IFAD, IMF, OECD, UNCTAD, WFP, the World Bank, the WTO, IFPRI and the UN HLTF.

6.1 ASEAN Food Security Information System

In market information, the ASEAN Food Security Information System (AFSIS) has set up its capability to gather market information on a few food staples, including rice. AFSIS remains an ASEAN project, and further actions are being undertaken to beef up the system with reliable, up-to-date, and demand-driven information.

The accurate interpretation of the information may be facilitated with a model of the rice market (e.g. Riceflow model), which is capable of assessing the impact on prices, production, consumption, and trade of the various shocks that the region may encounter. These include supply and demand shocks as well as policy changes. It is on the basis of this evidence that policy responses become more informed and useful. Any herding behavior that is based on inaccurate interpretation of market information can lead to an irrational price bubble. With the capability to analyze more accurately the impact of these shocks and to disseminate more precise information, such herding behavior can be cut at source before it develops into a self-fulfilling crisis.

6.2 Market Intelligence Through the ASEAN Rice Trade Forum

Another way of sharing information and increasing confidence in trade is through a platform where multi-stakeholders engaged in the rice sector can regularly meet and discuss market trends and emerging regional and global issues on rice. ASEAN, through the ASEAN Food Security Reserve Board, has thus initiated on a pilot basis the ASEAN Rice Trade Forum. The project can serve the role of sharing and analyzing market information as well as coordinating policy responses to developing events about the rice market.

Under the auspices of the ASEAN Rice Trade Forum, coordinated policy reforms and programs can be identified and agreed upon to rebuild confidence in and deepen rice trade. This may pave the way for making trade a more dependable basis for stabilizing rice prices in the region.

Through evidence-based analysis of policy issues, the forum can serve as the platform for policy debate. Preliminary actions toward this end and as suggested in this paper may include the following:

- an arrangement involving the reduction of rice self-sufficiency ratios by net rice importing countries in exchange for commitments by rice exporting countries to exempt forward contracts in rice from unilateral export restrictions;
- initiation of a discussion with India and Pakistan to secure their

commitment for sustained participation in rice trade. The two large rice exporting countries can be partners of ASEAN as well in the above deal;

- deeper integration of rice trade into ATIGA, i.e. accelerated reduction of preferential import tariffs and a clear set of criteria by which the CCCA may evaluate waiver requests for rice;
- investment programs for increasing the efficiency of the regional supply chain in rice, e.g. reduction of postharvest losses, accreditation of regional rice warehouses, and roll on–roll off (RORO) transportation system for rice for cheaper and faster delivery of stocks; and
- a trade facilitation program for rice, including the harmonization of product grades of rice and a certification system, which is important for regional rice futures trading in an existing regional commodity exchange.

7. RICE STOCKS

Another way of reducing price volatility is through rice stocks. ASEAN has established the ASEAN Plus Three Emergency Rice Reserve System (APTERR), which includes all ten ASEAN member states plus China, Japan, and the Republic of Korea. Each member country will maintain country reserves both for price stabilization and emergency purposes. As a regional rice reserve system, APTERR has three tiers of reserves; the first and second tiers are the more important for reducing price volatility. The APTERR agreement, signed in October 2011 in Jakarta, entered into force in July 2012 after the required number of ratifications.

The region has to yet to see how APTERR will actually operate, although during the time of the East Asia Emergency Rice Reserve (EAERR) which preceded APTERR, there were already Tier 3 (humanitarian) and Tier 1 (forward contracts) transactions that the EAERR facilitated. There is good reason to believe that APTERR will not take the same route as the ASEAN Emergency Rice Reserve (AERR), which was set up in 1979. For one, APTERR's size is tenfold more than AERR used to be and this is because of the commitments of the Plus Three countries. Secondly, APTERR has a modest level of capitalization and it is investing in developing standard operating procedures and the capability to predict possible rice emergencies in the region.

7.1 Conceptual Rationale of Rice Stocks

Wright[26] stressed the importance of food stocks in explaining the recent food crises in 2007–08. A low level of rice stocks-to-use ratios makes markets vulnerable to excessive price volatility even with only moderate supply or demand shocks, if such are accompanied with inaccurate information on the extent of the shock as what happened in 2007–08. Annual stocks-to-use ratios plummeted in the early 2000s. Just before the rice crisis in 2007–08, they were at their lowest level, 18 percent. Dawe[27] and Wright[28] – after controlling for the relatively large holding of rice stocks of China, which is not a major exporter – gave an even lower level of stocks-to-use ratio just before the 2007–08 rice crisis.

Several versions of food reserves have been proposed, including international coordinated grains reserves.[29] APTERR illustrates a multi-country effort of coordinating publicly held rice reserves at the regional level.

Timmer[30] proposed the same for rice stocks in Asia at four levels: (i) private stocks; (ii) public stocks in small importing countries; (iii) public stocks in large importing and producing countries; and (iv) international stocks. Private stockholdings respond to the seasonal nature of rice production. Traders accumulate stocks of rice at harvest time in anticipation of higher prices during the lean months of the year, or in the case of rice surplus countries, private traders do the same in anticipation of higher export prices. Private rice stocks tend to moderate the depressing effect on producer prices at harvest time and to smooth out the surges of prices in times where there is inadequate rice supply.

There is the continuing need for public rice stocks. It is likely that private traders play an important role only in smoothing intra-year fluctuations of prices, as costs and risks can be high for addressing multi-year price volatility, which publicly held rice stocks can address. Public storage may also be needed in intra-year volatility for the following reasons. Private traders tend to get the blame from rice consumers for rice price spikes. Under pressure, the government may consider penalizing those found holding rice stocks for hoarding when prices increase sharply, which

---

[26] See *supra* fn. 17.
[27] D. Dawe, 'The unimportance of "low" world grain stocks for recent world price increases', ESA Working Paper No. 09-01 (February 2009).
[28] See *supra* fn. 17.
[29] J. Lin, 'Prepared remarks presented at the roundtable on "Preparing for the next global food price crisis,"' (Center for Global Development, Washington, DC, 17 October 2008).
[30] See *supra* fn. 14.

introduces a disincentive to private storage and results in suboptimal amount of storage activity.

Additionally, relying completely on private stocks bears a risk to food security, since those stocks will be unloaded in the market at prices not affordable by the poor. Public rice stocks address these problems by releasing rice stocks in affected areas following an emergency situation and through targeted public distribution of rice stocks for the poor.

The size of rice stocks either in the hands of the private or the public sector depends upon the objective for which the stocks are held. In the case of the private sector, the profit motive is apparent. The private traders hold stocks for as long as the discounted expected price at which the stocks are unloaded in the market covers its procurement and holding cost (i.e. of storage and capital).

However, in the case of public stockholdings, governments have the other objective of insuring their respective countries against the risk of being without rice at any point in time. If there are available substitutes to rice, then it may hold a smaller volume of strategic stocks. This may also be the case if rice trade is deep so that even if there are domestic supply shocks in rice, governments can easily import rice from surplus countries. However, if the risk of export restrictions from traditional suppliers is high, then the strategic reserve can increase.

Holding and managing the public stocks can be expensive, since unlike those held by the private sector, these are released when the need arises. The holding time could be long. The manner in which these stocks are released can provide a disincentive to private stockholding, and therefore protocols of their release ought to be designed so as to minimize the disincentive.

Having international or regional stocks can reduce the holding cost. Operating an international rice stock program, however, is costly and runs a high risk of coordination failures. Lin's proposal for international coordinated grain reserves, for example, is estimated to cost about $1.05 billion a year. APTERR's regional reserve system, which is presently capitalized at over $3 million, may likely have a lower operating cost than the international coordinated grain reserves. However, its managers would need to pay attention to the coordination failure that had marked previous efforts in the past. The investment by APTERR in developing its standard operating procedures and in the capability to anticipate rice shortages is noteworthy.

Designed as a social protection measure, emergency reserves have only a small role in reducing food price volatility. These reserves, however, are important in meeting the food needs of the population in a given area hit by calamities or where the normal functioning of food markets are temporarily suspended due to the emergency. The proposal sets up a physical reserve, amounting to about 5 percent of current levels of food aid or about 300,000 metric tons of food in wheat units. The World Food Programme (WFP) is recommended to manage these food reserves strategically located throughout the world. The Group of 8 Plus 5 countries are being tapped for food stock contributions to the reserves and for financing.[31]

Other proposals focus on the operation of the food reserve system. Wright[32] suggested creating a system for information sharing regarding food stocks to improve policy responses to food shortages as they develop, and to allay the fears of stakeholders. While very useful for assessing as correctly as possible the impact of supply or demand shocks on the market, this information nonetheless is difficult to obtain. Incentives for disclosing information about food stocks need to be developed. An international food agency may be needed to coordinate the operations of the reserves and to gather and disseminate information about food stocks.

The debate, however, on the merits and demerits of rice stocks as a mechanism for reducing price volatility continues unabated. What is needed is a forum that can objectively assess the establishment of rice reserve stocks at national and regional levels through a more participatory and consultative approach. On the agenda is the determination of the appropriate levels of rice stocks at regional and country levels.

7.2 APTERR, AFSIS, and the ASEAN Rice Trade Forum

The ASEAN Rice Trade Forum can serve as the fulcrum for open dialogue in ensuring a more effective and transparent process for APTERR implementation. In coordination with APTERR, the forum can be the venue for determining the appropriate size of the regional rice reserves and the country reserves for small importing countries and for large producing and consuming countries. With climate change, there is greater need for reassessing the costs and benefits of holding larger stocks. Timmer[33] views a positive spillover of holding larger stocks in the form of improved confidence of countries and stakeholders in rice trade. Furthermore, in coordination with APTERR, the ASEAN Rice Trade Forum can consider initiating a dialog with Bangladesh, India, and Pakistan to expand the

---

[31] J. von Braun and M. Torero, 'Physical and virtual global food reserves to protect the poor and prevent market failure', Policy Brief 4, June 2008. Washington, DC: International Food Research Institute. http://www.ifpri.org/pubs/bp/bp004.pdf.

[32] See *supra* fn. 17.

[33] See *supra* fn. 14.

regional rice reserves, making this the ASEAN Plus Six Emergency Rice Reserve.

Additionally, AFSIS may use the ASEAN Rice Trade Forum activities in developing a system for sharing information about rice stocks and identifying the appropriate incentives for disclosure. The information on rice stocks is useful in assessing more precisely the impact of food shortages and developing policy responses to food shortages as they arise. Since the information may affect the price at which a trade transaction is made, the information can be difficult to obtain.

8.   CONCLUSION

ASEAN has taken major strides toward avoiding or mitigating the problem of extreme rice price volatility, starting with the ASEAN Integrated Food Security Framework and the Strategic Plan of Action for Food Security. In all three areas of strategic action – specifically, rice trade facilitation, market information and intelligence, and rice stocks – the regional organization has initiated steps toward building a set of institutions for attaining rice security, with the establishment of APTERR and the AFSIS project, and the pilot implementation of the ASEAN Rice Trade Forum.

This chapter suggests further actions toward enhancing ASEAN's resiliency to the problem of extreme rice price volatility. ASEAN is less vulnerable to this problem if it pursues deeper trade strategy, maintains an appropriate size of rice stocks at the regional and country levels, and if it is capable of gathering and interpreting correctly market information and intelligence.

Building confidence in trade remains a major task in ASEAN. Toward this end, this chapter suggests several actions, including: (i) pursuing arrangements whereby rice importing countries gradually reduce their rice self-sufficiency targets in exchange for import guarantees from the rice exporting countries; (ii) instituting clearer set of criteria for the use of rice waivers under ATIGA; (iii) decoupling Thailand's rice pledging program; and (iv) expanding coordinated rice policy with India and Pakistan. These actions include measures for enhancing the productivity of rice farming and processing, particularly in Cambodia and Myanmar.

Gathering, analyzing, and disseminating market information are important tasks for correcting cascades of wrong information about the situation of the market and preventing a self-fulfilling price bubble. The AFSIS project has been gathering and disseminating market information and developing an early warning mechanism regarding a developing crisis situation. While actions are needed to beef up AFSIS with reliable, up-to-date, and demand-driven information, it is also important to develop the capability of interpreting market information accurately. This can be facilitated with a rice market model capable of making not only a market situation and outlook but also policy analysis.

Besides smoothing intra-year or multi-year rice price volatility, rice stocks are needed in building the confidence of stakeholders in rice trade. Toward this end, the determination of the appropriate levels of rice stocks at the regional and country levels is needed. This may be an initiative under the ASEAN Rice Trade Forum in coordination with APTERR. To expand the regional rice reserve system, ASEAN may consider initiating a dialog with the Plus Three countries and with Bangladesh, India, and Pakistan on the proposal for an ASEAN Plus Six emergency rice reserve.

There is a need for continuing the pilot implementation of the ASEAN Rice Trade Forum. The forum can serve several roles, including: (i) gathering market information and intelligence as well as analyzing the impact of demand and supply shocks on the rice market; and (ii) providing a platform for discussing the proposals presented in this chapter, or any other ideas for deepening rice trade in the region and avoiding extreme rice price volatility. These policy actions may cover a trade facilitation program for rice, including the harmonization of product grades of rice and a certification system, which are important for regional rice futures trading, or an accelerated reduction of rice import tariffs to raise the level of integration of rice in ATIGA.

7. A private sector view of food security and pricing volatility

James McVitty

INTRODUCTION

Everyone must eat. A healthy active life has its foundation in a nutrition-ally balanced diet. Food is the fuel for life, an absolute non-negotiable, and as such food security is at the absolute apex of human concerns. Ensuring that basic food security needs are met, both now and in the future, is one of the world's most pressing issues.

Food security is a major, global challenge for the twenty-first century. The food security challenge is to provide improved nutrition to a global population with less impact on natural resources. Food security is not a single issue, but instead requires addressing a variety of factors.

Food security is too large of a mandate for one global organization such as the Food and Agriculture Organization (FAO) to address alone. Other organizations such as the WTO, WHO and APEC all have a critical role to play and without overarching political oversight and commitment, policy responses are likely to remain uncoordinated and piecemeal. Food is generally not very high on the global political agenda and often only emerges at times of crisis. This should not be the case; food policies need to be elevated to become part of the global sustainability debate.

Food security issues are often not well defined, with different institu-tions often using different language to talk about the same problem. Solutions need to be developed through a multi-stakeholder approach at local, regional and global levels. Key stakeholder groups include the private sector, public sector, institutions (academic, R&D, global, regional or local organizations), NGOs, consumers, and farmers. The food industry is well placed to contribute to policy discussions given that food companies interact with numerous stakeholders right across the supply chain.

COMPONENTS OF FOOD SECURITY

While food security is a problem for all of humanity, actual food security impacts occur at a localized level. There are geographies where food productive capability is in abundance, and geographies where it is not. It is also worth noting that access to food is fundamentally an income, rather than an agriculture production problem. Singapore is a good example: Singapore has no farms, but does not have an issue with access to food.

Ultimately food security is a function of farming efficiency, and of efficiency in moving food from areas of abundance to areas of need. However there are a variety of other related and significant factors which are crucial to food security, such as production efficiency, an open trade environment, food safety, nutritional security, and managing price volatility. The last of these is the primary focus of this chapter.

PRICE VOLATILITY IN AGRICULTURE

Food prices (in real terms) fell by an average of 0.7 per cent (increased by 1.7 per cent in nominal terms) a year during the twentieth century despite a significant increase in food demand. Higher prices play an important role in providing a signal to the market that a supply response is needed to meet rising demand. Food prices, as a percentage of income, have been declining since WWII, and low prices are one reason for under-investment in agriculture over the last few decades.[1]

However, a combination of falling yield growth, increases in demand for feed and fuel, supply-side shocks (due to droughts, floods, and variable temperatures), declines in global buffer stocks, and policy responses (e.g., governments in major agricultural regions banning exports) has contributed to a rapid rise in nominal food prices of almost 120 per cent (or 6.1 per cent annually) since the turn of the century.[2]

High and volatile food prices in recent years have led to serious concerns about food security and rising poverty in the world's poorest countries, where up to 75 per cent of income is spent on food.[3] It should be noted that a degree of agricultural commodity price volatility, as a result of

---

[1] OECD, *Water Use in Agriculture* (OECD 2013): http://www.oecd.org/environment/wateruseinagriculture.htm.

[2] Ibid.

[3] World Bank, *Agricultural Trade Policies and Food Security*. (World Bank conference presentation 2010). Found at: http://siteresources.worldbank.org/INTRANETTRADE/Resources/Internal-Training/287823-1 256848879189/6526508-1312911329405/8091228-1 321292670410/PPT_Martin.pdf.

natural conditions, demand shocks and time-lags for agricultural supply response, is a normal characteristic of agricultural commodity markets. The underlying cause of food price volatility is an imbalance between supply and demand. Key factors influencing this include supply shocks (resulting from factors such as weather, trade policy e.g., export restrictions, and disease), the long lag time in agriculture between increased demand and the supply response, and volatility in input costs.

MARKET INTERVENTION APPROACHES TO PRICE RISK MANAGEMENT

Over the past half-century, the international community and governments have attempted to manage commodity price risks by stabilizing price volatility or making the price distribution less variable through market interventions. Key among these mechanisms are compensatory mechanisms, stabilization mechanisms and international commodity agreements.

There are a number of problems associated with the use of intervention approaches. Policy responses which intervene in market prices act as a disincentive to the development of market based tools. The inefficiencies that such policy tools create are costly and slow the development of both the rural and the overall economy by masking price signals.

A further problem is that the global trade market for food, including dairy, is very thin. The FAO estimate that only 12 per cent of food is traded between countries.[4] A very thin global food market is dangerous because countries are more susceptible to local food production productivity swings. The food security problem will become more pronounced as global demand increases if the supply side is not free to respond.

There are a variety of examples of where government policies have acted to increase international market price volatility, or distorted market signals, thus discouraging investment in agriculture. Using dairy as an example, given the thin share of dairy traded on the global market, it has been particularly market distorting when these policies have been used by some of the world's largest producers. EU export subsidies, for example, undermined domestic producers in developing countries and depressed world market prices. The impact of these export subsidies, using international whole milk powder prices as an example, can be seen in Figure 7.1 below.

---

[4] FAO, *Agricultural Trade and Food Security* (FAO 2013) at http://www.fao.org/docrep/003/x6730e/X6730E03.HTM.

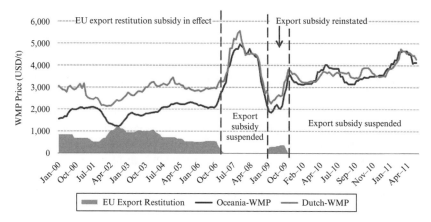

Figure 7.1   Impact of EU export restitution (subsidy) on international whole milk powder (WMP) prices

Figure 7.1 clearly demonstrates the impact which EU export restitution subsidies have had on the global market. The export restitution subsidies are variable export subsidies given to traders where there is a difference between the higher internal Common Agricultural Policy price of a commodity versus a lower world price. While the subsidies were in effect, international milk powder prices were artificially suppressed, and the suspension and subsequent reintroduction of these subsidies caused significant volatility in global prices for the affected commodities. Removal of the subsidies has moved international prices to parity with internal European and US prices.

India's volatile trade policy settings, as the world's largest producer and consumer of dairy, are another example. India has tariff barriers on dairy which are generally prohibitive to trade, and may also periodically impose export bans on certain dairy products. In the event of a poor monsoon season however, tariff barriers are sometimes relaxed to facilitate imports, causing upward pressure on global dairy prices. Argentina's export bans are another example of government policies which have the effect of exporting price volatility onto the international market.

The use of food reserves as a means to manage price volatility is currently being considered in a number of markets. Although food reserves for emergency humanitarian use have their place, if used as a price risk management policy tool they have the same distortionary impacts on agriculture markets as identified above. Stocks should not be so large as to suppress market price signals and investment in agriculture.

MARKET-BASED PRICE RISK MANAGEMENT TOOLS

Organized commodity futures exchanges have existed for more than a century. For agriculture, some of the primary exchanges are the CME, Eurex, NYSE Euronext, and in New Zealand, the NZX.

The development of market-based price risk management tools (derivative markets) and liquid futures markets is important for managing the inherent volatility in agricultural markets and ensuring that global food markets function effectively. Policy responses which intervene in market prices act as a disincentive to the development of market-based tools.

Market-based price risk management instruments have a number of advantages over 'interventionist' approaches:

- Market-based instruments, such as futures contracts, provide certainty of future revenues and/or expenditures. Dairy farmers in the US for example can use CME futures contracts to effectively lock in feed costs as well as milk price. Knowing what their margins will be provides farmers with the ability to make productivity increasing investments with confidence.
- Market-based instruments rely on market prices rather than administrative prices, which pass risk to viable financial markets that are better able and willing to assume risks. In most cases, they cost less than government price intervention programmes.[5]
- Commodity futures markets remain the most efficient price formation mechanisms, providing reliable benchmarks for physical trade. Because a wide group of participants can use the market, each participant brings into the price formation process the information possessed on future demand and supply conditions. In contrast to cash markets, futures markets are highly transparent yet anonymous, making price manipulation more difficult.[6]
- Another important benefit of exchange-traded instruments is the low cost of executing transactions, liquidity and also standardized requirements regarding quality, quantity and delivery dates, etc.[7]

---

[5] Myong Goo Kang and Nayana Mahajan, *An introduction to market-based instruments for agricultural price risk management* (FAO 2006).
[6] Ibid.
[7] Ibid.

THE ROLE OF LIQUIDITY PROVIDERS

Liquidity providers are a necessary part of a developed financial market as they plug the gap when hedging requirements of commercial buyers and sellers do not coincide, offering a counterparty for trades that might otherwise have no takers. It has become increasingly popular to blame speculators for run-ups in commodity prices, however empirical studies have found little evidence to support this, instead indicating that they may actually reduce price volatility.

Cash-settled and physically delivered futures derive their price from the commercial price references. While liquidity providers play a massive role in liquid financial markets, they are all but absent from physical markets. Commercial participants use derivative markets to hedge and thus transfer risk – somebody else has to take on this risk and liquidity providers play a key part in this.

Derivative markets exist to facilitate the transfer of risk from one party to another. Commercial players (producers and consumers of the physical commodities) use derivative markets to mitigate their exposure to volatile prices via hedging. By hedging their risk on the underlying physical exposures, producers and consumers can access capital at a lower cost, thereby facilitating economic growth and improving the capital formation process. However, for this to occur the risk needs to be transferred to someone else. Speculators, or liquidity providers, fulfil this role by taking on the risk with the expectation of making a return for doing so. Liquidity providers help to improve the efficiency of markets. With the motivation to make a profit they both buy and sell in the financial markets acting as an intermediary agent and narrowing the bid-ask spread. Liquidity providers cover a range of market participants from the banks at one end, through sovereign wealth funds and insurance companies, to both government and public pension funds at the other end.

Liquidity providers are both buyers and sellers when participating in derivative markets, both buying and selling futures positions for all commodities. If they were truly responsible for price increases they would only be on the buy side in order to bid prices up. A number of studies have been undertaken to determine what impact liquidity providers have on commodity prices. The results suggest that speculation is not the main source of price volatility:

- Irwin, Sanders and Merrin (2009)[8] found that markets without index fund participation (fluid milk and rice futures) and commodities without futures markets (apples and edible beans) showed price increases over the 2006–08 period in the absence of speculators. In addition Over the Counter (OTC) derivative markets, which do not have speculators involved, are more volatile than the exchange traded markets which do include speculators (Irwin and Sanders, 2010).[9] These findings are contrary to the traditional view about liquidity providers.

- Jeffrey and Harris (2009)[10] employed Granger Causality tests to analyse the lead and lag relations between the price and trading position of various types of traders in crude oil futures market. Their findings show that the change in liquidity providers' position is unlikely to stimulate the price over-shooting. Instead, the price changes precede liquidity provider's position change indicating they are responding to the market fundamentals.

- In one example study, Irwin and Sanders (2010)[11] summarize the results from a preliminary study on index and swap funds in both agricultural and energy commodity futures markets. They conclude that index and swap funds did not cause the bubble in commodity futures prices and that they did not increase market volatility.

- *The Economist* concluded that 'there is almost no evidence to connect speculators to the commodity-price spikes that they are routinely blamed for creating', consistent with the above results suggesting that there is little relationship between speculative positions and movement in commodity futures market. (Stoll and Whaley, 2009;[12] Harris and Buyuksahin, 2009;[13] Sanders and Irwin, 2010;[14] Aulerich, Irwin, and Garcia, 2010[15]).

---

[8] S.H. Irwin, D.R.Sanders and R.P. Merrin, 'Devil or angel? The role of speculation in the recent commodity price boom (and bust)' [2009] *Journal of Agricultural and Applied Economics*, 41:393–402.

[9] S.H. Irwin and D.R. Sanders, 'The impact of index and swap funds on commodity futures markets: Preliminary results' (OECD Food, Agriculture and Fisheries Working Papers, No. 27, 2010).

[10] J.H. Harris and B. Buyuksahin, 'The role of speculators in the crude oil futures market' (Working Paper, 2009). Available at SSRN: http://ssrn.com/abstract=1435042.

[11] *Supra* fn.9.

[12] H.R. Stoll and R.E. Whaley, 'Commodity index investing and commodity futures prices' (Working Paper, 2009).

[13] *Supra* fn.10.

[14] *Supra* fn.9.

[15] N.M. Aulerich, S.H. Irwin, and P. Garcia, 'The price impact of index funds in commodity futures markets: Evidence from the CFTC's daily large trader reporting system' (Working Paper, 2010).

PRICE VOLATILITY IN THE DAIRY INDUSTRY – THE NEW ZEALAND EXAMPLE

Dairy is a significant industry in New Zealand, making up around one-quarter of New Zealand's annual merchandise exports. The New Zealand dairy industry is predominantly pasture-based, with a temperate climate ensuring adequate feed for herds year-round. New Zealand is unique in that it exports approximately 95 per cent of the milksolids produced domestically.

On-farm Price Risk Management

Importantly, New Zealand farmers receive no government subsidies. This has encouraged a focus on low-cost, high-productivity farming systems. New Zealand has a very liberalized tariff policy, and dairy products receive little or no tariff protection. The combination of these factors means that New Zealand farmers are very responsive to trends in the international market. As an example of this, Figure 7.2 below provides an indication of the relationship between NZ farmer milk payouts and milk production.

As demonstrated previously, the removal of export subsidies (post-2007

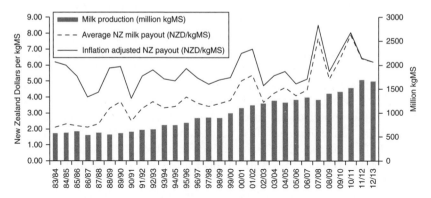

Source: Livestock Improvement Corporation (2013) New Zealand Dairy Statistics 2012–13.[16]

Figure 7.2   New Zealand farmer milk payouts and total New Zealand milk production

---

[16] Livestock Improvement Corporation (2013) New Zealand Dairy Statistics 2012–13. Available from http://www.lic.co.nz/lic_Publications.cfm.

for EU) has been an important factor in the convergence of international milk prices with EU/US domestic prices. In the past, depressed international prices suppressed farmers' confidence to invest in the New Zealand dairy industry. Higher international milk prices have resulted in higher New Zealand milk prices (which are around 95 per cent dependent on returns in the international market) and encouraged investment into dairy production in efficient producers like New Zealand – despite the price volatility they face from year to year. As a result of ongoing investment, dairy production within New Zealand has continued to increase (see Figure 7.2 above). Of course other factors have influenced international milk prices, such as growing demand for dairy in regions such as Asia, but the impact that policy settings, such as EU subsidies, have had on international dairy prices is significant.

In New Zealand's experience, exposure to the international market and price volatility has encouraged innovation and efficiency across the supply chain from farm to consumer. This innovation is pursued both by the cooperative and privately owned dairy companies operating within New Zealand, as well as via DairyNZ. DairyNZ is an industry with good organization, representing New Zealand's dairy farmers, and funded by farmers through a levy on milksolids. DairyNZ's purpose is to secure and enhance the profitability, sustainability and competitiveness of New Zealand dairy farming by leading innovation in world-class dairy farming.[17]

As a result of exposure to international markets, New Zealand farmers have become adept at controlling their on-farm costs from one season to the next to help manage market price volatility. However in addition to this, other market based solutions are being explored in the New Zealand context. Fonterra, for example, has developed a programme to offer farmers the option of increased certainty of returns with a guaranteed milk price. This voluntary pilot programme began in the 2013/14 season, offering farmers the opportunity to lock in a fixed (or 'guaranteed') milk price for a portion of their milk supply for the season. Such a programme allows a farmer to plan, budget, invest in, and manage their business with greater certainty. On the other side of the ledger, it allows Fonterra to lock in contracts with customers at a set price to hedge against commodity price movements for an equivalent volume of product.

---

[17] See DairyNZ.co.nz.

PRICE RISK MANAGEMENT FOR DAIRY CUSTOMERS

The primary steps in price risk management are to *identify*, *measure and forecast*, and *manage*. The key elements in these steps are presented in Figure 7.3 below.

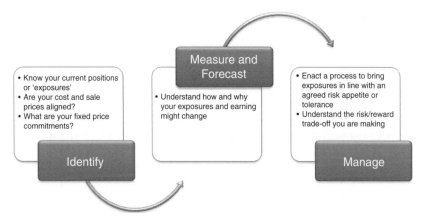

Figure 7.3   The price risk management process

Key to identifying your risk exposures is the basic understanding of the alignment between your costs and sales prices, and to what extent price changes can be passed through. For agricultural commodities with a high degree of price volatility, and a limited ability of food manufacturers to respond quickly through pricing, price risk management is an important tool (see Figure 7.4 below).

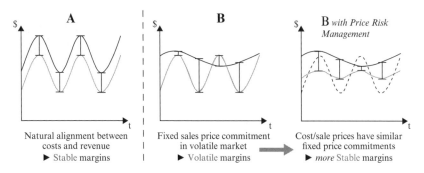

Figure 7.4   Cost and revenue alignment scenarios

EXAMPLES OF MARKET-BASED INSTRUMENTS FOR DAIRY – *GLOBAL*DAIRYTRADE AND THE NZX

Price volatility in the dairy industry has been unprecedented in recent years and this creates risk for all market participants. This volatility is expected to continue, driving demand for price risk management tools. One such tool is *global*Dairytrade (GDT). GDT is an internet-based electronic auction trading platform for cross-border trade in commodity dairy products, which include bulk milk powders, butter and milkfat, bulk cheese, and protein products. The auctions, or 'trading events' are held twice each month. GDT is a credible and responsive price reference point for the products being traded, as well as an efficient sales channel.

Trading events are conducted as ascending-price clock auctions run over several bidding rounds. In each auction a specified maximum quantity of each product is offered for sale at a pre-announced starting price. Bidders bid the quantity of each product that they wish to purchase at the announced price. If the price of a product increases between rounds, to ensure their desired quantity a bidder must bid their desired quantity at the new, higher price. Generally, as the price of a product increases, the quantity of bids received for that product decreases. The trading event runs over several rounds with the prices increasing round to round until the quantity of bids received for each product on offer matches the quantity on offer for the product (see Figure 7.5 below).[18]

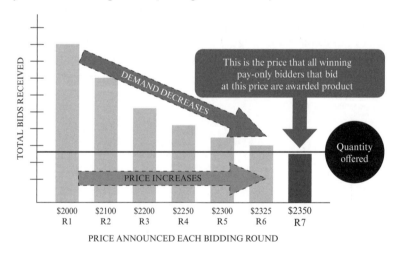

Figure 7.5   Global Dairy Trade (GDT) auction process

---

[18] See http://www.globaldairytrade.info/AboutGdt.aspx.

Aside from Fonterra, other sellers also now sell dairy products on GDT, including Murray Goulburn Cooperative Co Ltd, Arla Foods, Amul, EUROSERUM, Dairy America, and Land O'Lakes. Adding sellers leads to more trust in the marketplace, as well as a more robust reference price. A robust price supports credible derivative financial products.

The key benefit for food manufacturers participating in GDT is that it provides greater control over exposure to commodity price risk, as bidders choose their desired mix of contract maturities and hence their own exposure to commodity price risk. There are six contract periods to choose from: contract Period 1 will ship during the first month after the month that the trading event was held; contract Period 2 will ship during the second month after the month that the trading event was held; and so on. The regular auction events allow purchasers to fix prices in advance for as much or as little of their portfolio as they wish. GDT also provides customers with a quick sales process and a purchase process with lower transactions costs for both buyer and seller.[19]

The NZX now offers price risk management tools in the form of Futures and Options contracts settling against GDT results. Dairy Futures and Options are designed to manage risk and smooth out volatility, creating price certainty, transparency and a forward view of market sentiment. By trading on the futures and options market, dairy participants create price certainty. For a processor, hedging can provide certainty for themselves and the farmer over prices paid for liquid milk. It also means purchasers can secure supply and manage their own price risk, providing certainty over future purchase prices.[20] Futures contracts are currently offered for whole milk powder, skim milk powder, and AMF. An options contract is available for whole milk powder.

CONCLUDING REMARKS

Food security is a major, global, challenge for the twenty-first century. Ultimately food security is a function of farming efficiency and of efficiency in moving food from areas of abundance to areas of need. However it is also influenced by the trade environment, food safety considerations, price volatility, and nutritional security.

Food security is not a single issue, but a variety of factors require to be addressed.

---

[19] See http://www.globaldairytrade.info/QAs.aspx.
[20] See NZX website: http://www.nzxfutures.com/dairy/learn_more.

Rising price volatility in food has been felt in particular in the world's poorest countries, where often a significant percentage of income is spent on food. Increased volatility in food prices since the turn of the century has prompted a variety of policy responses by governments to deal with the issue. Market intervention approaches have some appeal in stabilizing price volatility or making the price distribution less variable. However, policy responses which intervene in market prices act as a disincentive to the development of market based tools, discourage investment in agriculture, and are generally much more costly than market approaches.

Fonterra believes that the development of market-based price risk management tools that all participants in the supply chain can use, as well as the development of responsive pricing signals (like GDT) are essential for managing the inherent volatility in agricultural markets and ensuring that global food markets function effectively.

PART III

8. Food security and limits to resources

Lee Ann Jackson[*]

INTRODUCTION

Changing global climate conditions are creating new stresses on agricultural producers and new demands on policymakers. Given the decreased predictability in the agricultural economy, policymakers are increasingly called upon to intervene to address food security concerns. Food security policy interventions often target agricultural production to increase supply, including by creating incentives to intensify production, such as through increased input use or expansion of cultivation. In attempting to address current food needs, policy interventions that influence the decisions of agricultural producers may have consequences on the state of the resources that are integral to future agricultural production. The challenge for policymakers is to create conditions that provide appropriate incentives for producers in the short term without leading to long-term degradation of resources.

This chapter discusses how resource constraints in food production affect food security and emphasizes the need to adopt policies to strengthen the resilience of agricultural production systems. This chapter begins by briefly describing the current state of global food security and resource constraints in the context of global agricultural production. It then describes predicted future food security outcomes, highlighting implicit economic assumptions about resource constraints and how these influence model results. The concept of resilience is described, including how this concept is useful in terms of focusing attention on the medium- and long-term impacts of food security interventions. This chapter then concludes by highlighting policy approaches that encourage sustainable food security outcomes.

---

[*] The views expressed in this chapter are solely the author's responsibility and do not purport to be an official position of the WTO.

THE STATE OF GLOBAL FOOD SECURITY

The Food and Agriculture Organization (FAO) defines food security as 'a situation that exists when all people at all times have physical, social and economic access to sufficient, safe and nutritious food that meets their dietary needs and food preferences for an active and healthy life'. Food security depends on three main factors: food availability, food access (ie. economic affordability), and food utilization, all of which are influenced by climate change.

Statistics from both the FAO and the International Food Policy Research Institute (IFPRI) indicate a declining hunger trend, however one in eight people continue to suffer from chronic hunger, with most of these living in the developing world. The FAO's State of Food Insecurity in the World reports that 805 million people in 2012–14 were suffering from chronic hunger, which is a 209 million lower than in 1990–92. IFPRI's measurement of food insecurity, the Global Hunger Index (GHI), aggregates three indicators (the proportion of people who are undernourished, the proportion of children less than five years old who are underweight and the mortality rate of children less than five) (IFPRI 2013). The world GHI fell 39 per cent in 2014 as compared to the GHI from 1990.

These global averages mask dramatic differences across regions. The FAO reports that most of the world's undernourished live in Southern Asia, followed by Sub-Saharan Africa and Eastern Asia. Africa is the region with the highest prevalence of undernourishment. In most countries in Asia the proportion of people undernourished has decreased, however improvement in South Asia has been relatively slow. IFPRI's GHI indicates that hunger is a persistent problem in Asia, mostly due to sustained under-nutrition in children caused by low nutritional, educational and social status of women in the region.

PREDICTING FUTURE FOOD SECURITY

Future looking simulations indicate that the prevalence of chronic hunger may recede in most countries by 2050, but hunger is not expected to disappear.[1] These simulations suggest that the prevalence of chronic hunger in developing countries would decrease to an average of 5 per cent of their population; however this average result hides the specific outcomes

---

[1] G.C. Nelson, M. Rosegrant, I. Gray, C. Ingersoll, R. Robertson, and S. Tokgoz, *Food Security, Farming and Climate Change to 2050* (IFPRI 2010).

on hunger. Indeed, 7 per cent of the population of Sub-Saharan Africa would still be expected to suffer from chronic hunger, and some individual countries in that region could have prevalence rates over 15 per cent.

Food security outcomes will be a result of changing agricultural supply and demand. The affordability of food also determines who will have economic access. Therefore the impact of food security policies on prices is a key component of determining outcome of these interventions. Modelling efforts to explain and predict food security outcomes include assumptions about basic economic relationships. Models often highlight the importance of supply-side interventions, because many of the key factors that determine demand are less amenable to policy intervention.

On the demand side, the key variables that determine market behaviour include population, income and preferences. Because these variables are predictable they do not contribute to short-term volatility of agricultural prices. Global population is expected to increase to 9.6 billion by 2050 and global food demand is expected to increase 60 per cent in the same amount of time.[2] Consumption of many agricultural commodities in developing countries is expected to increase in the next decade due to growing populations and increasing incomes.[3] It is expected increasing incomes will also lead to diversification of developing country diets, moving from consumption of basic staple crops to meat and dairy. This in turn contributes to a higher demand for grains and protein meal as inputs into the production of livestock and meat.

While the demand side of agricultural markets has traditionally been considered to be relatively predictable, some structural changes to agricultural markets can affect predictability of demand. Recent increased production of biofuels has created links between fuel markets and agricultural markets, which means that agricultural demand is also influenced by the price of fuel. As fossil fuel prices increase, demand for biofuel increases, which in turn increases the demand for agricultural crops as inputs to the production of biofuels. Thus, the demand side of global food security has become less predictable due to the introduction of biofuel production.[4]

Global food supply also has predictable elements, such as the distribution of global arable land. Yet food supply remains more variable than global demand due to several factors. Weather affects agricultural

[2] Center for Global Development working group on food security, 'Time for FAO to shift to a higher gear' (Center for Global Development 2013).

[3] OECD-FAO, *Agricultural Outlook* (OECD 2015).

[4] S. Tokgoz, W. Zhang, S. Msangi, P. Bhandary, 'Biofuels and the future of food: Competition and complementarities', (2012) *Agriculture* 2(4): 414–35: Doi:10.3390/agriculture2040414.

production, and in the current climate context extreme weather events, such as droughts and flooding, are more likely to occur. The climate impacts will be distributed unevenly among regions and the level of agricultural production and integration with the world markets will influence the food security impacts.

OECD and FAO jointly produce forecasts for agricultural commodity outlook on an annual basis. The OECD-FAO 2015 Agricultural Outlook (the Outlook) forecasts that production of commodities included in the annual outlook simulates global agricultural will increase 1.5 per cent on average during the period 2015–24. In the previous decade production grew on average 2.2 per cent annually. This decline in growth reflects expected rising costs, increasing resource constraints, and increasing environmental pressure. All of these factors limit the expected potential supply response to growing demand.

The Outlook is based on a partial equilibrium model, the Aglink-Cosimo, which allows an examination of the main agricultural commodity markets. In this model, world markets for agricultural commodities are competitive and prices are determined through a global or regional equilibrium in supply and demand. The OECD has incorporated elements into the model to allow for the analysis of the impacts of weather and macroeconomic changes on agricultural production and trade. The standard price projections that OECD produces using this model are predicated on the assumption of normal production conditions and the absence of unforeseen market shocks such as droughts and animal disease outbreaks. The Outlook modelling for 2013 examined the impact of relaxing this assumption, showing that agricultural commodity price prospects become much more variable when these type of market shocks are introduced.[5]

In terms of limits on water availability the model does not directly incorporate the possibility of changing availability of water inputs, but captures the potential impact of these changing resource constraints by assuming their impact on yield. For example, the 2013 Outlook examined the impact of the 2012 drought in the US. In order to introduce the effect of the drought, simulations included a negative shock on yields of particular commodities based on the difference between actual yields during the drought year and the forecast yields for that year. With lower yields, production drops significantly and the resulting price increases are correlated with the size of the shock and the tightness of the market. Similarly, the amount of water available for agricultural production in non-irrigated systems is also fixed. Furthermore, irrigation moves water from one area

---

[5] OECD-FAO, *Agricultural Outlook* (OECD 2013).

to another, without increasing the total supply of water. As a result, interventions that increase the use of water more quickly than the water can be replaced will lead to a decrease in total supply.

Various international agencies, such as the World Bank and IFPRI have been examining the effect of risk on agricultural productivity using interdisciplinary models that incorporate both economic and biological interactions to see how various resource constraints limit production over time. Some interesting work in this area uses geographical information systems to develop maps that allow an examination of distribution of both economic and biological impacts associated with particular land productivity, water and climate risks. While useful in providing aggregate global results, the downside to this type of modelling is that the potential interaction among various risks may not be captured in modelling results. For example, there might be a compound impact from climate change if water availability changes and these changes alter the viability of particular insect groups. Still, a closer examination of the spatial distribution of key agricultural resources allows for a more nuanced understanding of how changes to the economic and biological system can influence food security outcomes.

Resource Constraints

Model simulations of future agricultural production include assumptions related to factors that affect agricultural supply, in particular related to agricultural yields, land availability and water availability. Whereas previously these factors could be considered to be relatively predictable, climate change will impact each of these factors and increase the uncertainty in the models' predictions.

Agricultural yields

Improving agricultural productivity can contribute to increasing food production. Some estimates show that in the past decade factor productivity growth accounted for about 75 per cent of global output growth. This figure was less than 7 per cent in the 1960s when increases in land and input use largely explained output growth. There is lack of consensus on whether agricultural productivity growth has been increasing or decreasing. According to USDA estimates, in the past two decades total factor productivity growth was greater than world population growth.[6] While

---

[6] K. Fuglie, 'Productivity growth and technology capital in the global agricultural economy' in K. Fuglie, S. Wang and V. Ball (eds), *Productivity Growth in Agriculture: An International Perspective* (CAB International 2012).

Table 8.1   Sources of growth for major cereals in developing countries

		Annual growth (% per year)			Contribution to growth (%)	
		Production	Harvested land	Yield	Harvested land	Yield
Wheat	1961–2007	3.62	0.68	2.92	19	81
	2007–2050	0.87	0.01	0.86	1	99
Rice, paddy	1961–2007	2.46	0.54	1.91	22	78
	2007–2050	0.58	−0.05	0.63	−9	109
Maize	1961–2007	3.55	1.05	2.47	30	70
	2007–2050	1.43	0.59	0.83	41	59

Source: FAO 2012.

rates of output growth have fallen, growth rates of input use have fallen even more.

Crop yields differ by regions. Sub-Saharan Africa and South Asia have crop yields that are much lower than other regions. For example, rice yields in India are only 2 MT/hectare as compared to 6 MT/hectare in East and West Asia.[7]

There is also substantial variability among commodities regarding the sources of growth. Table 8.1 above illustrates the differences across several cereal crops with respect to the contribution of area of harvested land and yields to growth in production. The table illustrates that, for paddy rice in particular, yield will have an increasingly important role in production in the future.

Climate change will also have unexpected ecological impacts on agricultural systems. Changes in temperature can alter the geographical distribution of insects, for example, creating new threats for agricultural production from pest and disease. Milder winters have been shown to increase the survival of some insects, and rising temperatures could lead to faster insect growth and movement.[8] Thus climate change can fundamentally alter ecosystem structure by altering the composition of species in space and in time and the ultimate impact will be less predictable production.

[7] OECD, *Global Food Security. Challenges for the Food and Agricultural System.* (OECD 2013).

[8] J.S. Bale, et al., 'Herbivory in global climate change research: Direct effects of rising temperature on insect herbivores' [2012] *Global Change Biology* 8(1): 1–16.

Land constraints

Land quality and soil conditions are critical determinants of agricultural production. Land degradation, including soil erosion, water logging and contamination, has in some regions decreased the total amount of productive land available for crop cultivation. This degradation has been the result of intensification practices that extract nutrients from the soil without replenishing them and lead to the overuse of water. The OECD notes that it is estimated that 25 per cent of all agricultural land is highly degraded.[9] While soil loss and degradation may not represent a significant constraint for global agricultural production, it can be a serious constraint for fragile resource areas. Yield constraints due to soil erosion and degradation, for example, may be significant in arid regions of Sub-Saharan Africa where soils are more fragile.

Land degradation from intensification of production is possible in many regions. Some indicators provide a snapshot of the global state of land degradation. FAO has identified, for example the following characteristics as relevant:

- Net primary productivity
- Rainfall use efficiency
- Aridity
- Rainfall variability
- Erosion risk

Based on these indicators, the FAO has developed maps that provide a visual overview of the factors that affect land degradation.

Most modelling efforts looking at the future food security scenarios include factors that determine the share of land that is allocated to food production.[10] Traditional non-food agricultural production has included cotton, rubber, tobacco or forestry, but in the past decade an increasing amount of land has been used for production of feedstocks for biofuels.[11] As noted above, there are huge uncertainties relating to the impact of biofuel production on overall land use, particularly due to uncertainties about future fuel prices and technological developments in the area of biofuels.[12]

---

[9] OECD 'The economic rationale of public policies to enhance resilience and adaptation in agriculture – a scoping paper'. Joint working party on agriculture and the environment (OECD 2013).

[10] D. Laborde, et al. *Long-term Drivers of Food and Nutrition security* (IFPRI 2013).

[11] T. Hertel, et al., 'Competition for land in the global bioeconomy' [2013] *Agricultural Economics* 68: 1–10.

[12] OECD, n 7 above.

The spatial distribution of arable land affects regional food security outcomes. Certain regions may be more susceptible to negative shocks, such as extreme weather conditions. Marginal lands may be, for example, more steeply sloped than more productive lands, implying that a disturbance of the soil will lead to increased erosion and decreased productivity. Given the increase in intensive farming in marginal lands and the new stresses from climate change such as droughts, these systems will have difficulty providing adequate agricultural production for the populations that depend upon output from these areas. In addition, demographic analyses indicate that the number of agricultural dependent people is likely to grow in many of these areas.[13]

In the long run, expansion of land into agricultural production is less likely to be a sustainable way of increasing global agricultural supply. According to the FAO a large proportion of arable land not yet being cultivated is concentrated in Latin America, Central Asia and Sub-Saharan Africa, however these locations are not necessarily where there will be the highest demand for food in the future. In addition, the type of land is suitable only for particular crops and some estimates show that 70 per cent of this land suffers from soil and terrain constraints. Land not yet in use may not be easily brought into cultivation due to climatic constraints, agro-ecological constraints, or infrastructure constraints.[14] Still, increased demand puts pressure on these fragile lands, and increases the chance of degradation.

Water constraints
On a global scale there is sufficient capacity to support agricultural production, however the global distribution of water is uneven. Approximately 80 per cent of the water requirements for global crop production are met through rainfall. Irrigation satisfies the remaining water requirements. North Africa, South Asia, North China plains and the US Great Plains regions rely heavily on irrigation for crop production.[15] According to the FAO,[16] irrigated agriculture covers 20 per cent of arable land and accounts for 50 per cent of crop production. The intensity of groundwater use by agriculture combined with competing urban demands for water and

---

[13] T.S. Jayne, et al., 'Land pressures, the evolution of farming systems, and development strategies in Africa: A synthesis' [2014] *Food Policy* 48: 1–17.

[14] Food and Agriculture Organization, *FAO Statistical Yearbook* (FAO 2012).

[15] M. Rosegrant, C. Ringler, T. Zhu, S. Tokgoz and P. Bhandary, 'Water and food in the bioeconomy: Challenges and opportunities for development' (2013) *Agricultural Economics* 44(1): 139–50.

[16] FAO, n 14 above.

changing climatic conditions is leading to water scarcity in many parts of the world.

FAO modelling estimates that harvested irrigated land would expand by 17 per cent by 2050, with all of this increase occurring in developing countries. As a result, pressure on renewable water resources from irrigation is likely to increase, particularly in North Africa and South Asia. Irrigation may also have negative impacts by creating spillover effects on agricultural production such as water logging and salinity due to excessive water use and poor drainage systems.[17]

The impact of climate change on the global, spatial and temporal distribution of water is difficult to predict. Studies often focus on annual time scales, ignoring the variability across shorter time frames. More information is needed on the potential variability of water availability, including seasonal variations and extremes of water availability, in order to allow for an in-depth analysis of the impacts on agricultural production. The impacts of climate change on water quality will also be complex, given the possibility that increased flooding can lead to erosion and increased sediment loads, while severe droughts could lead to higher concentrations of toxins in the water system. The OECD initiated work on this topic to identify policies that create an enabling environment for on-farm adaptation.[18]

Resilient Agriculture for Food Security

Agricultural systems face new shocks and stressors in the context of climate change. As systems face increasing amounts of stress, they may not be able to recover from a particular shock. For example, fragile land that is already characterized by poor soil conditions or the steepness of the slope may not be able to recover from severe weather events. Because the changes in natural systems are happening more rapidly due to climate change, there is increasing risk that these types of thresholds could be breeched.

Given the important linkages that exist within agricultural systems and the potential for disturbance from climate change, an understanding of how these systems behave is critical to choosing policy interventions that will lead to desired results in the short and long term. One key consideration regarding agricultural systems is how they react to stress, especially whether they can recover from negative shocks. The concept of resilience

---

[17] V. Ruttan, 'Productivity growth in world agriculture: Sources and constraints' (2002) *Journal of Economic Perspectives*, 16(4): 161–84.
[18] OECD, n 9 above.

provides one useful framework for explaining the way systems find new equilibrium in the face of changing conditions.

The definition of resilience was first introduced to help explain nonlinear behaviour in ecological systems. Resilience of ecological systems was understood to be the amount of disturbance that an ecosystem could withstand without changing self-organized processes and structures. Ecological resilience often depends upon the existence of feedback loops that allow a natural system to achieve stable healthy equilibrium after the introduction of a new stress. The concept has since been adopted in other policy arenas, including the field of food security and development (see for example the IFPRI conference in 2014 on resilience in agriculture).[19] However these fields adopt a modified definition of the term resilience recognizing that in the context of discussions of food security improved equilibrium states are preferred to the status quo condition of poverty and hunger. For example, IFPRI describes resilience in the following way:[20]

> Building resilience means helping people, communities, countries, and global institutions prevent, anticipate, prepare for, cope with, and recover from shocks and not only bounce back to where they were before the shocks occurred, but become even better-off.

As highlighted in previous sections, policy interventions to improve food security will need to focus on resource constraints associated with agricultural production. In response to short-term crises, governments may take actions to address short-term objectives that, by degrading the resource base, compromise their ability to achieve sustainable improvements in the future. For example, in managing water inputs, policies that are intended to increase agricultural production by decreasing the cost of water can lead to overuse of water which will have spillover effects to other parts of the agricultural system. While these policy interventions may be necessary in the short term to address situations where vulnerable populations are at risk, the challenge for food security is to give attention to the potential spillover outcomes from specific interventions. More effective policies would promote resilience by strengthening the underlying system.

Government interventions can take many forms, and are often targeted at influencing farmer behaviour directly by altering land use incentives at the household and community levels. Changes in how land is used in agricultural production may alter the potential outputs that can be generated

---

[19] For further details of the conference can be found at http://www.2020resilience.ifpri.info.

[20] IFPRI *Building Resilience for Food and Nutrition Security*. (IFPRI 2014): http://www.ifpri.org/sites/default/files/publications/2020resilience_brochure.pdf.

in the future and the magnitude of these changes will be influenced by the quality of the land. Intensification of land use may lead to agricultural practices that exacerbate soil erosion. As noted above, this is particularly an issue for marginal lands that already have lower soil fertility, or that have a slope that leads to increased soil erosion if land use is not managed to avoid excessive run-off. While intensification does not inevitably lead to degradation of these types of marginal lands, care is needed to ensure that policies create incentives for farmers to adopt practices that reinforce resilience rather than detract from it.

IFPRI's Global Food Policy Report 2013 highlights the importance of developing strategies for sustainable intensification. Some researchers suggest that incremental changes, such as the use of improved varieties and the adoption of precision agriculture, could have important food security impacts without creating negative impacts on the environment. Studies have shown that the adoption of appropriate technologies could lead to yield gains in Sub-Saharan Africa, South Asia, Latin America and the Caribbean.

Governments can create a policy environment that encourages investment in the natural resource base for agriculture. With appropriate interventions, food systems can maintain stability in the face of additional pressures on the natural resource base. Some direct agricultural policy interventions may contribute to enhanced productivity without creating negative spillover effects on natural resource quality. These include incentives to implement improved input use, for example, combining organic and inorganic inputs or integrated pest management practices. In addition, policies that support alternative farm management practices particularly in marginal lands can moderate the likelihood that agricultural production excessively stresses the system leading to further degradation. Diversification of production can also contribute to spreading risk, particularly in the context of changes in insect populations.

Focusing on resilience draws attention to the importance of interaction among various parts of the system. The approach also focuses attention on various physical and economic feedback loops that affect the agricultural system by either enhancing stability or amplifying instability. Policies that are based on an understanding of these complex interactions are necessary to avoid unintended negative consequences.

CONCLUSION

In order to have a sustained positive impact on food production and food security outcomes, policy interventions addressing supply side constraints are essential. In some instances policies that seek to promote intensification may be optimal. In others, more attention may be needed to limit the impact on fragile systems and to achieve sustained increases in production. The policy options for sustainably addressing resource constraints in agriculture will need to be developed based on a clearer understanding of how these constraints vary over time and space.

With respect to variable impact over time, policymakers should also be cognizant of the potential time lags between policy interventions and economic and physical outcomes. Some interventions that work well in the short term may have long-term repercussions that will alter the robustness of the resource base for agricultural production. This is the case, for example, of policies that lead to the overuse of water in agricultural production. In the short run, these measures can enhance agricultural productivity by ensuring an adequate water supply to crops. However, in the long run, these measures may lead to overuse of water resources that will then constrain agricultural productivity in the future.

With respect to the physical distribution of policy impacts, since land and soil quality will vary, policies that are focused on addressing resource constraints need to ensure that interventions are made at the appropriate scale. Targeting policies to particular contexts will increase the chance that they will address the immediate food security needs without jeopardizing future food production. Therefore the possible impact of policy interventions should be considered at various physical scales, including at the farm and watershed levels.

Given variability in quality and quantity of land and water resources, rather than pursuing policies that mandate particular types of outcomes, public sector interventions should contribute to creating conditions that support farmers adopting sustainable practices. Government investments, for example, in R&D for stress tolerant crops and stronger livestock breeds would create the possibility for farmers to have alternative choices in the future to manage climate risks. Policies can also create an enabling environment for farm level adaptation by providing options for education and training for farmers. Incentives for farmers to share knowledge and contribute to collective action that encourages flexibility and problem solving are also key.

Finally, clearly defined property rights, which may be allocated to communities rather than individual producers, have been shown to be one way to encourage a longer term planning horizon for producers and motivating investments to ensure sustainable use of resources. Policy interventions to address resource constraints to achieving food security could target markets where property rights are ambiguous.

These types of interventions can generate incentives for farmers to invest in long-term land management strategies and ensure that they have access and ability to implement sustainable land-use strategies. In the context of resource constraints and climate variability, policymakers will need to develop a clear understanding of how interventions affect options and incentives at the farm level and create a policy environment in which agricultural producers can respond flexibly to changing economic and physical conditions. Given these changing conditions, investments in improved data on land use, land quality and water-use patterns and increased interdisciplinary research will facilitate a deeper understanding of how to ensure sustained improvements in food security in the context of resource constraints.

9. Environmental change, food security and trade in Southeast Asia

J. Jackson Ewing

I. INTRODUCTION

Environmental changes in Southeast Asia are creating pronounced food security challenges. The region is deeply endowed with natural resources valuable for agriculture, yet environmental stresses continue to threaten the region's future food production potential. These challenges are accelerating during a period of transformative change in regional food systems and impacting livelihoods, nutritional profiles and – in some cases – regional food trade dynamics.

This chapter reviews the intersection of environmental change, food security and trade challenges in Southeast Asia through three primary sections. First, the chapter explores the relationship between urbanisation, environmental change and shifting food systems, and introduces a related debate over what food production strategies are most apt for the region. Second, the chapter reviews the causes and implications of environmental stresses in ecosystems essential for agriculture – namely forests, freshwater sources and coastal/marine zones – and examines the ways that climate change is amplifying these challenges. Third, the chapter questions what environmental change may mean for regional food trade dynamics, and presents trade as both imperilled by environmental change and as a partial solution to it. The chapter concludes by challenging environmentally-driven food crises narratives as well as calls for reduced trade and greater food sovereignty, and argues for the continuing application of innovative agricultural inputs and trade policy instruments.

II. URBANISATION, ENVIRONMENTAL CHANGE AND FOOD SYSTEMS DEBATE

The significance of urbanisation for food security in Southeast Asia is difficult to overstate. Throughout the region's history the lure of social connectivity and economic opportunity has brought people to cities and peri-urban areas, and these movements have hastened in real and relative terms during the twentieth and twenty-first century.[1] Environmental changes are amplifying urbanisation for numerous reasons, and the resulting more urbanised populations in-turn create new demands on regional environments. Cities offer logical destinations for many people compelled to move in part because of protracted environmentally-related challenges (such as droughts) or abrupt events (such as storms). As centres of culture, commerce, trade and family relations, cities are places where the immediate and longer term needs of such populations can be most readily met.[2] In Southeast Asia, the pull of urban locations is drawing rural populations grappling with changing agricultural trends, declining small-scale farming profitability, and systemic shifts in the ways food is most readily accessed.

From farms to cities, urbanisation is being accompanied by rapidly modernising distribution chains, wholesaling, food processing, retail and supermarkets, and other midstream and downstream segments of regional food systems.[3] This is fundamentally altering the pathways by which citizens access food and the foods they choose to consume. While urbanisation and value chain modernisation is bringing with it many human development improvements, feeding growing and increasingly urban and affluent populations poses challenges. Inescapable development trends mean that more food must be produced by rural communities that continue to decline in size relative to their city-dwelling neighbours. This is true both domestically, where rural hinterlands feed urban centres, and internationally, where countries with high rural agricultural capacities supply countries with significant food importing needs.[4] Globally, arable land shrank from 0.45 hectares (ha) per person in the mid-twentieth century to 0.25 ha per person at its conclusion.[5] While perhaps alarming, this trend is unsurprising given the world's rapid population growth, mercurial gains in global economic production and the attendant land conversions that these changes necessitated. The trend is set to continue and estimates suggest that arable land per person will drop to 0.15 ha by

---

[1] A. Reid, *Charting the Shape of Early Modern Southeast Asia* (Silkworm Books, 1999).

[2] J. Jackson Ewing, 'Contextualising climate change as a cause of migration in Southeast Asia' in Lorraine Elliot (ed.), *Climate Change, Migration and Human Security in Southeast Asia* (RSIS Monograph No. 24, 2012) 13–27.

[3] T. Reardon and C. P. Timmer, 'The economics of the food system revolution' (2012) 4 *Annual Review of Resource Economics* 225–64.

[4] J. Jackson Ewing, 'Food production and environmental health in Southeast Asia: The search for complementary strategies' (2011) May *NTS Policy Brief* 1–6.

[5] H. Spiertz, 'Food production, crops and sustainability: restoring confidence in science and technology' (2010) 2 *Current Opinion in Environmental Sustainability* 439–43.

the mid-twenty-first century.[6] Moreover, as populations in Southeast Asia become more urban and affluent, diets are changing to include more meats, fish and processed foods, which can intensify the environmental footprint of food production.[7]

These developments frame a fundamental question surrounding food production in Southeast Asia: how can greater amounts of more diverse food be produced on less land and with acceptable environmental and social impacts? The region already has a substantial agricultural foundation, with some of the world's largest rice exporters and significant production and exportation of a range of fruits, vegetables and processed foods. Unlike the modern agricultural zones of Europe and North America, a significant portion of this food is produced at local levels and on relatively small scales, which leads to agriculture playing a weighty role in the economic and social fabric of the region. As such, continuing to make farming economically viable, warding off pervasive hunger problems and responding to the changing food value chains of a growing and developing region are paramount goals for governments and other regional stakeholders. While environmental considerations can easily get lost in the shuffle of these pursuits, there is a growing recognition that mitigating environmental stresses is necessary for future agricultural progress. Such recognition amplifies an already clamorous debate on what role technology and advancing agricultural methods should play in regional food production, the answers to which will have major environmental implications.

Environmentally-focused voices call attention to the high greenhouse gas emissions, degradation and depletion of freshwater systems, and conversions of valuable ecosystems that accompany many modern food production and distribution systems.[8] Decades of agricultural intensification have had serious effects, with the overuse of nitrogen-based fertilisers and high inputs of phosphorus, insecticides, fungicides and heavy metals creating lasting problems for soil and freshwater systems and for overall nutrient flows throughout food chains. These conditions give space to arguments for a return to or perpetuation of more 'traditional' small-scale farming techniques, with a focus on 'sufficiency' and preventing harmful environmental externalities.[9] Such approaches dovetail with strategies

---

[6] Ibid.

[7] S. Friel and P. I. Baker, 'Equity, food security and health equity in the Asia Pacific region' (2009) 18(4) *Asia Pacific Journal of Clinical Nutrition* 620–32.

[8] L. G. Horlings and T. K. Marsden, 'Towards the real green revolution? Exploring the conceptual dimensions of a new ecological modernisation of agriculture that could 'feed the world'' (2011) 21(2) *Global Environmental Change* 441–52.

[9] Ibid.

seeking to reduce global and regional food trade in favour of domestic, often localised, production growth.

Countervailing voices argue that agrotechnology provides environmentally prudent tools for managing the ecological footprint of the food sector.[10] Bourgeoning new technologies, the logic goes, can reduce water usage through targeted low-volume irrigation systems, combat soil erosion through less invasive tilling practices, and increase yields so that less land must be brought under cultivation. New approaches also present opportunities to mitigate greenhouse gas emissions and genetically modified plants that can require fewer external inputs such as fertilisers and insecticides. Such approaches often tacitly or overtly acknowledge that smaller percentages of developing country populations will be involved in agriculture, and call for food to be produced in consolidated areas where it is most environmentally and economically prudent to do so. Such arrangements necessitate trade.

These seemingly polemical positions on meeting food system needs in environmentally and socially sustainable ways are not mutually exclusive, and Southeast Asia will continue to host a mishmash of farming methods and distribution strategies that meld the traditional with the modern.[11] However, the trajectory of these strategies at subnational, national and regional levels, and the shifting supply and demand trends at their foundation, will affect key ecosystems throughout the region. These environmental effects will consequently impact the future of Southeast Asian food systems in fundamental ways.

III.   KEY ECOSYSTEMS

Forests

The primary traditional means for increasing food production in Southeast Asia, as with much of the world, has been to expand cultivation. Likewise, the expanding infrastructure that accompanies urbanisation brought alongside it the substantial conversion of formerly undeveloped lands. These and other drivers have led to the large-scale felling of Southeast Asian forests, with significant implications for agriculture.

Forests house primary watersheds which act as a linchpin for irrigation,

---

[10] Spiertz, n 5 above and Ewing, n 4 above.
[11] For an argument supporting the combination of modern and traditional farming methods see: The Royal Society, *Reaping the Benefits: Science and the Sustainable Intensification of Global Agriculture*, (The Royal Society, 2009).

energy generation, and commercial and individual freshwater needs. The degradation of forests can lead to deteriorating water quality and availability, threatening agricultural and industrial productivity as well as household access to freshwater. Forest root systems play an essential role in preventing soil erosion, particularly in highland areas such as the large swathes of tropical and equatorial regions of Southeast Asia. When left unchecked, soil erosion can further degrade freshwater resources and leave behind land with little agricultural or otherwise strategic value.[12] Such challenges increase further when forest conversions alter hydrological cycles and local weather patterns that forests help to regulate.

Despite the wide-ranging roles that forests play in both natural and social systems, they have traditionally been valued only for their commoditisable resources and the opportunities presented by their clearance.[13] As less quantifiable ecosystem services have not traditionally been reflected in these values, governments, companies and farmers 'often decide that forests are worth more cut down than standing'.[14] Southeast Asia has accordingly witnessed consistent forest losses throughout its modern history. Current regional deforestation rates are acute, but pale in comparison to annual net losses of 2.4 million ha from 1990–2000.[15] While forest management strategies and mechanisms should be praised for contributing to regional improvements; part of the decrease in deforestation rates is attributable to the fact that much of the easily accessed forested lands of the region have already been cleared for agriculture. Deforestation rates remain particularly severe in areas with expanding agricultural, palm oil, and pulp and paper sectors, and by some measurements Indonesia – Southeast Asia's largest country – had the highest rate of forest loss in the world in 2014.[16] If forest clearance is not pursued more judiciously, and confined to areas outside of key catchment zones, the region's food production potential will diminish.

---

[12] P. Dauvergne, 'Environmental insecurity, forest management and state responses in Southeast Asia', (1998) 2 Working Paper No. 1998/2, National Library of Australia.

[13] M. Poffenberger and K. Smith-Hanssen, 'Forest communities and REDD climate initiatives' (2009) 91 *Analysis from the East-West Center* 1–8.

[14] K. Lawlor and D. Huberman, 'Reduced emissions from deforestation and forest degradation (REDD) and human rights' in J. Campese (ed.) *Rights-based Approaches: Exploring Issues and Opportunities for Conservation*, (Center for International Forestry Research, 2009) 269–85.

[15] FAO, *State of the World Forests: 2014*, (Food and Agriculture Organization of the United Nations 2014); and FAO, *State of the World Forests: 2011*, (Food and Agriculture Organization of the United Nations 2011).

[16] T. Toumbourou, 'Indonesia's forests disappearing at record rates' (2015) *In Asia*, February 25. Accessed 22 April 2015 at: http://asiafoundation.org/in-asia/2015/02/25/indonesias-forests-disappearing-at-record-rates/.

Freshwater

Water problems in much of Southeast Asia result from poor management rather than natural vulnerabilities. As previously discussed, deforestation impacts freshwater systems by altering precipitation patterns and contributing to erosion and watershed degradation. Agriculture, meanwhile, is far and away the largest source of water usage in the region and inefficient irrigation practices cause significant water wastage. Through much of the region, however, these challenges occur in the context of relative water abundance. Average annual per capita water resources in Southeast Asia are almost double the world average, and this despite the region having a population density some 2.6 times higher than the global mean.[17] Problems arise not from overall supply shortages, but from localised water management deficits that leave areas of the region prone to flooding, salt-water intrusion and dry-season water deficits. Damming and water diversion strategies partially drive these problems, and scores of dams in the vital Mekong River Basin are changing river flow volume and timing, water quality and biodiversity.[18] Major agricultural zones such as Vietnam's Mekong Delta risk exhausting local water availability during the dry season, and the pressures on these resources continue to climb. Industrial pollution and agricultural run-off compound water challenges in some of the region's key basins, and industrial growth, population pressures and greater food demands create more pollution sources.[19]

Marine Environments

Several of the challenges posed by coastal resource degradation relate to the environmental stresses occurring inland. Deforestation and resultant soil erosion and the siltation of inland waterways can degrade coastal ecosystems.[20] The destruction of Southeast Asia's upland areas during the periods of major deforestation and land conversion has led to increased turbidity and pollution in the fresh water bodies emptying into nearby seas. Altered turbidity reduces light penetration into the water and, when

---

[17] UNEP, *Freshwater Under Threat: South East Asia* (UNEP, 2009).

[18] For an overview and case study relating to this dynamic see: C. Baker, 'Dams, power and security in the Mekong: A non-traditional assessment of hydro-development in the Mekong River Basin', (2012) 8 NTS-Asia Research Paper.

[19] MRC, 'Diagnostic study of water quality in the Lower Mekong Basin', (2007) 15 MRC Technical Paper, Mekong River Commission.

[20] E. D. Gomez, 'Status report on research and degradation problems of the coral reefs of the East Asian Seas' (South China Seas Fisheries Development and Coordinating Programme, Food and Agriculture Organisation (FAO), 1980).

these heavily silted waters reached the coast, damage and in some cases destroy the offshore seagrass beds and coral reefs that are essential fish habitats. Such habitat destruction has the corollary potential to alter the breeding patterns and lifecycles of aquatic fauna, leading to pronounced and lasting shifts in coastal ecosystems.

Coastal environmental changes also reflect population pressures and unsustainable coastal resource exploitation methods that have been the norm in parts of the region for decades.[21] Similarly to land-based shifts, previous decades of development have witnessed pronounced growth in commercial fishing operations in the seas throughout the region. These operations have significantly altered regional fish stocks and reduced yields for many small-scale municipal fishermen. A vicious cycle often results, in which poor communities are compelled by increasing numbers to degrade coastal environments while seeking the necessities of life, which further degrades coastal ecosystems and perpetuates the communities' impoverished plight.[22]

Regional data are confronting these points, with fish populations, reefs and mangroves all exhibiting signs of significant stress. Asia accounts for well over half of global fish production and consumption and much of the expansion in aquaculture and fish catches in recent decades has occurred in East and Southeast Asia.[23] More specifically, annual per capita fish consumption in Southeast Asia has risen from 12.8 kg in 1961 to 32 kg in 2009, and consumers continue to increase and diversify their fish consumption as the region becomes more affluent.[24] Unsurprisingly, such expanding consumption has placed aquatic resources under considerable pressure. By the turn of the twenty-first century much of the nearshore fishing territories of Southeast Asia had been overfished, and total world catches of marine fish continue to flatten as many of the major fishing areas of the region are either fully exploited or overexploited.[25]

Habitat destruction is occurring in tandem with, and at times as a causal

---

[21] I. C. Stobutzki, G. T. Silvestre, and L. R. Garces, 'Key issues in coastal fisheries in South and Southeast Asia, Outcomes of a Regional Initiative' (2006) 78 *Fisheries Research* 109–18.

[22] For analysis of such cycles see: Thomas F. Homer-Dixon *The Environment, Scarcity and Violence* (Princeton University Press, 1999).

[23] L. R. Garces, M. D. Pido and R. S. Pomeroy, 'Fisheries in Southeast Asia: Challenges and Opportunities' in A. Pandya and E. Laipson (eds), *Transnational Trends: Middle Eastern and Asian Views*, (The Henry L. Stimson Center, 2008).

[24] FAO, *State of World Fisheries and Aquaculture 2012* (Food and Agriculture Organization of the United Nations, 2012).

[25] G. T. Silvestre, et al., 'Assessment, management and future directions for coastal fisheries in Asian countries', (WorldFish Center Conference Proceedings, 2003, 1–40); FAO, ibid.; and Garces, Pido, and Pomeroy, n 23 above.

underpinning of, these decreasing fisheries. The destruction and degradation of key habitats such as reefs, mangroves and grassbeds means that fish and other marine species have fewer areas in which to reproduce and grow. Activities leading to the widespread destruction and alteration of important aquatic habitats in coastal zones include the reclamation of intertidal areas, destruction of mangrove forests for fuelwood or to build aquaculture ponds, damming of rivers and subsequent disruption of flooding cycles, extraction of corals and sand for construction materials or to create navigation channels, and the use of destructive fishing methods.[26] As a result, during the last century Southeast Asia lost some 70 per cent of the region's mangrove forests, 11 per cent of its coral reefs, and at least 20 per cent and as much as 60 per cent of seagrass beds.[27] These valuable ecosystems continue to come under threat of coastal developments and the physical changes accompany shifting climatic conditions. This final point is germane to many of the environmental challenges facing Southeast Asia, as it has the potential to compound existing levels of environmental stress and create emergent difficulties.

Climate Change

Climate change is amplifying many of the food-related challenges facing Southeast Asian communities. Much of the region exhibits the dual vulnerabilities of relying directly on natural resources for livelihood and sustenance, and possessing relatively low capacities for responding and adapting to climate shifts (particularly if they occur abruptly).[28] These vulnerabilities impact the region on land and at sea.

Escalating global temperatures are projected to increase extreme ocean weather events, coastal erosion, rising sea surface temperatures and an accelerated rise in global sea levels.[29] Rising ocean temperatures can lead to coral bleaching and mortality, more frequent flooding in low-lying areas, and greater coastal wetland and mangrove degradation; all of which would pose acute challenges to many of Southeast Asia's

---

[26] Garces, Pido, and Pomeroy, ibid.

[27] UNEP, Report of the Thirteenth Meeting of the Coordinating Body on the Seas of East Asia (COBSEA) on the East Asian Seas Action Plan, (UNEP, 1998).

[28] IPCC, Fourth assessment report, climate change 2007: A synthesis report, (IPCC Plenary XXVII, 2007).; M. L. Parry, et al., 'Technical summary', in M. L. Parry, O. F. Canziani, J. P. Palutikof, and P. J. Van der Linden (eds). *Climate Change 2007: Impacts, Adaptation and Vulnerability*, (Cambridge University Press, 2007); and D. Smith, and J. Vivekananda, 'A climate of conflict: The links between climate change, peace and war' 2007 (November) *International Alert*.

[29] IPCC, n 28 above.

coastal food production zones.[30] Higher ocean temperatures also affect fish breeding patterns, aquatic plant cycles and may cause more frequent and powerful coastal storms. Rising sea levels are particularly dangerous for low-lying coastal areas which can be rendered uninhabitable through inundation, saltwater intrusion into freshwater systems and untenable flood risks.

Inland, parts of Southeast Asia face risks to freshwater availability and agriculture deriving from warming temperatures and changing precipitation patterns. Warmer temperatures for longer durations can alter germination periods and growing cycles in agricultural zones such as those in the Mekong Basin and the large islands of the archipelagic states.[31] Changing precipitation patterns may lead to dry periods that are drier, wet periods that are wetter, and rains that accelerate erosion and runoff. Existing weather fluctuations, such as the El Niño phenomenon, already contribute to droughts during the dry season and floods during the wet, and these effects may become more acute in a changing climate.[32]

The physical manifestations of climate change that are threatening Southeast Asia are acting in conjunction to create multiple stresses that are greater than the sum of their parts.[33] For example, precipitation changes coinciding with sea-level rise and greater storm intensity can result in hydrological changes that prove catastrophic for coastal ecosystems and the strategic resources present within them. The contemporary state of land and coastal degradation in parts of Southeast Asia increases the potential for climate change to exacerbate already present agricultural challenges, as these degraded conditions reduce the ecological resilience of natural systems. Whether by affecting water quality or availability, degrading agricultural lands through drought, flooding or erosion, or rendering entire lands unviable by an encroaching sea, climatic changes create risks for the region, and these risks will likely become more formidable.

---

[30] A. A. Yusof and H. Francisco, *Hotspots! Mapping Climate Change Vulnerabilty in Southeast Asia* (EEPSEA, 2010).

[31] B. Rerkasem, 'Climate change and GMS agriculture' and N. T. H. Thuan, 'Adaptation to climate change in rice production in Vietnam Mekong River Delta' both in K. Rayanakorn (ed.), *Climate Change Challenges in the Mekong Region*, (Chiang Mai Press, 2011).

[32] IPCC, n 28 above.

[33] Parry, et al., 'Technical Summary', n 28 above.

IV. INTERSECTIONS BETWEEN ENVIRONMENTAL CHANGE AND THE REGIONAL FOOD TRADE

The shifting characteristics of Southeast Asian food systems both cause and respond to regional environmental challenges, and trade is no exception. Water and arable land are ostensibly 'traded' in the form of food from countries that have these resources in abundance to those that do not.[34] Countries with physical impediments to producing food, such as those in arid North Africa and the Middle East, are acquiring land in Southeast Asia through purchase and/or long-term leases to produce food, as are countries such as China that have overrun their production capacities.[35] Other countries including Singapore deal with intrinsic limits to food production through foreign direct investment into regional hinterlands that is geared towards creating more resilient food supplies.[36] Such relationships exist within countries as rural production zones produce food for growing cities and across boundaries in Southeast Asia as countries seek comparative advantages that will enable profitable food exports. These processes are fluid and open to interpretation – a project framed as a symbiotic investment relationship by some may be viewed as exploitative neo-colonial 'land-grabbing' by others.[37]

Regardless of the context, however, production has an *a priori* presence in food trade and depends upon a modicum of health and predictability in key environmental systems. Where regional environmental trends impinge on food production needs, whether through climate change, resource exhaustion, pollution, or a combination of factors, food trade will likely be impacted. Areas that combine large-scale production and environmental vulnerability are particularly salient to future regional food trade trends. The region's primary rice growing regions in the Ayeyarwady, Chao Praya, and the Red and Mekong Deltas each depend upon the monsoon rains from the Indian Ocean and fairly specific temperature ranges during various cropping periods.[38] Recent years have seen these temperature ranges exceeded by long stretches of high temperatures alongside

---

[34] For a detailed analysis of these dynamics see: Tony Allen, *Virtual Water: Tackling the Threat to our Planet's Most Precious Resource*, (L. B. Tauris, 2011).

[35] For details see: I. A. Kuntjoro and P. K. K. Hangzo, 'The challenges and opportunities of farmland acquisition in Southeast Asia', (2011) 7(July) *NTS Perspectives*.

[36] P. Teng, et al., 'Feeding Asia in the 21st century: building urban-rural alliances: summary of the main findings of the international conference on Asian food security held in Singapore on 10–12 August 2011', (2012) 4 *Food Security*, 141–46.

[37] Kuntjoro and Hangzo, n 35 above.

[38] Rerkasem, n 31 above, 35–75.

more erratic rainfall patterns.[39] These production zones supply rice to Southeast Asian importers such as Malaysia, Indonesia, the Philippines and Singapore as well further afield to Africa, western states and, increasingly, to China.[40] If the environmental conditions enabling rice production in these zones become less robust, price increases and supply crunches may become more likely. Fruit plantations in Mindanao, fisheries in the South China Sea and vegetable plots in Malaysia are likewise at the centre of trade relationships and vulnerable to similar environmental challenges.

However, caution is warranted on predictions of food shortages and price spikes arising directly from environmental change. For one, technological advancement and markets both add flexibility and resilience to regional food systems. Quantified claims about future production declines resulting from climate change and resource stresses often suffer from environmental determinism and fail to account for adaptation, innovation and demand shifts.[41] Rice, for example, is gradually declining in Southeast Asian diets and as a percentage of the total cropped land in the region. This shift is being driven by a complex mix of changing profitability assessments in the rice sector, demand changes occurring alongside urbanisation and economic growth and the policies of rice importers and exporters. Environmental changes, at this point, are peripheral by comparison. Moreover, efforts to ensure that rice production can continue under environmentally stressful conditions are longstanding and progressing, with the International Rice Research Institute and regional institutions pursuing promising research into drought, flood and heat resistant rice inputs and cropping strategies.[42] Similar efforts focusing directly on environmental changes are ongoing in vegetable, fruit, fishery and other food sectors.[43] Such advances have the potential to bring new areas of land under cultivation and increase yields in areas with more tenable environmental characteristics.

While such production advances could boost trade, real and perceived volatilities in regional food markets continue to drive campaigns for greater food self-sufficiency in Southeast Asia – particularly since the

---

[39] Ibid.

[40] For analysis of recent regional rice trade dynamics see: J. J. Ewing and Z. Hongzhou, 'China as the world's largest rice importer: Regional implications' (2013) 166, *RSIS Commentary*.

[41] For a selection of such quantified predictions see: N. V. Nguyen, *Global Climate Changes and Rice Food Security*, (FAO, 2005).

[42] FAO/IRRI, 'Advanced technologies of rice production for coping with climate change: 'No Regret' options for adaptation and mitigation and their potential uptake', (FAO/IRRI 2011).

[43] RSIS, 'Impact of climate change on ASEAN food security: Downscaling analysis and response', (2013) *NTS Issues Brief*.

2008 food crisis. This crisis saw international prices for wheat climb in response to production decreases, and corn prices rise primarily because of crop diversions to the biofuel industry. The prices of rice and subsequently other foods spiked in Asian markets in response as exporters such as India and Thailand reduced outflows and imposed minimum export prices. Importing countries sought to rapidly increase rice stocks through purchases on the international market, which in turn drove the prices ever higher in a compounding cycle of panic buying and climbing prices. 'Nervousness' in Asian rice markets led to skyrocketing prices that saw rice move from USD375 per tonne at the beginning of 2008 to over USD1,100 per tonne by April of that year, and had wider effects on food price indexes.[44]

This market instability has contributed to moves by traditionally large importers such as the Philippines and Indonesia towards self-sufficiency. This has both logic and political appeal when framed as an attempt to secure domestic supplies and stabilise domestic rice prices. It is far from clear, however, if it is in the long-term economic or environmental interests of these large archipelagic countries to dedicate increasing labour, land and water resources to rice cultivation. Outside of major river basins the ecological limits for agricultural production can be reached quickly, and aversions to trade may bring marginal lands under cultivation with long-term environmental consequences.[45] Rice is not wholly unique here, as bringing new lands under cultivation in the name of domestic crop diversification and sufficiency brings similar economic and ecological challenges.

Regional resistance to trading food may therefore exacerbate environmental stresses. The forces underpinning such resistance are not confined to Southeast Asia, and on international levels groups such as Greenpeace, Friends of the Earth and La Via Campesina are driving critiques of both modern agricultural techniques and market integration.[46] These groups seek to protect rural farming populations from the dangers of liberal markets and exploitative practices, and often trumpet 'food sovereignty' as a pathway for countries, communities and individuals to gain power over the food systems affecting them. They cite environmental stresses from large-scale agriculture alongside the economic and social exploitation

---

[44] C. P. Timmer, 'Reflections on food crises past', (2010) 35(1) *Food Policy* 1–11.

[45] For examples from Indonesia see: J. J. Ewing, 'Forests, Food and Fuel: REDD+ and Indonesia's land-use conundrum', (2011) 19, MacArthur Asia Security Initiative Paper No. 19.

[46] H. I. Miller and D. L. Kershen, 'Politics and the poor man's plate', (2013) January *Defining Ideas*, 1–5.

of rural communities to argue for less trade, more local production and greater support for traditional agrarian lifestyles.[47]

Protecting farmer interests and warding off exploitation are laudable goals, and civil society groups have bolstered these arguments in Southeast Asia while political forces use them as a pathway to electoral success.[48] However, such agendas do not necessarily jibe with the stated interests of small- and medium-scale farmers, nor do they offer a clear pathway towards greater regional resilience in the face of environmental change. On the contrary, a combination of more robust regional trade mechanisms and the continued modernisation of value chains and agricultural techniques have demonstrable environmental and social value.[49]

V.   CONCLUSION: GROWTH UNDERMINING GROWTH?

Clearly, Southeast Asian food systems face daunting environmental challenges. These challenges vary widely in their physical and social causes, and will be met with responses of widely divergent effectiveness. However, the common thread running through these dynamics is that rapid development and social change have been the primary drivers of regional environmental stress, and it is likely that many such stresses are becoming more pronounced.

This somewhat gloomy thesis should not, however, lead automatically to dystopian narratives of a region on the precipice of food crises and set to devolve into social instability and greater human suffering. Regional developments in agricultural production and trade have helped pull millions of people out of poverty and contributed to fantastic, if often uneven, improvements in quality of life. In this vein the nascent efforts to create an ASEAN Economic Community (AEC), with reduced trade barriers, stronger regional development, and increased global competitiveness, may improve the workings of the regional food trade and the lives of many Southeast Asian citizens.[50] The potential of such shifts should not be

---

[47] For a more extensive discussion of these forces see: J. J. Ewing, 'Supermarkets, iron buffalos and agrarian myths: exploring the drivers and impediments to food systems modernisation in Southeast Asia', (2013) 26(5) *The Pacific Review* 481–503.

[48] Ibid.

[49] Ibid.

[50] J. Jackson Ewing and Sandra Silfvast, 'Regionalism and food market interventions: Lessons from ASEAN and the EU', in *Food Security: The Role of Asia and Europe in Production, Trade and Regionalism*, (Singapore: Konrad-Adenauer Stiftung and European Union 2014).

discounted or subverted by environmentally-based critiques, nor should future agricultural goals fall victim to radical or overzealous environmental constrictions.

On the contrary, there is a need to recognise that the nature of environmental systems dictates that short-term actions can have intergenerational implications, and that balancing development ambitions with sober and strategic longer-term food security assessments is essential. Trade and markets do not and will not provide 'silver bullet' solutions, but they are tools for enabling the regional production zones capable of sustainably producing food surpluses to benefit wider regional food security. In this pursuit, the judicious application of new agricultural inputs and methods along with innovative and evidence-based trade policy instruments may prove invaluable.

10. Is there a role for international law in supporting systemic solutions to the food security challenge?

Melanie Vilarasau Slade

The role of international law – and in particular international economic law – in supporting food security is a source of division and controversy. It is criticized both for leaving inadequate domestic policy space for the implementation of effective food security policies and for failing to effectively constrain governments to put these policies in place. Trade and investment law in particular are seen variously as the problem and the potential solution to many of the food security challenges we face.

Given this, it is interesting to note that, of the many of the international initiatives that have taken place since the 2008 food crisis, few if any advocate significant reform of international law beyond trade reform envisaged in 2001. To explore this apparent contradiction further, this chapter aims to outline the principal international initiatives in the field of food security, identify areas of proposed reform where collaborative solutions are required and encourage discussion of the limitations and potential for international law to support a systemic approach to food security.

TOWARDS POLICY COHERENCE: A GLOBAL STRATEGIC FRAMEWORK

The 'perfect storm' of the 2008 food crisis has had a profound effect on the food security policy landscape. With the vulnerabilities of the global food system brutally revealed, governments have sought to reduce their population's exposure to them. These efforts have gone in seemingly contrasting directions: on the one hand there have been numerous unilateral initiatives aimed at securing sources of supply, nationally and internationally; on the other hand there have been highly visible efforts towards international cooperation on the topic of food security.

These cooperative efforts have taken different forms, some at institutional level such as the UN High-Level Task Force on global food and nutrition security[1] and others at intergovernmental level, such as those at the G8[2] and G20 level.[3] The most comprehensive and inclusive of these initiatives is the reformed Committee on World Food Security (CFS).[4] The CFS has been touted as 'a new breed of global governance emerging, in which [civil society] are co-authors of international law with governments and international agencies'.[5] Its mandate includes coordinating a global approach to food security and encouraging policy convergence. As part of its mandate, the CFS has prepared the Global Strategic Framework on food security and nutrition (GSF), which 'aims to reflect – not exhaustively – the existing state of consensus across governments'.[6]

In the GSF, the CFS has highlighted several emerging challenges: meeting the food and nutritional needs of growing urban and rural populations, with changing dietary preferences; increasing sustainable agricultural production and productivity; enhancing resilience to climate change; and finding sustainable solutions to the increasing competition for natural resources.[7] The imperative for cooperation in these areas is clear: these systemic challenges require systemic solutions, as the impact of national policy choices is rarely constrained by national borders.

Intuitively, the current fragmentation of international law would seem to undermine a systemic approach to food security. Yet while the GSF identifies governance failures at both national and international level as factors contributing to food insecurity, the role of international law is not directly mentioned.[8]

We know that several contributing factors to food insecurity singled out for attention in the GSF, such as insufficient investment, an inadequate system of international trade, and inadequate access to food, are policy

---

[1] The UN HLTF has espoused the zero-hunger challenge. Further details available at http://www.un.org/en/zerohunger/foodsecurity.shtml.

[2] This included the creation of the G8 Global Partnership on Agriculture, Food Security and Nutrition.

[3] This included the 2011 G20 Action Plan on Food Price Volatility, and more recently in 2014 the G20 Food Security and Nutrition Framework.

[4] Created in 1974, in 2009 the CFS underwent reform to open it to a wider range of stakeholders and enhance 'its ability to promote polices that reduce food insecurity'.

[5] Olivier de Schutter Press Release (10 October 2010), on the occasion of the first session of the CFS. Available at http://www.srfood.org/en/in-rome-the-committee-on-world-food-security-reinvents-global-governance. It should be noted that whilst agencies and civil society are represented, the decisions of the CFS are adopted on the basis of consensus among Member States, who have sole voting rights.

[6] See CFS Global Strategic Framework for Food Security and Nutrition (3rd version 2014), p. 6.

[7] Ibid., p. 11.

[8] Ibid., p. 8.

areas governed by specific areas of international law: international investment law, trade law, and human rights law respectively. All three have a direct impact on the scope of national policy space in different ways, with little connecting them.

These fields of international law are potentially critical to meeting the challenges identified by the CFS. The aim of this chapter is to explore the potential for these areas of international law to support the kind of systemic solutions required to address the food security challenges we face, as well as those that lie ahead.

THE PRODUCTION CHALLENGE: THE ROLE OF INVESTMENT LAW

There is a general consensus that enhanced investment in agriculture will be required in order to feed a growing global population.[9] The GSF sets out the importance of investment both in infrastructure[10] and agriculture, and for this investment to be responsible.[11] The term 'responsible investment' is one which has received greater attention since 2008, when as part of their drive to ensure security of supply, countries invested in self-sufficiency efforts domestically and internationally through large-scale purchases of land, with a number of private actors following suit in search for investment opportunities. International purchases in particular have generated controversy, as many have taken place in countries with weak governance structures and unclear systems of land ownership. The negative effects of these 'land grabs' have made headlines[12] and led to voluntary guidelines[13] designed to define and support 'responsible' investment.[14]

---

[9] For an overview of the case for investment in agriculture see the FAO State of Food and Agriculture Report 2012.

[10] See *supra* fn. 6 at p. 24.

[11] See *supra* fn. 6 at p. 10 'The importance of increased as well as responsible investment in agriculture as an economic activity, and in particular the role of small-scale food producers as investors, needs to be recognized and promoted.'

[12] See inter alia M. Sochua and C. Wikström, 'Land Grabs in Cambodia' *The New York Times* (18 July 2012) and BBC 'Analysis: Land Grab or Development Opportunity' *BBC News* (22 February 2012) at http://www.bbc.co.uk/news/world-africa-17099348.

[13] These have taken the form of voluntary guidelines, as there is very little if any appetite to negotiate changes to the legal framework in order to define the responsibilities of investors. See S. M. Lundan, 'Human rights issues in multinational value chains' in *Research Handbook on Global Justice and International Economic Law*. (Edward Elgar Publishing 2013).

[14] Two high-profile initiatives in this regard include the Principles for Responsible Agricultural Investment (PRAI) and Voluntary Guidelines on the Responsible Governance of Tenure

At its heart, this controversy concerns control over natural resources.[15] The starting point for any discussion of resource ownership under international law is the fundamental principle of State sovereignty, encompassing the permanent sovereignty of a State over all its wealth, natural resources and economic activities.[16] Regulation of these investments is thus primarily a domestic issue.

Yet the apparent simplicity of this legal principle fails to reflect the multiplicity of binding obligations affecting a State's ability to manage the resources within its national territory. Over time, States have created an increasingly complex and interlinked network of international agreements that regulate the way in which their sovereignty is exercised. These international treaties have increasingly blurred the distinction between international law and domestic law and classical separation between public and private law. Even basic questions of jurisdiction are rarely straightforward and 'a simple model that looks only to territorial delineations among official state-based legal systems is now simply untenable (if it was ever useful to begin with)'.[17] This is particularly visible in the field of international investment law. In a bid to develop an attractive investment environment,[18] States have entered into a plethora of international investment agreements (IIAs), such as bilateral investment treaties (BITs) and Investment Chapters in Free Trade Agreements (FTAs), which are influencing the way in which States regulate and manage their resources.

International investment law recognizes the principle of State sovereignty and contemporary international law recognizes the right of every State to nationalize foreign-owned property, even if a predecessor State or a previous government engaged itself by treaty or contract not to do so.[19] Yet the ability of States to make full use of this right depends on their ability to effectively compensate for any damages caused to the investor in accordance with their obligations under the relevant IIA, and their level of

---

of Land, Fisheries and Forests in the Context of National Food Security (VGGT), which are variously described as complementary or antithetical.

[15] The tensions caused by land grabs are not specific to agricultural investments and could apply to any investment affecting rights over land and other supply-side resources (e.g., water).

[16] See UN Resolution 1515 (XV) of 15 December 1960, and proclaimed in successive UN Resolutions.

[17] P. S. Berman, *Global Legal Pluralism: A Jurisprudence of Law Beyond Borders* (Cambridge University Press 2012).

[18] See, inter alia, 'The facilitation of trade by the rule of law: the cases of Singapore and ASEAN', M. Ewing-Chow, J. J. Losari and M. Vilarasau Slade in *Connecting to Global Markets Challenges and Opportunities: Case Studies Presented by WTO Chair-Holders*, M. Jansen, M. Sadni Jallab and M. Smeets (eds) (WTO Publications 2014).

[19] E. Jimenez de Arechaga, 'State responsibility for the nationalization of foreign owned property' [1978] *New York Journal of International Law and Politics*, 11, 179–95.

sensitivity – or vulnerability – to any negative effect on further investment in the country.

Any curtailment of a State's policy discretion in the regulation of natural resources that are critical and limited – and in the realm of food security there are many aspects, particularly on the supply-side, which are either or both 'rival' and 'excludable'[20] – will inevitably generate tensions. This renders the nature of the rules and systems regulating the ownership and use of these critical resources singularly important to their effective management.

One of the principal criticisms of IIAs is that they are skewed too heavily towards the protection of investors, to the detriment of the public interest. The systemic bias of IIAs towards investment protection becomes particularly problematic when dealing with large-scale agricultural investments in weak States with systems of property ownership that fail to protect existing or traditional land use.[21] As argued by Häberli and Smith, once an investment is made, 'governance of agri-FDI at regional and international level unevenly distributes obligations and responsibilities between the weak host state, the investor and the investor's home state in such a way that there is over protection of the investor and under regulation of the investment'.[22]

Attempts to redress this balance seek to bolster States' policy space by expanding and/or clarifying the scope of public interest 'exception' clauses in the IIAs.[23] Proponents suggest this could to take place in different ways, some advocate changes to individual IIAs, expanding general public interest clauses through affirmations of the right to regulate or the insertion of public policy exceptions[24] or the inclusion of a public interest clause

---

[20] Put simply, rival goods are goods where consumption by one consumer prevents simultaneous consumption by another consumer. An excludable good is one where consumers can be excluded from using the good.

[21] By way of example, 'the central role of the state in land relations, legal devices for the state to allocate resource rights to large-scale investors, and varying, but overall limited, protection for local resource rights are recurring features of national legal systems in Africa'. See L. Cotula, '"Land grabbing" in the shadow of the law: Legal frameworks regulating the global land rush' in *The Challenge of Food Security: International Policy and Regulatory Frameworks*. (Edward Elgar Publishing 2012).

[22] C. Häberli and F. Smith, 'Food security and agri-foreign direct investment in weak states: Finding the governance gap to avoid 'land grab' (2014) *Modern Law Review* 77(2), 189–222.

[23] Put simply, where such exceptions are included in IIAs, even where damage has been caused to the investor, compensation will not be due if the government's action is deemed to be in the public interest.

[24] For example, see recently concluded Japanese, Canadian and US BITs available on UNCTAD's online IIA database at unctad.org/iia.

for food security,[25] whereas others advocate for multilateral agreements introducing an equivalent of Article XX GATT,[26] or the issuing of multilateral declarations,[27] which would be applicable to all IIAs. The ASEAN Comprehensive Investment Agreement (ACIA) provides an example of a public interest exemption agreed at regional level that is intrinsic to the definition of 'expropriation'.[28]

However, simply widening the scope for State discretion does not promote a systemic approach to food security nor does it necessarily result in sustainable or responsible use of resources. Indeed, widening the scope for unilateral State action too much would create uncertainty for investors and potentially allow for protectionist actions by States, which could in turn undermine efforts to promote investment in agriculture.

Other proposals seek instead to promote responsible investment by defining investor responsibilities. There is movement towards this, as evidenced by the inclusion of obligations to respect national laws and reference to CSR initiatives in several recent IIAs.[29] In addition to the practical difficulties involved (e.g., providing for obligations to suit all nature of investments) there are significant disadvantages to using the investment law system to define investor responsibilities. These obligations would be partial at best as they would only apply to foreign investors, and the quality of the obligations would be at the mercy of relative negotiating power of the signatory States to the IIAs. Further, these obligations would again encroach on domestic policy space via an investment law system that is currently not equipped to interpret, monitor, decide on or enforce them.

Common to most of IIAs is an acceptance that disputes under them will be subject to binding Investor-State Arbitration (ISA). The justification for resorting to arbitration is investor confidence, as it provides greater certainty of the enforceability of the terms of the IIAs than might be available under national legal systems.[30]

---

[25] Ibid.

[26] R. Sappideen and L. L. He, 'Dispute resolution in investment treaties: Balancing the rights of investors and host states' (2015) *Journal of World Trade* 49(1), 85–116.

[27] UNCTAD *World Investment Report 2010: Investing in a Low-Carbon Economy* (UNCTAD 2010).

[28] Annex 2 of ACIA at para. 4 provides that 'non-discriminatory measures of a Member State that are designed and applied to protect legitimate public welfare objectives, such as public health, safety and the environment, do not constitute an expropriation of the type referred to in sub-paragraph 2(b)'.

[29] W. Alschner and E. Tuerk, 'The role of international investment agreements in fostering sustainable development' in *Investment Law within International Law: Integrationist Perspectives* F. Baetens (ed.) (Cambridge University Press 2013).

[30] See ICSID Convention, Report of the Executive Directors on the Convention on the Settlement of Investment Disputes between States and Nationals of Other States (International Bank for Reconstruction and Development 1965) stated:

Yet as the use of ISA by investors affected by domestic regulation has increased it has generated controversy, pitting as it does governments and their definition of public interest against market actors and their legitimate expectations and protection from discrimination in fora which are often less transparent and accountable than national courts. The legal uncertainty generated for States has prompted high-profile criticisms of the ISA system[31] and even withdrawals by certain States.[32] Ultimately, use of ISA under IIAs generates results that are by their very nature binary and bound to generate controversy through 'winner takes all' outcomes without recourse for appeal.[33]

To render investment law a useful tool for promoting sustainable investment in agriculture there is a need to rebalance the international investment system, as well as to enhance its accountability,[34] but it is a fine line to tread: the greater the bias towards the 'public interest' and therefore State policy discretion within investment law the less significant its role is likely to be in incentivizing investment. It remains to be seen whether the

---

private capital will continue to flow to countries offering a favorable climate for attractive and sound investments, even if such countries did not become parties to the Convention [. . .] adherence to the Convention by a country would provide additional inducement and stimulate a larger flow of private international investment into its territories.

Furthermore, at para. 9 it highlights the value of ICSID itself: 'The creation of an institution designed to facilitate the settlement of disputes between States and foreign investors can be a major step toward promoting an atmosphere of mutual confidence and thus stimulating a larger flow of private international capital into those countries which wish to attract it.'

[31] Such as those by Australia (see Sappideen and He, *supra* fn. 24) and Indonesia (See M. Ewing-Chow and J. J. Losari, 'Pacific Rim investment treaty practice: Regional considerations – reflective or reactionary? Indonesia's approaches to International Investment Agreements and recommendations for the future' [2015] *TDM* 1).

[32] Bolivia, Ecuador and Venezuela have withdrawn from ICSID because of their negative perceptions of the system.

[33] ICSID Convention, art. 53:

(1) The award shall be binding on the parties and shall not be subject to any appeal or to any other remedy except those provided for in this Convention. Each party shall abide by and comply with the terms of the award except to the extent that enforcement shall have been stayed pursuant to the relevant provisions of this Convention.

[34] There are already international efforts in this direction with the approval of the UN Convention on Transparency in Treaty-based Investor-State Arbitration in December 2014. The press release announcing its adoption acknowledged 'The Transparency Rules represent a fundamental change from the status quo of arbitrations conducted outside the public spotlight. Indeed, confidentiality is often a valued feature of commercial arbitration. However, in investor-State disputes, the arbitration involves a State and often issues of public interest, as well as taxpayer funds.' See UN Press Release 'General Assembly Adopts the United Nations Convention on Transparency in Treaty-based Investor-State Arbitration' UNIS/L/210 11 December 2014.

public policy carve-outs provided for in more recent IIAs can provide this balance within the existing system.

INEQUITABLE DISTRIBUTION: WHAT ROLE FOR THE RIGHT TO FOOD?

Food insecurity exists despite the fact that sufficient food is produced to feed the global population. It is clear that focusing on increased production alone will not be sufficient to ensure effective distribution to the most vulnerable and food insecure. Barriers to access and enjoyment currently prevent a significant proportion of the global population – and many in Asia – from achieving a state of food security. Yet international law already guarantees the right of individuals to a food security via the existence of a 'Right to Food' which States are obliged to respect, protect and fulfil (i.e., provide and facilitate).[35]

This right is enshrined in several international human rights instruments including the Universal Declaration of Human Rights 1948 which recognized that, 'Everyone has the right to a standard of living adequate for the health and well-being of himself and his family, including food (. . .)' (Art.25);[36] the International Covenant on Economic, Social and Cultural Rights (ICESCR) 1966,[37] which provides a right to an adequate standard of living and freedom from hunger (Article 11);[38] and the Convention on the Rights of the Child, 1989.[39] The Universal Declaration of Human Rights is widely understood to be part of customary law, and the bulk of East, Southeast and South Asian countries have ratified the ICESCR.[40] Having entered into these obligations voluntarily, one might assume that

---

[35] UN Committee on Economic, Social and Cultural Rights (CESCR), General Comment No. 12: The Right to Adequate Food, 40–41, UN Doc. E/C.12/1999/5 (May 12, 1999).

[36] The article in full reads:

> Everyone has the right to a standard of living adequate for the health and well-being of himself and of his family, including food, clothing, housing and medical care and necessary social services, and the right to security in the event of unemployment, sickness, disability, widowhood, old age or other lack of livelihood in circumstances beyond his control.

[37] UN General Assembly, *International Covenant on Economic, Social and Cultural Rights*, 16 December 1966, United Nations, Treaty Series, vol. 993, p. 3.

[38] Article 11 'Everyone has the right to an adequate standard of living for himself and his family, including adequate food, clothing and housing. Everyone has the right to be free from hunger.'

[39] See UN General Assembly, *Convention on the Rights of the Child*, 20 November 1989, United Nations, Treaty Series, vol. 1577, p. 3.

[40] Exceptions are Bhutan, Brunei, Malaysia, Myanmar and Singapore.

the human rights framework, coupled with the political will of the signatory State governments, would together form a powerful impetus for the promotion of food security. Moreover, the ICESCR places an obligation on States 'to take steps, individually and through international assistance and co-operation, especially economic and technical, to the maximum of its available resources, with a view to achieving progressively the full realization of the rights recognized in the present Covenant by all appropriate means'.

As with other 'progressive' rights, both implementation and enforcement of the Right to Food is weak as the ICESCR establishes that these positive rights should be achieved over time, within the limits of available resources and in particular via implementing legislation.[41] From a legal perspective, this creates formidable barriers to its effective enforcement. Indeed, despite the recognition of a Right to Food in international law, there are few instances when the Right to Food has been invoked successfully, or even invoked at all.[42]

For effective enforcement, the Right to Food relies on action and implementation into national legal systems by the very governments that it is intended to hold to account. Where this has taken place, there are examples of Public Interest Litigation (PIL) cases successfully galvanising courts to effectively enforce these rights. India offers an often-cited example[43] where several national food distribution programs were classified as 'entitlements' under the relevant Constitutional provision.[44] While the extent to which the court legislated in this instance is debatable,[45] this

---

[41] The ICESCR at its art. 2(1) states that each party has the obligation 'to take steps . . . to the maximum of its available resources with a view to achieving progressively the full realization of the rights recognized in the present Covenant by all appropriate means, including particularly the adoption of legislative measures'.

[42] M. McDermott, 'Constitutionalizing an enforceable right to food: A tool for combating hunger', (2012) *Boston College International and Comparative Law Review*, 35(2), 543–74.

[43] *People's Union for Civil Liberties v. Union of India & Others (PUCL)*, Writ Petition (Civil) No. 196 of 2001 (India) described in detail in L. Birchfield and J. Corsi, 'Between starvation and globalization: Realizing the Right to Food in India', (2010) *Mich. J. Int'l L.* 31, 691. The orders issued by the Indian Supreme Court as a result of a PIL on the Right to Food including those distributing grain to poor families, allowing poor workers to act in work-for-food programs, and giving schoolchildren access to lunch during the school day, into legal entitlements. The court set up a commission to monitor compliance and to make policy recommendations.

[44] Ibid.

[45] Some argue its principal focus on legal entitlements and the legislative process fall within its remit. See N. Lambek, 'Respecting and protecting the Right to Food: When states must get out of the kitchen' in N. Lambek, P. Claeys, A. Wong, and L. Brilmayer (eds), *Rethinking Food Systems: Structural Challenges, New Strategies and the Law* (Springer 2014).

form of judicial activism, which takes over functions traditionally reserved for the legislative branch of government, is controversial.[46] It is a role the judiciary is arguably ill suited to, as it requires courts to determine the priority and allocation of budgetary resources, necessitating an assessment of information and balancing of competing interests that go beyond the facts of the case before it. As a result, this level of judicial activism is rare, even in those countries where the Right to Food is a constitutional right.

In order to enhance the effective implementation of the Right to Food some advocate a greater focus on the obligation to 'respect' existing access to adequate food – requiring State parties not to take any measures that result in preventing such access – and the obligation to 'protect' – ensuring that enterprises or individuals do not deprive individuals of their access to adequate food.[47] The proposal does not ignore the positive element to the right, but notes that many of the criticisms of its justiciability and enforceability would not apply to these 'negative' rights and that in addition, they 'ensure that the state does not undermine progress in reducing food insecurity in one area, by engaging in violations of the right to food in another'.[48] Particularly where it has been transposed into national constitutions, the Right to Food can be key to guaranteeing the food security of those disenfranchised from the political system, seeking accountability from governments who fail to meet their obligations. This is a critical role, in particular for the most vulnerable and food insecure.

Yet there are significant limitations to the application of human rights as a legal framework for supporting a systemic approach to food security challenges. Under the current framework, reliance on judicial enforcement at national level would be likely to lead to piecemeal solutions and a fragmented policy landscape based on largely voluntary transposition and implementation by national governments and on individual enforcement initiatives at State level.

There is potential however, as advocated by the CFS itself, for a human rights framework or approach to support policy coherence at both national and international level, and avoid States entering into commitments that would undermine their Right to Food obligations.[49] This Right to Food

---

[46] D. Landau, 'A dynamic theory of judicial role' (2014) *Boston College Law Review* 55(5), 1501–62.

[47] CESCR, *supra* fn 34.

[48] Lambek, Claeys, Wong and Brilmayer, *supra* fn 44.

[49] To this end, human rights advocates propose *inter alia* that States carry out impact assessments. See for example Oliver De Schutter, UN Special Rapporteur on the Right to Food, *Guiding Principles on Human Rights Impact Assessments of Trade and Investment Agreements*, U.N. Doc. A/HRC/19/59/ Add.5, at principle 2 (19 December 2011).

approach focuses on retaining (and allowing others to retain) adequate domestic policy space for implementation of human rights compliant policies. In the GSF the CFS takes this a step further and cites the Right to Food in support for the obligation of States to cooperate to address issues such as pricing volatility and climate change.[50] Yet while this approach by the CFS is supported by the ICESCR, which advocates international cooperation in realising the Right to Food, the human rights framework provides little if any policy direction[51] to guide a systemic approach.

Part of the challenge both investment law and human rights law face in supporting a systemic approach is that while they are international in nature, their focus is on the domestic policy space. Both grant protections that share common elements with those afforded by effective rule of law within national territories: legal certainty; equality and non-discrimination; and effective systems of accountability (access to justice and judicial review).[52] The potential for strengthened rule of law at national level to support both enhanced investment and effective protection for human rights is clear. So too is the potential for a clash of the current fragmented international law systems brought to the forefront: international investment law restricts the domestic policy space, which human rights rely on for their effective implementation and enforcement. The CFS' approach, which is to focus on country-driven policies to strengthen the rule of law would, if implemented, go a long way to bolstering these protections in a more sustainable way than enforcement through dispute resolution or litigation can afford.

A SYSTEMIC SOLUTION UNDER INTERNATIONAL LAW – RELYING ON INTERNATIONAL TRADE LAW

The potential for the international trade system to support a systemic approach to food security was explicitly acknowledged at the 1996 World Food Summit 'Plan of Action' which contained a specific commitment

---

[50] *Supra* fn 5.

[51] Food Sovereignty advocates for instance would argue that the Right to Food is not clear enough to adequately guarantee the right of people to adequately feed themselves. See by way of example R. Dunford, 'Human rights and collective emancipation: The politics of food sovereignty'(2015) *Review of International Studies* 41, 239–61.

[52] In some ways the IIAs seek to provide a 'shortcut' – albeit with additional protections – to the lengthy process of building 'efficient, accountable and transparent institutions and structures and decision-making processes to ensure peace and the rule of law, which are essential elements of a conducive business environment' as identified by the CFS (see Global Strategic Framework for Food Security and Nutrition, p. 10).

to 'strive to ensure that food, agricultural trade and overall trade policies are conducive to fostering food security for all through a fair and market-oriented world trade system'; and to implement this in 'cooperation with the international community'.[53] The need for the trade liberalization process to take into account food security is also explicitly acknowledged in the preamble to the multilateral Agreement on Agriculture (AoA),[54] which states that 'commitments under the reform programme should be made in an equitable way among all Members, having regard to non-trade concerns, including food security'. A framework within which countries can rely on each other for the stable supply of basic commodities has the potential to relieve the pressure that would otherwise be placed on limited resources by the need for each country to ensure its 'self-sufficiency' in this regard, as well as mitigating the risk of relying principally on national production for food security. This is crucial as it is not only the effectiveness of these policies in providing for the immediate needs of a national population that must be assessed, but also their sustainability over time in the face of challenges including climate change.[55]

The current framework for trade in agriculture leaves much to be desired from a global or 'collective food security' perspective. OECD studies draw the conclusion that the immediate quantitative effects of the AoA on trade and protection levels, as well as the developing countries' level of penetration in world agricultural markets have been modest.[56] Indeed, '[d]espite on-going reforms there are still significant barriers to trade in agricultural commodities among developing countries and between developing and OECD countries'.[57] Protectionism on agricultural products is

---

[53] World Food Summit, 1996, World Food Summit Plan of Action, Rome Declaration para. 4.

[54] Agreement on Agriculture, Apr. 15, 1994, Marrakesh Agreement Establishing the World Trade Organization, Annex 1A, *The Legal Texts: The Results of The Uruguay Round of Multilateral Trade Negotiations* 33 (1999), 1867 UNTS 410. [Not reproduced in ILM].

[55] FAO (2008) 'Climate change and food security: A framework document', Rome: FAO:

Rising sea levels and increasing incidence of extreme events pose new risks for the assets of people living in affected zones, threatening livelihoods and increasing vulnerability to future food insecurity in all parts of the globe. Such changes could result in a geographic redistribution of vulnerability and a relocalization of responsibility for food security – prospects that need to be considered in the formulation of adaptation strategies for people who are currently vulnerable or could become so within the foreseeable future.

[56] OECD, Agricultural Policies in OECD Countries: Monitoring and Evaluation (2001 and 2002) and OECD, The Uruguay Round Agreement on Agriculture (2001) cited in C. Breining-Kaufmann 'The right to food and trade in agriculture' in T. Cottier, et al., *Human Rights and International Trade* (OUP 2005), p. 30.

[57] See Interagency Policy Report (2011) 'Price Volatility in Food and Agricultural Markets: Policy Responses'. The report was requested by G20 leaders at their summit meeting in

not only higher than on non-agricultural products (by a factor of four), it is also much more volatile.[58] In addition, the framework governing export restrictions was shown to be ineffective during the 2008 food crisis.

The negative impact of the failings of the current framework on food security only serves to emphasize the critical importance of trade reform. This reform has been a long time coming. Kicking off in 2001, the Doha Development Round or Agenda (DDA) is the latest negotiating round at WTO level. Under its actions to reduce pricing volatility the CFS notes the need to 'maintain focus on building an accountable and rules-based multilateral trading system taking into account food security and nutrition concerns, in particular those of the least developed and net food importing developing countries' and supports 'an ambitious, balanced and comprehensive conclusion of the Doha Development Round, in accordance with its mandate'.[59] It is encouraging that a consensus driven organization such as the CFS is this clear in its recommendation, adding to the widespread recognition that the current international trade system requires reform. Yet despite this there is no agreement in sight on reform of trade in agriculture.

The 2013 Bali Package which was intended to include agreement only on what was considered the 'low hanging fruit' of AoA reform almost collapsed due to differences over the treatment of national food security policies, and in particular India's insistence that it be allowed to fund public stockholding at above market price.[60] The agreement reached in Bali does not resolve but instead postpones a difficult discussion: at issue is the defi-

---

November 2010 and submitted to the French Presidency of the G20 on 2 June 2011. The report was undertaken by FAO, IFAD, IMF, OECD, UNCTAD, WFP, the World Bank, the WTO, IFPRI and the UN HLTF.

[58] A. Bouët and D. Laborde, 'The potential cost of a failed Doha Round, IFPRI Issue Brief 56' (IFPRI 2008) and 'Assessing the potential cost of a failed Doha Round', (2010) *World Trade Review* 9(2), 319–51.

[59] The CFS notes that a transparent and predictable international trade in food is crucial for reducing excessive price volatility. See *supra* fn. 6 at p. 19.

[60] India argued that the procurement of public stocks from low-income resource-poor farmers at prices higher than the market price, is an essential part of their efforts to secure food security as this is the only way to ensure that the quantities needed for distribution to more than 800 million food insecure can be acquired. In addition, as farmers often face reduced prices during the harvest period, a guaranteed price would significantly contribute to their food security.

See FAO Trade Policy Briefs on issues related to the WTO negotiations on agriculture No. 16 The Bali Package – implications for trade and food security (February 2014).

nition of food security initiatives and their potentially damaging impact on stability of international trade.[61]

Given the significant sensitivities involved it has been suggested that, where staple goods are traded regionally, it may be that this is a better level to begin to build confidence in stable trade flows. The CFS places significant emphasis on the potential for advances at the regional level, citing regional investment for fostering national efforts, and tackling specific issues such as lifting intraregional trade barriers, reinforcing regional value chains, harmonizing information systems, coordinating monitoring systems for food emergencies and mobilizing resources.[62] Yet when it comes to the sensitive issue of food security policies and their effects, stumbling blocks arise at both international and regional level. The ASEAN free trade agreement ATIGA, part of wider regional efforts to build the ASEAN Economic Community, contains an explicit dispensation for rice and sugar.[63]

Furthermore, though slow, progress is being made at WTO level. The Bali package[64] includes strict transparency obligations for food security policies wishing to benefit from the temporary reprieve of the 'peace clause'. States must have provided, and continue to provide on an annual basis, additional information by completing the template contained in the Annex for each public stockholding programme to be included under the exemption, as well as statistical data broken down per crop.[65]

As countries continue the difficult process of multilateral negotiation by consensus, ways in which international trade law could provide systemic support include:

---

[61] During the talks, 'developing countries such as Thailand, Pakistan, and Uruguay – all of which, like India, are major exporters of rice – contended that overpaid farmers in India could undercut producers in their own countries' P. McClanahan, 'Why the WTO agreement in Bali has finally helped developing countries' *The Guardian* (6 December 2013).

[62] As supported by the CFS:

> In accordance with their mandates, regional bodies can have an important role to play in developing regional policies to address the cross-border dimensions of food security and nutrition, and build strong regional markets. Such policies are based on the strong intraregional complementarities between ecology, production and consumption. They address the need for shared management of transboundary resources such as rivers and river basins, aquifers, pastoral lands and marine resources as well as shared management of transboundary pests.

See *supra* fn. 5 at p. 45.

[63] ASEAN Trade in Goods Agreement 'Protocol to provide special consideration for rice and sugar'.

[64] Public Stockholding for Food Security Purposes, Ministerial Decision (WT/MIN(13)/38 or WT/L/913).

[65] Ibid., see annexes.

- Supporting legal coherence: we have already seen that the WTO Dispute Settlement Panels will take international law beyond trade law into account when making their decisions. Making food security (and the Right to Food obligations of many WTO members) a recognised feature of WTO negotiations would be a useful step in promoting a harmonised approach.[66]
- Transparency: reporting obligations such as those included in the Bali Package could be a powerful support for a systemic approach to food security.
- Accountability: Strengthening notification procedures, such as those contemplated for export controls, would help to promote a system whereby countries are accountable to one another for the impact of national policies beyond national borders.

The above initiatives fall squarely within the WTO's mandate. However, there have been strong pressures for the WTO to go beyond this. Many have seen in international trade law the ideal support for systemic application and enforcement of other international obligations, and seek to promote greater cohesion within international law through the WTO.

There is some support for this notion within current WTO practice. WTO Dispute Settlement Understanding obliges WTO Panels and the Appellate Body to apply customary rules of treaty interpretation including having consideration to other international law rules applicable between the parties.[67] Further, a WTO panel held that the relationship between WTO agreements and customary international law is broader than the rules of interpretation, and that customary international law applies generally to economic relations between WTO members.[68] This has led commentators to conclude that through 'a coherent interpretation of state obligations in both international trade law and human rights

---

[66] This approach would acknowledge the need for flexibilities but also that international trade law should provide effective support for stability of trade (of course, this would not in itself provide a solution: for an insight into the complexities involved in reconciling legal frameworks see R. Howse 'Human Rights in the WTO: Whose Rights, What Humanity? Comment on Petersmann' (2002) *Eur J Int Law* 13(3), 651–9). Some commentators recommend going further and formally recognizing the legal relationship between human rights and international trade law. See B. Choudhury, et al. 'A call for a WTO ministerial decision on trade and human rights' in *The Prospects of International Trade Regulation*, T. Cottier and P. Delimatsis (eds) (1st ed., Cambridge University Press 2011).

[67] K. R. Gray, 'Right to food principles vis-à-vis rules governing international trade' (British Institute of International Comparative Law December 2003) available at http://www.cid. harvard.edu/cidtrade/Papers/gray.pdf.

[68] See *Korea – Measures Affecting Government Procurement*, WTO/DS163?R, Report of the Panel, 19 June 2000, para. 7.96.

instruments',[69] international trade law should be agreed and applied in a manner compatible with human rights and supportive of food security. Equally there is scope for deference to the concept of sustainable development. WTO jurisprudence provides precedent for deference to sustainable development goals in the resolution of disputes. In *Shrimp/ Turtle*[70] the Appellate Body acknowledged the 'objective' of sustainable development is generally accepted as a concept that integrates economic and social development and environmental protection, and argued that WTO members can and should act to protect the environment. However, it is important to note though that even if human rights rules or provisions of environmental protection are acknowledged within WTO rules it does not imply that a WTO Panel will *apply* human rights or environment law provisions. These rules may constitute a defence against an allegation of breach of WTO provisions, but do not serve to initiate a legal claim under the WTO Dispute Settlement Mechanism (DSM).[71]

There has been strong pushback against attempts to widen the WTO mandate beyond this, with disparaging warnings by former DGs against using the WTO as a 'Christmas tree on which to hang any and every good cause that might be secured by exercising trade power.'[72] Beyond the concerns that this overextension would damage the WTO's ability to further trade reform, it is clear that the WTO DSM is not suited to deciding on these issues[73] and the trade remedies it provides are not appropriate. Imposing trade measures would not directly address any existing violation of a State's international obligations but could potentially aggravate an existing situation.

Must the role of international trade law therefore be limited to ensuring a stable supply of trade and minimizing trade-distorting protectionism? The WTO is at a crucial juncture where failure to scale up ambition and take leadership on issues of critical relevance to trade in agriculture such as food security and sustainability could seriously erode its legitimacy

---

[69] Breining-Kaufmann, *supra* fn 55, pp. 21–22.

[70] *United States — Import Prohibition of Certain Shrimp and Shrimp Product* (6 November 1998) WT/DS58/AB/R.

[71] E. Blanco and J. Razzaque, 'Legal framework guiding natural resource management' in *Globalisation and Natural Resources Law: Challenges, Key Issues and Perspectives*, Blanco and Razzaque (eds) (Edward Elgar 2011), p. 200.

[72] Joint Statement by Arthur Dunkel (Director-General, GATT, 1980–93), Peter Sutherland (Director-General, GATT/WTO, 1993–95) and Renato Ruggerio (Director-General, WTO, 1995–99) at WTO Press Release 'Joint statement on the multilateral trading system' (1 February 2001). The quote continues: 'Nor can its branches be lopped off because it might sometimes tackle trade issues which have other public policy components.'

[73] G. Marceau, 'WTO Dispute Settlement and Human Rights' (2002) *Eur J Int Law* 13(4), 753–814.

and relevance. Currently, the WTO system can only provide an imperfect shield against protectionist tendencies that undermine market-based solutions for collective food security. Yet systemic solutions, particularly to environmental challenges facing the agricultural system, will require greater support than this from the international legal framework.

SUSTAINABILITY OF THE GLOBAL AGRICULTURAL SYSTEM – THE NEED FOR A SEPARATE FRAMEWORK?

In addition to sufficient production and more equitable distribution, perhaps the greatest challenge facing the agricultural system: the imperative that it be sustainable. This was specifically mentioned in the CFS report, both as a challenge[74] and as an element critical to its proposed solutions.[75]

The UN High-Level Task Force on Global Food Security and Nutrition (UN HLTF) has defined a sustainable food system (SFS) as 'a food system that delivers food security and nutrition for all in such a way that the economic, social and environmental bases to generate food security and nutrition for future generations are not compromised'.[76]

It is also generally accepted that public policies will be required in order to build a resilient and sustainable agri-food system. While 'market mechanisms have shown themselves time and again to be effective means of promoting voluntary win-win transactions [. . .] [w]*here significant informational, coordination or external costs are involved, public assistance may be needed to facilitate them*' (emphasis added).[77]

Yet whereas informational costs – at least as regards production levels – are being directly addressed through international initiatives such as AMIS[78] and regional ones such as AFSIS,[79] addressing information,

---

[74] Under 'Climate / Environment' notably 'Unsustainable use of natural resources'. See *supra* fn. 6, p. 9.

[75] Ibid., p. 23 'Meeting the challenge calls for yield increases and overall productivity gains in food and agricultural production in the context of a more socially, economically and environmentally sustainable agriculture.'

[76] This echoes Bruntland's 1987 definition of sustainable development as 'development that meets the needs of the present without compromising the ability of future generations to meet their own needs'.

[77] Blanco and Razzaque, *supra* fn. 70, p. 105.

[78] Established at the request of the Agriculture Ministers of the G20 in 2011, the Agricultural Market Information System (AMIS) is an inter-Agency Platform to enhance food market transparency and encourage coordination of policy action in response to market uncertainty.

[79] The ASEAN Food Security Information System aims to strengthen food security in the region through the systematic collection, analysis and dissemination of food security related information.

coordination and external costs affecting agricultural sustainability at international level has been principally left to private sector initiatives and to the separate field of environmental law. Progress in this area is critical: experts note that 'only where specific international regimes have been developed, as in the management of fisheries and water resources, can it be said that the concept of sustainable use has acquired some normative content or could potentially be used to judge the permissibility of natural resource exploitations'.[80] In the absence of a specific treaty regime, States have considerable discretion on how to implement the principle.[81]

Setting aside the question of how and whether the international trade system could carve out sufficient flexibility to incorporate environmental agreements,[82] for this to take place it would require international agreement on sustainable agricultural policy, likely in a separate forum, before it could become integrated within the WTO system. Compared with the governance of economic activity in the context both of trade and of foreign investment, natural resource governance is poorly developed and scattered across a variety of agencies and programmes within the UN with overlapping mandates, international treaties secretariats and national government initiatives.[83] Furthermore, while it is clearly an environmental issue, the sustainability of the agricultural system cannot be addressed solely through environmental law – much like climate change, its ramifications are simply too wide-ranging.[84]

The wording of the Preamble to the Marrakesh Agreement would suggest there is room for incorporating the concept of sustainability in international trade law. It makes direct reference to:

> allowing for the optimal use of the world's resources in accordance with the objective of sustainable development, seeking both to protect and preserve the

---

[80] P. Birnie, A. Boyle and C. Redgwell, *International Law and the Environment* (Oxford University Press 2009) p. 216.

[81] Ibid.

[82] WTO Declaration on access to medicines, the WTO waiver for the 'Kimberley Process' on the control of conflict diamonds, and the WTO dispute settlement rulings on the right to make trade preferences for less-developed countries conditional on 'objective standards' (i.e., ratification and implementation of major UN human rights convention) are examples of the way in which initiatives with a significant impact on trade have been integrated into the WTO system in the past. For a detailed discussion of the integration of environmental agreements to the WTO system see R. Howse and A. L. Eliason, 'Domestic and international strategies to address climate change: An overview of the WTO legal issues' in *International Trade Regulation and the Mitigation of Climate Change*, T. Cottier, O. Nartova, and S. Z. Bigdeli (eds) (Cambridge University Press 2009).

[83] Blanco and Razzaque, *supra* fn. 70.

[84] C. Carlarne, 'Delinking international environmental law and climate change' (2014) *Mich J Envtl & Admin L* 4, 1.

environment and to enhance the means for doing so in a manner consistent with their respective needs and concerns at different levels of economic development.

Yet currently there seems to be no political appetite for inclusion of 'sustainable development' within the WTO framework. A major constraint to moving to concrete recommendations is the reluctance of many developing countries to accept trade restrictions to promote environmental objectives, beyond those already allowed in the WTO, especially where the proposed measures relate to production and processing methods.[85] This is despite significant efforts towards promoting environmental objectives at national level.[86] The explanation given by Neumayer in 2004 remains current, as does his warning:

> Perhaps the greatest challenge then is to reform the WTO rules in a way that is beneficial to developing countries and therefore acceptable to them. If environmentalists and developed country representatives do not succeed in convincing developing countries that more environmentally friendly trade rules need not be detrimental to their economic development aspirations, then any progress at the WTO will be relegated to the panels and appellate body in the resolution of environmentally relevant disputes.[87]

Even if the political will existed to include issues of production and processing in the negotiating agenda of the WTO, it would not be an easy task: the definition of what is 'sustainable' in the context of agri-food production and trade will in itself constitute a significant hurdle.

The interpretation of what constitutes sustainable agriculture remains fluid and particular to each national context.[88] This has significant disadvantages not only for the promotion of a systemic approach but to the effectiveness of WTO provisions in this area. Currently governed by the

---

[85] As succinctly explained by Neumayer:

> Practically all developed countries are in favor of some greening, partly by conviction, partly due to pressure from civil society. But their support is partial. For example, the US and Canada are most reluctant to assign any more prominent role to the precautionary principle and the EU is highly reluctant to reduce agricultural subsidies. But the greatest and almost unanimous opposition comes from the developing world. Their representatives do not *trust* the alleged idealistic intentions and suspect that the greening of WTO rules is old protectionism in new environmental disguise. (emphasis added)

See E. Neumayer, 'The WTO and the environment: Its past record is better than critics believe, but the future outlook is bleak' (2004) *Global Environmental Politics* 4.3, 1–8.

[86] Ibid.

[87] Ibid.

[88] P. Aerni, C. Häberli and B. Karapinar, 'Reframing sustainable agriculture' in Cottier et al, *supra* fn 65.

'Green Box' exemption, which provides no ceiling for programmes aimed at delivering public goods such as food security or sustainability,[89] there is concern that current definitions provide greater certainty to developed country programmes than to those suited to developing countries[90] and, more critically, that the exemption is being used for programmes with protectionist aims and that cause significant distortion to trade, at times with nil or even negative impacts on sustainability.[91]

In the absence of public regulation, the concerns sustainability raises for much of the global population is already being catered for – and monetized – principally in the case of consumers in developed countries through private regulation and the implementation of standards aimed at providing guarantees of sustainable production. These private standards are becoming increasingly pervasive, assisted by the significant global coverage and purchasing power of participating retailers and large multinational suppliers.[92] Concerns have been raised that developing country actors are underrepresented across these schemes and that, absent specific provisions and assistance, these standards block smaller suppliers, again in particular from developing countries, from accessing more profitable markets.

Even if these concerns were to be addressed, as some schemes have,[93] private standards cannot provide the level of systemic support that WTO rules could afford. Moreover, the sustainability of trade in agriculture is of such fundamental importance to the stability of agricultural trade,

---

[89] Provided they cause not more than minimal distortion of trade or production, and must be provided through a government-funded programme that does not involve transfers from consumers or price support to producers (for definition see Annex 2 of the AoA).

[90]   The G–33 is also proposing to expand the list of 'general services' under the 'Green Box', a call from the African Group dating back to 2006. This proved less controversial. Developing countries want more programmes that are relevant to them on the list, and the African Group and G–33 have identified: land rehabilitation, soil conservation and resource management, drought management and flood control, rural employment programmes, issuing land ownership titles and settlement programmes.

   See https://www.wto.org/english/thewto_e/minist_e/mc9_e/brief_agneg_e.htm.

[91] R. Meléndez-Ortiz, C. Bellmann, and J. Hepburn, *Agricultural Subsidies in the WTO Green Box: Ensuring Coherence with Sustainable Development Goals* (Cambridge University Press 2010). Findings summarized at http://www.ictsd.org/downloads/2012/02/agricultural-subsidies-in-the-wto-green-box-ensuring-coherence-with-sustainable-development-goals.pdf.

[92] The GSF notes under 'Chapter VI: Issues that may require further attention' (p. 55) that the effect of food standards 'including private standards' on production, consumption and trade patterns merits further attention.

[93] E.g., GlobalGap. For details see D. Fuchs, K. Glaab, A. Kalfagianni, and R. Meyer-Eppler, 'Food security in the era of retail governance' in *The Challenge of Food Security, supra* fn 20.

and vice-versa, that it would imply a critical failure of States to address the intrinsic link between the two if this were to be framed by rules and outcomes determined outside the international trade framework. Indeed, the greater the fragmentation of the two systems, the less likely that either can be effective.

Critically, as we have seen, the tensions involved in incorporating sustainability – and indeed food security – into the WTO system are also key to unlocking the agricultural chapter of the DDA.[94]

There is no simple way forward. The factors involved are complex, often differ widely between countries, and are increasingly linked to the greatest systemic challenge of our generation: climate change.[95] Sustainability policies will need to be implemented at domestic level, but these will not suffice to tackle the challenges ahead. Better international trade rules will be required to improve and build trust in the international trade system. The Bali Package may only be a small cautious step in this direction, but it is at least that.

CONCLUSION

The fragmentation of international law and of its systems of redress complicates the policy landscape for food security and does not support the pursuit of systemic solutions. Each system of law has its own biases and enforcement mechanisms tailored to their nature and goals, none of which are suitable for 'enforcing' food security policies on States.

There can be no international law substitute for the existence of peace, stability and the rule of law at national level. Where these are absent or weak, attempts to bolster protections for certain beneficiaries, as investment law does, have the potential to produce or exacerbate inequitable distribution of resources. The onus placed by the newly reformed CFS is, rightly, on the need for country-driven policies to create a stable business climate and promote food security in line with the Right to Food.

But ensuring the sustainability of the global agricultural system, critical

---

[94] See inter alia Aerni *supra* fn. 87: 'Thus the abuse of this term by the various domestic policy agendas that are associated with it may have prevented a breakthrough for the main issues on the Doha Development Agenda.'

[95] See Carlarne, *supra* fn 83, citing leading legal and political figures describing climate change variously as the 'biggest global-health threat of the 21st century', 'the greatest market failure the world has seen', the 'biggest human rights issue of the 21st century', the 'great moral challenge of our time', 'the new great threat to biodiversity', 'by far the most important and fundamental issue affecting all of our lives', 'the worst problem facing the world today', and, ultimately, 'the greatest challenge of our generation'.

to facing future food security challenges, will require international cooperation that national rule of law alone can support. While international trade law is not a panacea, it remains a critical starting point for promoting greater transparency and accountability for national food security policies at international level. To the extent the international trade system can contribute to these, and we have seen the potential for it, it will be a powerful support for a systemic approach by national governments. It is also the only guarantor against protectionist moves that promote 'beggar thy neighbour' policies that result in lose-lose propositions. Indeed, it is difficult to imagine an effective solution to the global food security challenge that does not involve international trade, and by extension international trade law. But to do so there must be trade reform, be it through building on regional integration efforts or through renewed multilateral negotiation.

If the current international trade system and the institutions that govern it fail to fulfil their potential to underpin the safe, stable and sustainable supply of food on a global scale, the call for specific regulation – and resort to private standards – is likely to grow. This could in turn lead to even greater fragmentation and complexity. The clear danger, however, is that solutions sought by individual States will bypass collective action altogether, resorting to carving out opt-outs in the pursuit of quick solutions to national food security challenges. This is a particularly risky option in light of the unpredictable effects on specific geographical agricultural yield caused by climate change.

It is urgent and imperative that policymakers create mechanisms to ensure an integrated approach at all levels. The institutional and policy initiatives taking place, particularly via the CFS, are encouraging, but they do not directly address the need for significant reforms of international economic law required in order to adequately address present and future food security challenges. Collective solutions take time, whereas food crises require an immediate response. We have already seen the proliferation of self-sufficiency policies in the aftermath of the 2008 food crisis. The potential for this default policy option to aggravate the resource challenge and fundamentally undermine the pursuit of a global food system to benefit all citizens should not be underestimated.

PART IV

11. The WTO and food security – and a possible step forward

Clemens Boonekamp

INTRODUCTION

I was asked by the organizers of the CIL Conference on Food Security and Trade and editors of this book to provide my thoughts on the agenda of the World Trade Organization (WTO) on food security – what it is and what it could be.

This chapter outlines my views as outlined at the CIL Conference in 2013. I served for many years in the GATT Secretariat and later the WTO where I was the Director, Trade Policy Review Division and later the Director, Agriculture and Commodities Divisions. Since my retirement in 2013, I have been a trade policy consultant to several countries and I have continued to be involved in the issues.[1] The opinions that I express below are my personal opinions but my hope is that they will be useful in stimulating debate on how the WTO could move forward in dealing with the issue of food security and trade.

Nearly one in eight people in the world go hungry, mainly in developing countries. This situation undermines the growth and development of both individuals and countries. Ensuring that people are appropriately fed is thus a moral, political and economic imperative. In consequence, food security has become an important item on the international agenda and it is central to the work of the WTO on agriculture.

Food security is a global challenge. In our system of nation states, the primary responsibility for meeting this challenge has devolved to individual governments. These governments are sovereign. They are free to implement those policies they deem necessary to ensure food security for their own populations, paying due attention to their international obligations. For the 160 Members of the WTO such obligations were negotiated in the WTO Agreement on Agriculture (AoA) and, more recently, in the

---

[1] I am now an Associate Partner with the IDEAS Centre in Geneva.

context of the Ninth WTO Ministerial Conference in Bali in December 2013.

The AoA seeks a more level field for trade in agriculture, which improves the two key elements of food security – accessibility and availability. Moreover the AoA is careful to ensure that governments retain policy choices to support their agricultural sectors. In addition, the decisions taken at the Bali Ministerial Conference have particular relevance, inter alia, for stock holding for food security purposes.

The AoA, as its Article 20 recognizes,[2] is a work in progress, as are the subsequent decisions taken under it. Negotiations are ongoing to improve the disciplines under the AoA, with of course implications for Member governments' food security policies. But under the present draft negotiating modalities[3] the new AoA would become more complex and perhaps more difficult and controversial to implement. It may be time to think of simplification. With the momentum built both at the recent Bali Ministerial and subsequently, simplification and agreement may be possible – to the benefit of food security.

This chapter continues with a brief section on the role of trade in food security. But trade is not enough on its own. It needs to be part of a coherent policy framework and to be embedded in an agreed, stable set of multilateral rules for its conduct. Framing and agreeing these rules is the role of the WTO. The next sections therefore deal with the AoA and related decisions, the negotiations to improve the AoA, and an overview of how simplification might be affected. A short concluding section looks at the adequacy of the present rules and explores potential rules, as well as what remains to be done.

FOOD SECURITY AND TRADE

Self-sufficiency is a policy choice available to governments to ensure food security. Few, if any, countries are naturally equipped to do so, particularly if a varied diet and consumer choice are to be achieved. Clearly, too, such policies are likely to divert resources from more efficient uses,

---

[2] Article 20 AoA entitled 'Continuation of the Reform Process' begins: 'Recognizing that the long-term objective of substantial progressive reductions in support and protection resulting in fundamental reform is an ongoing process . . . .'

[3] '"Modalities" are described by the WTO as 'ways or methods of doing something. Here, the ultimate objective is for member governments to cut tariffs and subsidies and to make these binding commitments in the WTO. The "modalities" will tell them how to do it, but first the "modalities" have to be agreed'.' See WTO website at: https://www.wto.org/english/tratop_e/dda_e/modalities_e.htm.

reducing potential purchasing power: the economy's ability to buy food is not optimized. Also, domestic prices in closed, self-sufficient markets have the potential to be more volatile than on world markets, where the risk of a sudden variation of supply is lower. Thus, perhaps counter-intuitively to some countries, less food may be available under self-sufficiency policies; and at a given price, a larger volume of food could be bought from more efficient (import) sources. A quest for self-sufficiency can thus undermine both accessibility to and availability of food. Trade improves both and, as such, is an essential element in achieving food security.

But trade alone is not nearly enough to guarantee food security. Rather trade is a necessary part of a comprehensive, coherent policy package to achieve food security. Accompanying policies, such as extension services, irrigation, transportation and storage infrastructure, research and development, access to seeds, fertilisers and credit, land policies, and appropriate sanitary and phytosanitary (SPS) requirements and facilities are also key factors; as is a social safety net to protect the more vulnerable. But many countries lack the needed financing, bespeaking the need for well-targeted support and investment policies. Here the international community and, above all, sound domestic macroeconomic and structural policies, including a liberal trade regime, can be invaluable.

In all of this, trade is a transmission belt. It provides price signals to improve resource allocation – enhancing purchasing power and hence access to food – and it connects 'the land of plenty to the land of the few' increasing the availability of food. Openness to trade in food can help both lower costs and better absorb shocks to domestic production. Restrictive measures encourage others to do the same. In this context, food security is supported by both stabilizing and freeing the interconnectedness between markets: between the sources of supply and demand. It is the role of the AoA to both facilitate the provision of price signals and to improve the interconnectedness between markets, thus fostering food security.

THE AGREEMENT ON AGRICULTURE AND RELEVANT SUBSEQUENT DECISIONS[4]

The WTO's AoA was a landmark achievement. Negotiated in the Uruguay Round of multilateral trade negotiations (1986–94), the AoA entered into

---

[4] Chapter 1, on *Food security issues and the multilateral trading system*, by Evan Rogerson and Diwakar Dixit, provides a more detailed review of the relevant WTO disciplines.

force with the establishment of the WTO on 1 January 1995, superseding the General Agreement on Tariffs and Trade (GATT).

The GATT had always covered agriculture but the disciplines were weak. The result was a proliferation of barriers to trade: markets were often unstable; surpluses in countries using domestic supports were dumped on world markets at subsidized prices; and incentives were reduced for countries, often developing countries, to use their comparative advantage in agriculture.

The AoA initiated a reform process aimed at a more equitable, efficient agricultural trading system through specific commitments to reduce protection in market access, domestic support and export subsidies and through strengthened rules and disciplines. Moreover, it also ensured that non- or minimally distortive support remained available as a policy option; and for developing countries certain agricultural and rural assistance measures integral to development strategies remain exempted from commitments. The AoA thus explicitly gave effect to the requirement in its Preamble that commitments have regard to food-security concerns.

In *market access* the AoA brought systemic change. All parties to the AoA bound (that is, placed an upper limit on) each of their agricultural tariffs. These upper limits were combined with reduction commitments, except in the case of Least-Developed Countries (LDCs). In addition, all agriculture-specific non-tariff barriers (NTBs) were prohibited; existing measures were 'tariffied' (that is, replaced with a tariff that provided an equivalent level of protection). For the 'tariffied' products, countries were required to maintain minimum and current access levels, to be expanded over time. These changes: (a) enhanced the role of prices as the main link between domestic and international markets, thus facilitating better resource allocation; and (b) improved the predictability and transparency of agricultural market access. The trade and investment climate was enhanced, promoting food security.

The AoA broke new ground in the area of *domestic support*. The fundamental consideration was to discipline and reduce trade-distorting support while leaving countries scope to design and implement agricultural policies based on their own needs. Thus, reduction commitments, leading over time to bound upper limits, were negotiated on the aggregate use of distorting measures such as market-price supports and direct production and input subsidies (Amber Box). Thirty-three WTO Members, including the EU, now have such a limit; all others are at zero (excluding the *de minimis* entitlements available to all WTO Members). Although potentially trade-distorting, certain direct payments under production limiting programmes were exempted from commitments (Blue Box), essentially because they serve to constrain the 'exportable surplus' which otherwise might be 'dumped'. Nor were limits put on non- or minimally distortive supports, such as extension, inspection and marketing services, infrastructural activities and could include stock-building and food-aid programmes (Green Box). In addition, as noted above, developing countries are not limited in their use of certain measures, including some investment and input subsidies (Development Box). Clearly the latter two boxes allow for measures that directly support food security; while the first two can encourage production in third markets, encouraging the diversification of supply, again enhancing food security.

Further, in the context of the Bali Ministerial and subsequent decisions it was agreed that the Green Box includes certain support for land reform and rural livelihood security; and that in developing countries, existing public stock-building programmes of staple foods for food-security reasons are allowed, de facto, to use administered prices.

In its third pillar, the AoA also significantly strengthened disciplines on *export subsidies*. Prior to the Uruguay Round, these measures had become prevalent, largely as a result of surplus production under domestic support programmes, thus undermining the opportunities of more efficient producers, often developing countries. The AoA served to curtail such behaviour, thus supporting food security. It also foresaw that international food aid should not be used to circumvent the export subsidy commitments and encouraged disciplines on export credits. In Bali, it was agreed that there would be utmost restraint in recourse to export subsidies and measures with equivalent effect. The AoA also took additional disciplines on export prohibitions on food, making it clear that that an exporter taking such a measure was to take into account the food security needs of importers.

Overall, the AoA was an important step in improving the international trading conditions for agriculture, particularly compared to those prior to the start of the Uruguay Round, to the clear advantage of food security. Nevertheless, even with the full implementation of the Agreement in the early 2000s, the actual trade environment for agriculture remains difficult. The Producer Support Estimate (PSE) averaged close to 19 per cent in the OECD countries in 2013; while this is down from some 26 per cent in 2006, the decline due at least in part to higher prices.[5] On the other hand the PSEs of some major non-OECD Members appear to be on a rising trend.

---

[5] OECD, 2013 Monitoring and Evaluation: Reference Tables: *Producer Support Estimate by Country*, www.oecd.org.

NEGOTIATIONS IN THE WTO

Much remains to be done. Negotiations to improve the AoA started in 2000 and became part of the new round of multilateral negotiations, the Doha Development Agenda (DDA) in 2001. Negotiations progressed steadily to the point that in December 2008 there were draft modalities with few remaining decision points for a significantly revised Agreement on Agriculture.[6] Subsequently the negotiations stalled, not least because of difficulties in other areas of the DDA, particularly Non Agricultural Market Access (NAMA). However, some momentum was regained at Bali and subsequently when in Agriculture, a number of decisions were taken with relevance for food security (see above), each of which are in line with the draft modalities.

The modalities would strengthen (and complicate) agricultural trade disciplines. In *market access* developed countries would lower bound tariffs by at least 54 per cent and developing countries would do so by at most 36 per cent; both would have flexibilities for 'sensitive' products. Developing countries would also have flexibilities for 'special' products and they would have available a Special Safeguard Mechanism (SSM) in the event of surges in import volumes or sharp declines in import prices. Tariff escalation would be reduced and, overall, access would improve, which is significant as it is estimated that agricultural market access barriers account for some 50 per cent of the costs of global trade protection.[7]

Under the draft modalities, WTO Members with Amber Box commitments would reduce their *trade-distorting support*, significantly in the case of most developed countries (traditionally the main providers). Also, the *de minimis* levels of developed countries would be halved and remain unchanged for most developing countries, which would also benefit from enhanced public stockholding entitlements. Blue Box support would be limited. Most countries would schedule a base 'Overall Trade-Distorting Support' (OTDS) but this would not constrain the use of *de minimis* support by the recently acceded Members to the WTO. Access to the Green Box would become somewhat easier and the Development Box would remain unchanged.

In the area of *export competition*, under the draft modalities, export subsidies would be eliminated, as agreed at the WTO's Sixth Ministerial Meeting, in Hong Kong, China in December 2005, and reaffirmed in Bali.

---

[6] WTO, Committee on Agriculture Special Session, 'Revised Draft Modalities for Agriculture', document TN/AG/W/Rev.4, 6 December 2008.
[7] D. Laborde and W. Martin, 'Agricultural trade: What matters in the Doha Round?' Policy Research Working Paper 6261, (World Bank, 2012).

In parallel, disciplines would be strengthened on export credits, food aid and agricultural exporting state trading enterprises. There also would be a marginal strengthening of rules for export restrictions.

Overall, agreement on the draft modalities would improve the agricultural trading environment: opportunities would improve for efficient producers and disciplines on distortions would be strengthened, particularly in the case of developed countries. Concurrently, flexibilities would be maintained for developing countries, allowing additional space for them to achieve their agricultural objectives. Potentially, each of these factors works to the advantage of food security.

SIMPLIFICATION

The question is whether agreement can, or indeed should, be reached on the basis of the present draft modalities. They may no longer be acceptable to a number of participants, especially as the environment has changed significantly since the start of the negotiations. For example, China's PSE rose from 3.96 per cent in 2001 to 16.81 per cent in 2012 while over the same period those of the EU and the USA fell by 68 per cent and 37 per cent, respectively. In absolute terms, China's PSE in 2012 exceeded the combined PSE of the EU and the USA by a significant margin.[8] Indeed, the value of agricultural production has increased very significantly in some major developing Members, entitling them under the draft modalities to high levels of (trade-distorting) support while that of many other Members, particularly developed country members, would decline markedly. Also, there are what many consider to be potential 'loop holes', like the developing-country exemption for public stock-building for food security. This leaves some to wonder whether the playing field would be made more level under acceptance of the modalities – as is the aim of the negotiations – or be skewed once again, as it was prior to the Uruguay Round, creating imbalances the like of which the AoA began to address.

Moreover, differences remain significant, including on the SSM for developing countries. It was agreed at WTO Ministerial meeting in Hong Kong that an SSM would be available to developing countries, but there is no agreement on how it will function. Also, under the modalities, notification requirements would increase considerably, both in number and level of complication. Under the present AoA few Members are up to date in their notifications and presentations differ; difficulties would

---

[8] OECD 2013, *supra* fn. 4.

be compounded under the proposed new system and monitoring and transparency could suffer.

Ultimately, the goal is a more market-oriented, transparent agricultural trading system that allows WTO Members the maximum amount of policy (and instrument) choice while minimizing the damage to others. To achieve this, and to overcome the differences and difficulties that now separate negotiators, and building on the momentum from Bali, a more simplified framework may be appropriate, perhaps as follows (in the same order as the three pillars appear in the draft modalities):

i) on *overall trade-distorting support* (OTDS): define the base OTDS, as per the modalities but with a more recent reference period (e.g., 2005–10), and bind it (except perhaps for LDCs, possibly with modest reduction commitments. Members would be allowed to use their OTDS in any way they wish, subject to a percentage per product, say 10 per cent, to avoid concentration (and which would be halved for cotton, to meet the commitment made at the Hong Kong, China Ministerial Meeting and reaffirmed in Bali that cotton would be addressed 'ambitiously, expeditiously and specifically' within the agricultural negotiations). The Development Box would remain unchanged, as 'Special and Differential' treatment, but all other trade-distorting outlays would be counted, including those for public stockholding. The Green Box would also remain (taking into account the Ministerial Decision in Bali on 'general services') but the need for the Amber and Blue Boxes and for *de minimis* would be obviated. Members would notify their OTDS expenditures every year – every two years for LDCs and perhaps for Net Food-Importing Developing Countries (NFIDCs) – to the WTO's Committee on Agriculture, ensuring transparency;

ii) in the area of *market access*: restrict the decision points to average tariff cuts and the SSM, dropping sensitive and special products and the like, but retaining the Bali Ministerial Decision on tariff quotas. With respect to the SSM, base it on GATT Article XIX (Safeguards), replacing 'serious injury' with 'injury'. Average tariff reductions should be reasonably low, both to compensate for the absence of flexibilities and such that they are doable without too much (political) difficulty – say, 18 per cent for developed and 12 per cent for developing countries, with an exemption for LDCs. Nevertheless, this would bring some improvement to market access in agriculture, especially to developed markets, where applied and bound rates are close: in fact, there has been little improvement in agricultural market-access among major traders since 2001, except in the case of

China, due to its accession to the WTO.[9] Also, encourage the EU to implement its tariff simplification proposal and seek to make multi-lateral the EU's deal on tropical products with a group of countries – but if these are elusive, put them into a 'built-in agenda' (BIN); and,

iii) in the third pillar, on *export competition*: the modalities are 'clean' (and the draft text is without brackets, suggesting that there was consensus amongst the Members at the time of drafting). However, even if this consensus is hard to retain, Members could repeat the Bali reaffirmed, Hong Kong, China agreement on export subsidies (reaffirmed in Bali), and seek consensus on export credits, leaving the remaining items (food aid and agricultural exporting state trading enterprises) in the BIN for future negotiations. This would prevent backtracking on previously agreed upon issues and will allow the Members to focus on the other areas. The BIN would also include other issues in the draft modalities, *namely*, export restrictions, differential export taxes and geographical indications.

Under the above framework, modalities would be simpler, an agreement could be easier to reach, and certainly easier to implement and track. Choice and access would be enhanced while limiting distortive support, all to the benefit of food security. But there would still be an obvious, significant 'gap': export restrictions. There has been a recent increase in their use, as confirmed by WTO monitoring reports.[10] Such measures can and do increase price-volatility, to the detriment of food security. But WTO disciplines on export restrictions are relatively weak and need strengthening, especially with respect to the justifications for, and the monitoring of, export prohibitions.

CONCLUSION

An agreement on the simplified modalities could be taken, at least provisionally, apart from the rest of the DDA. At the Eighth WTO Ministerial Meeting in 2011 in Geneva, Ministers expressed their readiness 'to advance negotiations, where progress could be achieved, including focusing on elements of the Doha Declaration that allow Members to reach provisional or definitive agreements based on consensus earlier than the full conclusion of the DDA as a single undertaking', that nothing is agreed

---

[9] WTO Statistics, Tariff Data available at www.wto.org.
[10] See, for example the WTO reports on G-20 Trade Measures on its home page under 'Implementation and monitoring' available at www.wto.org.

until everything is agreed.[11] It would be more efficient and more effective, however, to conclude the DDA in the context of a single undertaking, perhaps on the basis of similar simplification in the other areas, including NAMA, Rules and Services. This would immeasurably strengthen the WTO and allow it to plan for the future of the trading system. In either case, implementation of the agreement could be reviewed by Members within a relatively short period after its conclusion, after which the BIN would be activated, continuing the process of improving the AoA.

Food security is central to the WTO's Agreement on Agriculture. The AoA started a reform process towards levelling the playing field, improving accessibility and availability. More needs to be done. The elements are on the table; they could be the basis of another step forward, especially with simplification: access would be enhanced, disciplines strengthened, and flexibilities retained or increased for countries to implement their chosen food security policies. But important issues would remain unaddressed, including export restrictions. Food security benefits from an open, disciplined trading environment. Trade improves resource allocation, enhancing the ability to purchase food, and the transmission of food to where it is needed. The WTO process of improving trading conditions needs to continue.

---

[11] WTO 8th Ministerial Conference, Chairman's Concluding Statement, WTO document WT/MIN(11)/11, 17 December 2011.

12. Conclusion: Moving to collective food security

Michael Ewing-Chow and Melanie Vilarasau Slade

SELF-SUFFICIENCY: A FORM OF FOOD SECURITY?

A National Perspective

There were numerous policy responses to the 2008 food crisis, all of which ostensibly placed the achievement of food security front and center in the policy considerations of many governments. Many countries turned to self-sufficiency[1] as an answer. There are clear limitations to this policy option, particularly in the case of import-dependent countries in which the socio-political and/or geographical conditions for agricultural production are less than ideal.

Yet despite its high costs, food self-sufficiency represents a food security strategy followed by a wide range of countries. This is understandable given that it is the responsibility of national governments to ensure food security for their population. Self-sufficiency is in essence a very costly food insecurity insurance scheme, limited to the national level and one that not all States are able to afford.

Further, whilst it can ensure sufficient production (i.e., physical *availability*) in some States, it is not a guarantee against individual food insecurity (i.e., economic and physical *access*) within those States.

As noted by the FAO:

> Food self-sufficiency, or the provision of a level of food supplies from national resources above that implied by free trade, represents a strategy followed by a wide range of countries. While this approach implies the provision of sufficient domestic production to meet a substantial part of consumption requirements,

---

[1] The concept of self-sufficiency incorporates all policies aimed at ensuring the provision of a level of food supplies from national resources above that implied by free trade.

it does not necessarily imply that all households in the country have access to all the food they require.[2]

Indeed, it is not just that a policy of self-sufficiency does not go far enough to ensure food security for the most vulnerable sections of society. In certain cases such policies run counter to the attainment of food security. By way of example, the fact that it is the poorest sections of the population which are most dependent on rice for food security in many Asian countries 'makes a mockery of the strategy of most Asian countries of keeping rice prices stable by keeping them high, well above long-run levels in world markets.'[3] This policy would ensure food security only for those rural (rice-producing) households to the extent that they are self-sufficient in rice, and is clearly to the detriment of the food security of the urban (rice consuming) poor.

As reasoned by Timmer:

> When *food security* is equated with *food self-sufficiency*, this strategy may make sense, because it is easier to stabilize domestic food prices using domestic production — stimulated by high prices — than to follow and depend on the world market for rice, with its great price volatility. But this strategy forces poor consumers to pay high prices for rice, and it increases considerably the degree of poverty in a country. Self-sufficiency in rice is a political strategy, not a poverty strategy. If countries were more open to rice trade, they would be richer, not poorer.[4]

If the aim of these policies is to achieve a state of food security for individuals on a global scale, especially one that is sustainable over time, policies which focus solely on achieving food security at the domestic level may be ineffective and possibly even counterproductive.

A Global Perspective

The dramatic effect of the 2008 food crisis on rice market is a good illustration of the effect that focus on national self-sufficiency policies can have on global prices.

Whilst it is acknowledged that national food security policies alone cannot explain the food crisis, Dawe and Slayton[5] contend that policies

---

[2] FAO, *Trade Reforms and Food Security: Conceptualizing the Linkages*, (FAO, 2003).

[3] C. P. Timmer, 'The changing role of rice in Asia's food security', in *Food for All: Investing in Food Security in Asia and the Pacific – Issues, Innovations, and Practices* (Asian Development Bank, 2011).

[4] Ibid.

[5] See, inter alia, D. Dawe and T. Slayton, 'The world rice market crisis of 2007–08' in David

and panic are the only plausible explanation as to why rice prices increased so much faster than maize and wheat prices.[6] As they pointed out, rice markets do not need to contend with other fundamental challenges, such as biofuel policies and bad weather, as maize and wheat markets do. Also, rice is barely traded on futures markets, which arguably influenced maize and wheat markets.

As discussed below, increased trade liberalization has the potential to reduce market volatility by evening out supply fluctuations, incentivizing production diversification and, as a direct result, enhancing food security[7] now and in the future. However, '[t]o fulfill this beneficial pooling function to the maximum degree, trade has to be able to flow between nations and the tendency which has emerged, in recent crises, for countries to try to insulate themselves from international markets needs to be reversed.'[8]

Just as international trade is an essential element of a national food security policy; it is also an essential requirement of a properly functioning and sustainable global food trade system that could enable the achievement of food security for all. To pick a topical example, recognizing the value of collective food security policies will be vital in ensuring the successful completion of the Doha Development Agenda (DDA).[9] There have been calls from multiple stakeholders to modify the current structure of the international trade system in agriculture. To date, there has been little success in ensuring progress in trade reform via further multilateral agreement at WTO level. The DDA while wider than trade in agriculture, proposes

---

Dawe (ed.), *The Rice Crisis: Markets, Policies and Food Security* (FAO and Earthscan, 2010).

[6] D. Headey and S. Fan, *Reflections on the Global Food Crisis*, International Food Policy Research Institute (IFPRI) monograph 165 (IFPRI, 2010), p.18.

[7] It must be acknowledged that the overlap of food security policies with poverty alleviation policies in many countries, means that any moves towards greater trade liberalization must also be accompanied by displacement management policies implemented at national level. It is however beyond the scope of this chapter and the expertise of the authors to advise on the exact nature of the region-specific food security initiatives and / or country-specific displacement management policies to be implemented. These are likely to vary greatly between regions and countries and merit far more detailed analysis.

[8] See Interagency Policy Report, 'Price Volatility in Food and Agricultural Markets: Policy Responses' (OECD 2011).

[9] As described on the WTO website:

The Doha Round is the latest round of trade negotiations among the WTO membership. Its aim is to achieve major reform of the international trading system through the introduction of lower trade barriers and revised trade rules. The work programme covers about 20 areas of trade. The Round is also known semi-officially as the Doha Development Agenda.

http://www.wto.org/english/tratop_e/dda_e/dda_e.htm.

major reforms of the current food trade system. The DDA includes proposals for further reductions in distortive trade measures as well as safeguards for developing economies. This is an implicit acknowledgment that the distortions inherent in the current system are untenable.[10] However, negotiations have stalled partially due to some governments' insistence on self-sufficiency as their only food security strategy and there seems to be little hope of a new multilateral agreement on agriculture being agreed in the near future.

Agricultural subsidies in the form of trade distorting market price support or payments linked to production are not only inefficient in terms of bolstering farm incomes,[11] but also severely affect the ability of developing country farmers to sell their products at a fair price.[12] Price fixing also distorts the market suppressing incentives for domestic food producers to increase production or for consumers to reduce their consumption.[13] Conversely, export restrictions by individual countries, which are aimed at preventing the transmission of rising international prices into their domestic markets, inevitably reduce the world supply in cases where those countries are also food producers, pushing global food prices to rise even higher.[14] The current market distortions afforded by national food security policies affect the incentives for investment, production and diversification. In doing so, it can affect production incentives in ways which can run counter to long-term achievement of food security.

---

[10] Doha WTO Ministerial 2001: Ministerial Declaration WT/MIN(01)/DEC/1 (20 November 2001).

> Building on the work carried out to date and without prejudging the outcome of the negotiations we commit ourselves to comprehensive negotiations aimed at: substantial improvements in market access; reductions of, with a view to phasing out, all forms of export subsidies; and substantial reductions in trade-distorting domestic support. We agree that special and differential treatment for developing countries shall be an integral part of all elements of the negotiations.

[11] According to OECD figures, '[o]f every $1 in price support, only $0.25 ends up in the farmer's pocket as extra income. The rest is absorbed by higher land prices, fertiliser and feed costs and other factors'.

[12] See, inter alia, X. Diao, E. Diaz-Bonilla, and S. Robinson, *How Much Does it Hurt? The Impact of Agricultural Trade Policies on Developing Countries* (IFPRI, 2003).

[13] An OECD research on the potential market effects of price fixing found that the world food price spike was some 2–3 per cent higher than it would have been without this policy. See, W. Thompson and G. Tallard, 'Potential market effects of selected policy options in emerging economies to address future commodity price surges', *OECD Food, Agriculture and Fisheries Working Papers*, No. 35, (Paris: OECD Publishing, 2010), p.17.

[14] See generally, ASEAN Food Security Information System (AFSIS),; and S. Mitra and T. Josling, 'Agricultural Export Restrictions: Welfare Implications and Trade Disciplines', *IPC Position Paper / Agricultural and Rural Development Policy Series*, (International Food & Agricultural Trade Policy Council, 2009).

From a global food security perspective therefore the slow progress on the agricultural proposals in the DDA is particularly worrying, as the current system discourages production diversification both in terms of products and geography. Instead, production gravitates towards those areas most protected by tariffs and subsidies, encouraging a concentration of production in areas in which agricultural production – or at least current levels and types of agricultural production – would not be a natural choice.

With climate change poised to affect traditional farming regions in unpredictable ways[15] this is a dangerous policy that figuratively and perhaps even literally puts too many eggs in one geographical basket. Instead, market distortions should be reduced to ensure that one of the most limited global resources, land, is efficiently utilized.

TOWARDS COLLECTIVE FOOD SECURITY

In a liberalized system, the certainty which State initiatives provide to producers would need to be replaced with greater availability of information. The greater the transparency and the more effective the information-sharing initiatives accompanying this liberalization, the more inclusive and sustainable these food security gains can be.

Indeed many international food security initiatives are now focused on the need for accurate information. The Agricultural Market Information System (AMIS) is a G20 initiative which acknowledges that there is a need to 'enhance global food security by encouraging information sharing, improving data reliability and increasing transparency, and introducing a global early warning system.'[16] Currently such initiatives are principally inter-State. Effective participation by the private sector would require such initiatives be increasingly focused towards providing useful input for agricultural producers themselves.

For rice, as for other staple foods, '[t]he big question is how to make such openness possible when policy-makers and the general public distrust the world rice market, for reasons that are easy to

---

[15] FAO, *Climate Change and Food Security: A Framework Document* (Rome: FAO, 2008):

> Such changes could result in a geographic redistribution of vulnerability and a relocalization of responsibility for food security – prospects that need to be considered in the formulation of adaptation strategies for people who are currently vulnerable or could become so within the foreseeable future.

[16] See Interagency Policy Report, *supra* fn 9.

understand.'[17] As pointed out by Sarris, uncoordinated individualistic policies by each government destabilized the global markets. The perverse effect of this instability was that it made national concerns and overreactions further justified.[18] The challenges posed by climate change make it imperative to break this vicious cycle of instability and food insecurity.

Sarris suggested that confidence be enhanced by ensuring adequate supplies either through the international market or through some kind of mutual agreement.[19] To date no such initiative has appeared.[20] In this regard, the current international food aid system has shown itself to be dangerously lacking. During the 2008 food crisis the extremely rapid run-up in food prices eroded the capacity of the national and international relief organizations to purchase food in the most hard-hit countries and regions. With prices doubling or tripling within a few months, their purchasing power was dramatically reduced. Indeed the inability of the World Food Programme to meet all its food aid needs was 'largely due to the high prices of staple grains.'[21]

In a context in which the effectiveness of emergency responses cannot be guaranteed,[22] it is difficult to encourage countries to do away with the protectionist mechanisms which ensure their self-sufficiency, even when they are to the direct detriment of collective security.

The contributors to this book have within their respective chapters advocated several ways forward, which could contribute to forging collective food security policies. In Sections I and II of this publication we have

---

[17] C. P. Timmer, 'Did speculation affect world rice prices?' in Dawe (ed.), *supra* fn 6, pp.29–60.

[18] A. Sarris, 'Trade-related policies to ensure food (rice) security in Asia' in Dawe (ed.), ibid., p.82.

[19] Ibid.

[20] 'The world still does not have an adequate international emergency food reserve' as aid remains highly politicised and undersubscribed. Shaw cited in Briones et al., 'Climate change and price volatility: Can we count on the ASEAN Plus Three Emergency Rice Reserve?', *ADB* Sustainable *Development Working Paper Series*, No. 24 (ADB, 2012).

[21] G. Ziervogel, and P. Ericksen, 'Adapting to climate change to sustain food security', (2010) *WIREs Climate Change* 1: 525–40.

[22] As noted by UN agencies themselves:

While response to appeals made, for example, by the World Food Programme were both rapid and generous, crucial weeks and months were lost as international organisations and humanitarian NGOs scrambled to raise funds or divert monies from other uses to address the crisis. This situation revealed deficiencies in international readiness to deal with such a widespread problem.

See Interagency Policy Report, 'Price Volatility in Food and Agricultural Markets: Policy Responses' (OECD 2011).

seen that the contribution that the WTO has made to liberalizing trade in food, though imperfect, is significant. At present, efforts towards increased liberalization – be they international or regional – can and do co-exist with national food security policies, of varying effectiveness. Though WTO rules provide domestic policy space for these national initiatives, as we have seen these can have the unintended consequence of creating instability and volatility on international markets, which in turn undermines efforts towards greater liberalization. To move on from this impasse, the contributors to this book take the view that confidence building measures are key: whether buffer stocks; transparency mechanisms or forms of market-based risk management tools; the uncertainties of international trade must be managed if greater liberalization and investment – two key areas to reduce the impact of market shocks and pricing volatility – are to be encouraged.

Looking to the future, Sections III and IV of this publication highlight the importance of building resilience in the global food system, and point towards methods of achieving it. A resilient approach to food security policies and greater focus on supply-side constraints through impact assessments will become critical to unlocking production potential in a sustainable way. Greater trust in the international trade system will be required in order to allow for reliance on trade as a source of food security. Greater transparency and accountability must be achieved for this to take place. As pointed out in Chapter 10 on the role of international law, these are efforts that the international trade system has the potential to support.

There is a long way to go, and heightened cooperation will be required. Regional agreements, such as the ASEAN Plus Three Emergency Rice Reserve (APTERR)[23] regional rice stockpile initiative currently implemented at ASEAN+3[24] level, may show us a way.[25]

---

[23] The ASEAN Plus Three Emergency Rice Reserve Agreement was signed during the 11th Meeting of the ASEAN Ministers of Agriculture and Forestry and the Ministers of Plus Three Countries (AMAF+3) held in Jakarta, Indonesia in October 2011.

[24] ASEAN+3 includes all ASEAN members (Brunei Darussalam; Cambodia; Indonesia; Lao PDR; Malaysia, Myanmar; Philippines; Singapore; Thailand; Vietnam) plus People's Republic of China (PRC); Japan; and South Korea.

[25] Regional agreements and initiatives – by their very nature closer in geographical and often cultural terms than international initiatives – are able to provide a safety net which is not as vulnerable to the natural or economic circumstances which may cause a national food emergency, and which would render many national food security initiatives ineffective.

CONCLUSION

Famines are often a political, social or economic phenomenon rather than a climatic inevitability. Indeed, Sen asserted that famines were not just a consequence of nature, but also an economic and political catastrophe that is entirely avoidable.[26] The difficulty will be trying to chart a middle path to allow States the leeway necessary to protect their national populations from severe shortages and price spikes while discouraging protectionism. It is important to do so despite the challenges presented: in the long term, tariffs and domestic subsidies will disincentivize global production and diversification and ultimately reduce yield.

The FAO holds that 'a food security strategy that relies on a combination of increased productivity in agriculture, greater policy predictability and general openness to trade will be more effective than other strategies.'[27]

We agree and would go further – collective food security – understood as long-term food security measured at household level across the globe – cannot be achieved via self-sufficiency policies. The 2008 food price crisis is clear evidence of this. Free trade in food is the only way of effectively ensuring long-term food security on a global scale. A combination of national food security policies focused on sustainability and resilience, and greater reliance on international trade facilitated by trade reform is needed. Regional food security initiatives are a critical stepping-stone between the two. It is our view that these initiatives are not only crucial to ensuring food security at times of emergency but are also an essential first step to building confidence in the international trade system as a method for delivering collective food security.

Currently, it is the import-dependent countries and most vulnerable sectors of society that suffer most from our global failure to achieve collective food security. The challenges and uncertainties presented by climate change make this about more than just fairness towards countries facing food security challenges: it is about our collective global survival.

---

[26] Amartya Sen, *Poverty and Famines: An Essay on Entitlement and Deprivation* (Clarendon Press 1981).

[27] *The State of Food Insecurity in the World 2011: How does international price volatility affect domestic economies and food security?* (FAO, 2011).

Index